An IBM PC Business User's

Planning and Budgeting
for Higher Profits

Jeffrey R. Alves ▪ Dennis P. Curtin ▪ Anne K. Briggs

Curtin & London, Inc.   Somerville, Massachusetts

Van Nostrand Reinhold Company   New York Cincinnati Toronto Melbourne

Printed in the United States of America

Published in 1983 by Curtin & London, Inc.
and Van Nostrand Reinhold Company
135 West 50th Street, New York, NY 10020, U.S.A.

Van Nostrand Reinhold Limited
1410 Birchmount Road
Scarborough, Ontario M1P 2E7, Canada

Van Nostrand Reinhold Pty. Ltd.
17 Queen Street
Mitcham, Victoria 3132, Australia

VisiCalc® and VisiCalc® Advanced Version are registered trademarks of VisiCorp
IBM® is a registered trademark of International Business Machines Corporation
DIF™ is a trademark of Software Arts Products Corp.

Concept development: Dennis P. Curtin
Editor: Katherine Carlone
Managing editor: Nancy Benjamin

Interior design and cover design: Susan Marsh
Illustrations: Elisa Tanaka
Composition: York Graphic Services, Inc.
Printing and binding: Halliday Lithograph

10 9 8 7 6 5 4 3 2 1

Library of Congress Cataloging in Publication Data

Alves, Jeffrey R.
  Planning and budgeting for higher profits.

  Includes index.
  1. VisiCalc (Computer program) 2. IBM Personal
Computer. 3. Business—Data processing. I. Curtin,
Dennis. II. Briggs, Anne K. III. Title.
HF5548.4.V57A464 1983   658.1′54′02854   83-7219
ISBN 0-930764-61-7

Acknowledgments

The following "Business tips" are reprinted with permission from Bank of America, NT&SA, "Cash Flow/Cash Management," *Small Business Reporter*, Vol. 15, No. 9, Copyright 1982: page 20, "Raising cash"; page 35, "Credit collection"; page 44, "Borrowing funds"; page 45, "A checklist for cash management"; page 68, "Monitoring credit" and "Cash on hand"; page 69, "Monitoring inventory movement" and "Inventory control."

Disclaimer

Contents

Tips

Introduction

Planning and budgeting are important but frequently avoided tasks that confront every business manager or owner. Doing them well can be time-consuming and complicated, and you are in business to run the company, not to get buried in paperwork.

Both the time and paperwork normally associated with planning and budgeting can be greatly reduced by using a personal computer and off-the-shelf software. Business software, such as the VisiCalc® program, is simply an electronic version of the traditional business spread sheet. Within a few hours, you can be entering line items and formulas that give you a dynamic, working budget, one that is easy to update. And once the budget is on the computer, you can explore a whole range of "What Ifs" to see how your plan or budget will operate under a variety of business conditions. This is where the computer not only pays its way, but can also help pave the way to better planning and budgeting.

This book is for anyone who wants to do planning and budgeting by computer. It's a practical, how-to business book. We'll show you how to put three important financial tools—a cash budget, pro forma (projected) income statement, and pro forma balance sheet—on your personal computer. Almost every business decision you make affects these three statements. We'll explain these tools, their various line items, and how to estimate them. Then we'll show you how to adapt your computerized budgets to your company and use them to explore changes. With clear, sequenced instructions, we'll take you through the whole process, as further described in Chapter 1, "Planning and budgeting: Step by step."

Regardless of how you approach planning and budgeting—with enthusiasm or resignation—we think you'll discover, as we have, that doing these tasks by computer is a remarkably faster and better process than doing them by pencil and paper.

Acknowledgments

In the early stages of the Business User's Guide series, many people offered valuable suggestions and encouragement, including James Cash, Les Porter, and Eric Rosenfeld at the Graduate School of Business Administration, Harvard University; Hoo-min Toong at the Sloan School of Management, Massachusetts Institute of Technology; Ted Klein, Metropolitan College, Boston University; Lisa Underkoffler and Jack McGrath of Software Arts; and Jack Rochester and Stuart Allsop II of CW Communications. The authors are grateful to Philip Wharton, not only for his research skills and template work, but also for the insight and enthusiasm he brought to the series. John McGregor's critical comments and suggestions were enormously helpful to the series. Several other people provided support and assistance which helped immeasurably: Mary McCann at the Boston Computer Society, and the support staffs at IBM Corporation, and VisiCorp.

For their work on *Planning and Budgeting,* the authors would like to thank Christine Graunas for diligently copyediting the manuscript; Linda D'Anna, who patiently and carefully typed the manuscript on a personal computer; and Irene Cinelli, who aided in the final preparation of the manuscript.

Each of the authors wishes to personally thank a few special individuals: Dennis Curtin is grateful to Dave Grady and to Peggy Curtin; Jeff Alves, to Tina Gottesman-Alves and Dr. Joe Lavely; and Anne Briggs wishes to thank her husband Kenneth Bell, as well as George Bradt, Margaret Nelson, and Jim Hilderbrand.

1   Planning and budgeting: Step by step

Charting a course

Planning is charting the course of a business — how it will move from its current state toward a future condition. A plan is anticipated action and results; in written form it clarifies where the business expects to go in the future and how it's going to get there. Increased sales or profits, higher inventory turnover, or lower debts do not just happen. While some events are caused by external factors, internal actions and results also affect many business activities. Profits go up, inventory moves, or debts decrease as a result of management planning and action.

In a firm with varied operations there are many types of plans, but all are developed using the same basic approach. Planning starts with management's understanding of the business: its products or services, competition, customers, costs, and the other factors that make up a firm's current position. Objectives are then set based on this understanding. Meaningful goals or objectives are clear, specific, and practical; they are based on a realistic assessment of both the present and future.

Next, a course of action to meet the objectives is spelled out. Any significant developments that could affect or alter the plan must be taken into account, as well as the pros and cons of the course of action. Once the plan (with its goals and methods) has been set, milestones or dates are established for review of the plan and the firm's progress toward its goals. Based on this review, goals, anticipated actions, or the entire plan are updated or revised, and the cycle starts all over again. Planning is a continual process.

Why plan?

"You never know what's going to happen, so why plan?" "Plans always get fouled up, so why bother?" "I'm a nuts-and-bolts type. My gut feel for business has always served me well. Why change?" These are a few of the objections to planning raised by some people in business. Others question whether the end result — the plan — is worth the effort involved in collecting, organizing, and assessing the information needed for planning. For small businesses, perhaps the strongest argument for planning comes from Dun and Bradstreet's "Business Failure Record." One of the most frequently cited causes of business failure is the lack of financial planning and control. The studies are not referring to complex or sophisticated planning techniques. A large number of firms fail simply because managers don't set goals or track business performance in a clear, understandable manner, which would allow them to anticipate problems and avoid them.

There is also a strong correlation between goal setting and success. Goals give a focus to efforts; actions are undertaken or resources are allocated because a certain result is desired. Less energy and money are wasted if goals are set. Reasonable goals also imply that managers have thought through a situation so that they can take advantage of opportunities and avoid or minimize unprofitable risks. So, you can plan to avoid failure and you can plan to achieve success. One manager started with the former, planning only to solve problems like cash crises, and ended up with the latter, planning to achieve profits and firm growth. The improvement, he found, was not only in profits but also in peace of mind. Having information about the expected future, in the form of a plan, he felt better prepared to face it. Once you make the decision to plan, the next issue to face is *what* you should plan.

What to plan

Planning takes many forms. There are plans for products, personnel, equipment, training, market development, promotion, pensions, taxes, production, distribution, and finances. All of these plans can help a business become a successful enterprise. The type and amount of planning that a firm undertakes and needs is largely a function of its size, industry characteristics, and management's attitude toward planning. In most large corporations, planning is specialized, formal, and highly structured. In many small and medium-sized businesses, planning is less formal, and often directly involves a larger proportion of the organization's staff. All firms need to plan; but what they plan, and the detail involved, varies.

In any business, the results of all actions and plans eventually show up on three financial "scorecards": the cash flow statement, income statement, and balance sheet. These statements can explain what happened in the past. But they can also be used to plan for the future when you make a *forecast*. Forecasting by using these tools can help a manager chart the future direction of a company. Another reason for preparing a financial forecast is that should you need to apply for a loan, a bank manager or other lender will want to see evidence of your financial planning. A cash budget and financial statements show that you have thought through your future needs.

In this book, we'll examine these tools in detail and explain how you can use them with your computer to forecast and budget for your business. Together, they can help you to keep last-minute decisions and surprises to a minimum, to set standards of performance for various activities of your business, to anticipate financial needs, and to assess the effects of policy changes. They can help you answer questions such as:

- Can I pay my bills?

- Will I need additional money and when will I need it?

- What profits do I expect, and are they enough to stay in business?

- Am I financially strong enough to expand operations?

- What will be the short- and long-term effects of growth?

- Can action be taken to make more cash available?

- If so, what will yield the most cash in the shortest amount of time with the least adverse impact?

We'll show you how to answer these questions and others by using the personal computer with the tools of the cash budget and a projected income statement and balance sheet.

Our step-by-step approach

Our approach to planning and budgeting is, first of all, computer-based. We provide a sample cash budget and pro forma (projected) income statement and balance sheet that are linked by formulas to create a dynamic, working model. You can enter a change in one line item of the model (which we call the example) and immediately track the effect of this change on other related line items. The computer does a lot of the necessary calculations for you. You've undoubtedly made plans or budgets before by some other method, such as using a pencil and paper. Our purpose is to show you how to do the same thing by computer.

Specifically, we'll show you how to enter the three parts of the example on your computer. The entering of each part is broken down into specific steps with accompanying detailed, how-to instructions. All line items that make up the budget or statements are defined, and guidelines on how to forecast or estimate these line items are given. You don't need extensive computer experience to follow the steps in entering the example. We do assume that you have gone through the owner's manual for your computer model and the VisiCalc version you plan to use. All you need is a basic familiarity with the computer and the VisiCalc program; we provide additional instructions on the essential computer procedures and when to use them. By the end of this book, you'll know how to:

- Set up a model cash budget and pro forma income statement and balance sheet on the computer.

- Adapt or customize the models to your business.

- Use your models as working tools to explore changes and update your plans or budget.

- Forecast or estimate individual line items (using basic principles).

- Continue working with the computer to further refine your plans or budgets.

- Assess how changes in sales and expenses, and the timing of these changes, affect cash flow, profits, and financial position.

To meet these objectives, you need to go through the entire book in sequence. Here is a brief overview of what you'll be doing as you follow the step-by-step instructions in each chapter.

Courtesy of IBM Corporation

The computer system you need *Chapter 2 describes the IBM PC, the VisiCalc program, and the diskettes that you use with this book.*

```
Part 1: Cash budget
```

Item:	What if column	1 1984	2 1984	3 1984	4 1984	5 1984	6 1984	7 1984	8 1984	9 1984	10 1984	11 1984	12 1984
Seasonal pattern*	100	8	8	8	8	8	8	8	8	8	8	8	8
Net sales; monthly*	450000	37500	37500	37500	37500	37500	37500	37500	37500	37500	37500	37500	37500
Cash receipts:													
% collected within 30 days*	60	22500	22500	22500	22500	22500	22500	22500	22500	22500	22500	22500	22500
% collected within 60 days*	20	7500	7500	7500	7500	7500	7500	7500	7500	7500	7500	7500	7500
% collected within 90 days*	20	7500	7500	7500	7500	7500	7500	7500	7500	7500	7500	7500	7500
Other cash receipts*	0	($)	($)	($)	($)	($)	($)	($)	($)	($)	($)	($)	($)
Total cash receipts		37500	37500	37500	37500	37500	37500	37500	37500	37500	37500	37500	37500
Inventory purchases*	60	22500	22500	22500	22500	22500	22500	22500	22500	22500	22500	22500	22500
Gen. & admin.*	20	7500	7500	7500	7500	7500	7500	7500	7500	7500	7500	7500	7500
Selling expenses*	10	3750	3750	3750	3750	3750	3750	3750	3750	3750	3750	3750	3750
Interest expense*	15	500	500	500	500	500	500	500	500	500	500	500	500
Other expense*	0	($)	($)	($)	($)	($)	($)	($)	($)	($)	($)	($)	($)
Taxes*	40	2400			2400			2400			2400		
Total cash disbursements		36650	34250	34250	36650	34250	34250	36650	34250	34250	36650	34250	34250
Net cash flow		850	3250	3250	850	3250	3250	850	3250	3250	850	3250	3250
Opening cash balance		20000	20850	24100	27350	28200	31450	34700	35550	38800	42050	42900	46150
Loans required	0	0	0	0	0	0	0	0	0	0	0	0	0
Ending cash balance*	20000	20850	24100	27350	28200	31450	34700	35550	38800	42050	42900	46150	49400

Building a cash budget You'll begin the business section of this book in Chapter 3, by building a sample cash budget on your computer. As you proceed through the steps, all line items or terms are explained, as well as some principles to use in estimating these items.

A budget is a plan in numbers. A cash budget (or cash flow projection) forecasts cash surplus or deficit for a future period. It covers the expected cash inflows, cash outflows, and cash position of the company. Cash position includes the opening and ending cash balance and the financing required during the period of time covered by the budget.

By figuring out your cash needs and cash resources ahead of time, you put yourself in a better position to:

- Make the most efficient use of cash.
- Finance your seasonal business needs.
- Develop a sound borrowing program.
- Develop a workable program of debt repayment.
- Provide funds for expansion.
- Plan for the investment of surplus cash.

```
Part 2: Pro forma income statement
```

		1	2	3	4	5	6	7	8	9	10	11	12
Net sales	450000	37500	37500	37500	37500	37500	37500	37500	37500	37500	37500	37500	37500
Cost of goods sold	270000	22500	22500	22500	22500	22500	22500	22500	22500	22500	22500	22500	22500
Gross profit	180000	15000	15000	15000	15000	15000	15000	15000	15000	15000	15000	15000	15000
General & administrative	90000	7500	7500	7500	7500	7500	7500	7500	7500	7500	7500	7500	7500
Selling expenses	45000	3750	3750	3750	3750	3750	3750	3750	3750	3750	3750	3750	3750
Depreciation	15000	1250	1250	1250	1250	1250	1250	1250	1250	1250	1250	1250	1250
Operating income	30000	2500	2500	2500	2500	2500	2500	2500	2500	2500	2500	2500	2500
Interest expense	6000	500	500	500	500	500	500	500	500	500	500	500	500
Other income/expense*	0	($)	($)	($)	($)	($)	($)	($)	($)	($)	($)	($)	($)
Income before taxes	24000	2000	2000	2000	2000	2000	2000	2000	2000	2000	2000	2000	2000
Taxes	9600	800	800	800	800	800	800	800	800	800	800	800	800
Net income	14400	1200	1200	1200	1200	1200	1200	1200	1200	1200	1200	1200	1200

Building a pro forma income statement In Chapter 4, you'll be shown how to build a projected twelve-month income statement, step by step, on your computer. You will also see how it relates to the cash budget entered in the previous chapter. This statement forecasts the expected performance, as measured in profits, of your company over an annual period.

```
Part 3: Pro forma balance sheet
==================================================================================================================
Assets:
------------------------------------------------------------------------------------------------------------------
<Current assets>
Cash                       20000   20850   24100   27350   28200   31450   34700   35550   38800   42050   42900   46150   49400
Accounts receivable        60000   60000   60000   60000   60000   60000   60000   60000   60000   60000   60000   60000   60000
Inventory                  30000   30000   30000   30000   30000   30000   30000   30000   30000   30000   30000   30000   30000
Prepaid expenses            2000    2000    2000    2000    2000    2000    2000    2000    2000    2000    2000    2000    2000
------------------------------------------------------------------------------------------------------------------
Total current assets      112000  112850  116100  119350  120200  123450  126700  127550  130800  134050  134900  138150  141400

<Fixed assets>
Buildings & equipment      50000   50000   50000   50000   50000   50000   50000   50000   50000   50000   50000   50000   50000
Less accum.depreciation    30000   31250   32500   33750   35000   36250   37500   38750   40000   41250   42500   43750   45000
Land                       10000   10000   10000   10000   10000   10000   10000   10000   10000   10000   10000   10000   10000
------------------------------------------------------------------------------------------------------------------
Net fixed assets           30000   28750   27500   26250   25000   23750   22500   21250   20000   18750   17500   16250   15000

Total assets              142000  141600  143600  145600  145200  147200  149200  148800  150800  152800  152400  154400  156400
==================================================================================================================
Liabilities:
------------------------------------------------------------------------------------------------------------------
<Current liabilities>
Accounts payable           22500   22500   22500   22500   22500   22500   22500   22500   22500   22500   22500   22500   22500
Accrued wages & taxes       5500    3900    4700    5500    3900    4700    5500    3900    4700    5500    3900    4700    5500
Other current liabilities   4000    4000    4000    4000    4000    4000    4000    4000    4000    4000    4000    4000    4000
------------------------------------------------------------------------------------------------------------------
Total current liabilities  32000   30400   31200   32000   30400   31200   32000   30400   31200   32000   30400   31200   32000

Long term debt             40000   40000   40000   40000   40000   40000   40000   40000   40000   40000   40000   40000   40000

Total liabilities          72000   70400   71200   72000   70400   71200   72000   70400   71200   72000   70400   71200   72000

<Owner equity>
Common stock               50000   50000   50000   50000   50000   50000   50000   50000   50000   50000   50000   50000   50000
Retained earnings          20000   21200   22400   23600   24800   26000   27200   28400   29600   30800   32000   33200   34400
------------------------------------------------------------------------------------------------------------------
Total owner equity         70000   71200   72400   73600   74800   76000   77200   78400   79600   80800   82000   83200   84400

Total liab. & owner equity 142000  141600  143600  145600  145200  147200  149200  148800  150800  152800  152400  154400  156400
==================================================================================================================
```

▲
Building a pro forma balance sheet *The projected balance sheet, covered in Chapter 5, forecasts the expected financial condition of your company. It includes asset, liability, and equity sections, which we'll describe. You will see how it is structured and how the information it contains is derived from both the cash budget and income statement entered previously.*

▶
Exploring changes in plans and budgets *After you have built a sample cash budget and pro forma financial statements, in Chapter 6 you learn how to use them to explore different financial possibilities and decisions. This is done by entering "What If" questions on the computer. What if, for example, you expect sales to have a strong seasonal pattern? How will that affect your financing needs? The questions are translated into figures and entered into the What If column and/or row 6 on the example. You see the results instantly.*

These exercises are helpful both in developing plans and budgets and in using them to control operations. Even the most well-thought-out plans and budgets need to be tracked and updated. The computer makes that easier because it saves considerable calculation time. The parts of the example are linked together, so you can, for example, enter a change in the cash budget and see its effect on line items of the pro forma income statement and balance sheet. Exploring changes by computer is useful, easy, and fun.

Part 1: Cash budget

Item:	What if column	1 1984	2 1984	3 1984	4 1984	5 1984	6 1984	7 1984	8 1984	9 1984	10 1984	11 1984	12 1984
Seasonal pattern*	100	5	5	5	5	5	5	10	10	10	10	10	20
Net sales; monthly*	450000	22500	22500	22500	22500	22500	22500	45000	45000	45000	45000	45000	90000
Cash receipts:													
% collected within 30 days*	60	22500	13500	13500	13500	13500	13500	13500	27000	27000	27000	27000	27000
% collected within 60 days*	20	7500	7500	4500	4500	4500	4500	4500	4500	9000	9000	9000	9000
% collected within 90 days*	20	7500	7500	7500	4500	4500	4500	4500	4500	4500	9000	9000	9000
Other cash receipts*	0	($)	($)	($)	($)	($)	($)	($)	($)	($)	($)	($)	($)
Total cash receipts		37500	28500	25500	22500	22500	22500	22500	36000	40500	45000	45000	45000
Inventory purchases*	60	13500	13500	13500	13500	13500	27000	27000	27000	27000	27000	54000	13500
Gen.& admin.*	20	7500	7500	7500	7500	7500	7500	7500	7500	7500	7500	7500	7500
Selling expenses*	10	3750	3750	3750	3750	3750	3750	3750	3750	3750	3750	3750	3750
Interest expense*	15	500	500	500	500	500	500	500	500	500	500	709	709
Other expense*	0	($)	($)	($)	($)	($)	($)	($)	($)	($)	($)	($)	($)
Taxes*	40	2400			-4800			-4800			6000		
Total cash disbursements		27650	25250	25250	20450	25250	38750	33950	38750	38750	44750	65959	25459
Net cash flow		9850	3250	250	2050	-2750	-16250	-11450	-2750	1750	250	-20959	19541
Opening cash balance		20000	29850	33100	33350	35400	32650	16400	4950	2200	3950	4200	0
Loans required	16759	0	0	0	0	0	0	0	0	0	0	16759	0
Ending cash balance*	20000	29850	33100	33350	35400	32650	16400	4950	2200	3950	4200	0	19541

Part 2: Pro forma income statement

	What if column	1 1984	2 1984	3 1984	4 1984	5 1984	6 1984	7 1984	8 1984	9 1984	10 1984	11 1984	12 1984
Net sales	450000	22500	22500	22500	22500	22500	22500	45000	45000	45000	45000	45000	90000
Cost of goods sold	270000	13500	13500	13500	13500	13500	13500	27000	27000	27000	27000	27000	54000
Gross profit	180000	9000	9000	9000	9000	9000	9000	18000	18000	18000	18000	18000	36000
General & administrative	90000	7500	7500	7500	7500	7500	7500	7500	7500	7500	7500	7500	7500
Selling expenses	45000	3750	3750	3750	3750	3750	3750	3750	3750	3750	3750	3750	3750
Depreciation	15000	1250	1250	1250	1250	1250	1250	1250	1250	1250	1250	1250	1250
Operating income	30000	-3500	-3500	-3500	-3500	-3500	-3500	5500	5500	5500	5500	5500	23500
Interest expense	6419	500	500	500	500	500	500	500	500	500	500	709	709
Other income/expense*	0	($)	($)	($)	($)	($)	($)	($)	($)	($)	($)	($)	($)
Income before taxes	23581	-4000	-4000	-4000	-4000	-4000	-4000	5000	5000	5000	5000	4791	22791
Taxes	9432	-1600	-1600	-1600	-1600	-1600	-1600	2000	2000	2000	2000	1916	9116
Net income	14149	-2400	-2400	-2400	-2400	-2400	-2400	3000	3000	3000	3000	2874	13674

Part 3: Pro forma balance sheet

Assets:

	What if column	1 1984	2 1984	3 1984	4 1984	5 1984	6 1984	7 1984	8 1984	9 1984	10 1984	11 1984	12 1984
<Current assets>													
Cash	20000	29850	33100	33350	35400	32650	16400	4950	2200	3950	4200	0	19541
Accounts receivable	60000	45000	39000	36000	36000	36000	36000	58500	67500	72000	72000	72000	117000
Inventory	30000	30000	30000	30000	30000	43500	57000	57000	57000	57000	84000	70500	30000
Prepaid expenses	2000	2000	2000	2000	2000	2000	2000	2000	2000	2000	2000	2000	2000
Total current assets	112000	106850	104100	101350	103400	114150	111400	122450	128700	134950	162200	144500	168541
<Fixed assets>													
Buildings & equipment	50000	50000	50000	50000	50000	50000	50000	50000	50000	50000	50000	50000	50000
Less accum.depreciation	30000	31250	32500	33750	35000	36250	37500	38750	40000	41250	42500	43750	45000
Land	10000	10000	10000	10000	10000	10000	10000	10000	10000	10000	10000	10000	10000
Net fixed assets	30000	28750	27500	26250	25000	23750	22500	21250	20000	18750	17500	16250	15000
Total assets	142000	135600	131600	127600	128400	137900	133900	143700	148700	153700	179700	160750	183541

Liabilities:

	What if column	1 1984	2 1984	3 1984	4 1984	5 1984	6 1984	7 1984	8 1984	9 1984	10 1984	11 1984	12 1984
<Current liabilities>													
Accounts payable	22500	22500	22500	22500	22500	36000	36000	36000	36000	36000	63000	22500	22500
Accrued wages & taxes	5500	1500	-100	-1700	1500	-100	-1700	5100	7100	9100	5100	7016	16132
Other current liabilities	4000	4000	4000	4000	4000	4000	4000	4000	4000	4000	4000	20759	20759
Total current liabilities	32000	28000	26400	24800	28000	39900	38300	45100	47100	49100	72100	50276	59392
Long term debt	40000	40000	40000	40000	40000	40000	40000	40000	40000	40000	40000	40000	40000
Total liabilities	72000	68000	66400	64800	68000	79900	78300	85100	87100	89100	112100	90276	99392
<Owner equity>													
Common stock	50000	50000	50000	50000	50000	50000	50000	50000	50000	50000	50000	50000	50000
Retained earnings	20000	17600	15200	12800	10400	8000	5600	8600	11600	14600	17600	20474	34149
Total owner equity	70000	67600	65200	62800	60400	58000	55600	58600	61600	64600	67600	70474	84149
Total liab. & owner equity	142000	135600	131600	127600	128400	137900	133900	143700	148700	153700	179700	160750	183541

```
Templa:Forecasting unit sales, sales revenue, and cost of goods
=========================================================================================================
Detail of line item:  Total    1     2     3     4     5     6     7     8     9     10    11    12
Unit sales forecast    units  1984  1984  1984  1984  1984  1984  1984  1984  1984  1984  1984  1984

Product number 1       1200    96    96    96   120   120   120   120   120   120    72    48    72
Product number 2       1200    24    24    24    48    48    48    60    96   180   216   216   216
Product number 3        500  (#  ) (#  )  250   250  (#  ) (#  ) (#  ) (#  ) (#  ) (#  ) (#  ) (#  )
Product number 4       2000  (#  ) (#  ) (#  ) (#  ) (#  ) (#  ) (#  ) (#  ) (#  ) (#  ) (#  )  2000
Product number 5       4000   333   333   333   333   333   333   333   333   333   333   333   333
Product number 6        100     8     8     8     8     8     8     8     8     8     8     8     8
Product number 7          0  (#  ) (#  ) (#  ) (#  ) (#  ) (#  ) (#  ) (#  ) (#  ) (#  ) (#  ) (#  )
Product number 8          0  (#  ) (#  ) (#  ) (#  ) (#  ) (#  ) (#  ) (#  ) (#  ) (#  ) (#  ) (#  )
Product number 9          0  (#  ) (#  ) (#  ) (#  ) (#  ) (#  ) (#  ) (#  ) (#  ) (#  ) (#  ) (#  )
Product number 10         0  (#  ) (#  ) (#  ) (#  ) (#  ) (#  ) (#  ) (#  ) (#  ) (#  ) (#  ) (#  )
Product number 11         0  (#  ) (#  ) (#  ) (#  ) (#  ) (#  ) (#  ) (#  ) (#  ) (#  ) (#  ) (#  )

Total unit sales       9000   462   462   712   760   510   510   522   558   642   630   606  2630
=========================================================================================================


=========================================================================================================
Detail of line item:  Total    1     2     3     4     5     6     7     8     9     10    11    12    Net   Dis-   List
Sales revenue forecast sales  1984  1984  1984  1984  1984  1984  1984  1984  1984  1984  1984  1984  price count  price

Product number 1       4800   384   384   384   480   480   480   480   480   480   288   192   288  4.00 (   %)  4.00
Product number 2       7200   144   144   144   288   288   288   360   576  1080  1296  1296  1296  6.00 (   %)  6.00
Product number 3       1200     0     0   600   600     0     0     0     0     0     0     0     0  2.40    20   3.00
Product number 4       9000     0     0     0     0     0     0     0     0     0     0     0  9000  4.50 (   %)  4.50
Product number 5      32700  2725  2725  2725  2725  2725  2725  2725  2725  2725  2725  2725  2725  8.18    50  16.35
Product number 6        735    61    61    61    61    61    61    61    61    61    61    61    61  7.35 (   %)  7.35
Product number 7          0     0     0     0     0     0     0     0     0     0     0     0     0  9.25 (   %)  9.25
Product number 8          0     0     0     0     0     0     0     0     0     0     0     0     0  0.00 (   %) ($  )
Product number 9          0     0     0     0     0     0     0     0     0     0     0     0     0  0.00 (   %) ($  )
Product number 10         0     0     0     0     0     0     0     0     0     0     0     0     0  0.00 (   %) ($  )
Product number 11         0     0     0     0     0     0     0     0     0     0     0     0     0  0.00 (   %) ($  )

Total sales revenue   55635  3314  3314  3914  4154  3554  3554  3626  3842  4346  4370  4274 13370  6.18
=========================================================================================================
```

Forecasting sales and expenses *How to actually forecast
sales and expenses is covered in detail in Chapter 7. This
information supplements that in previous chapters, since
realistically projecting sales and expenses affects the usefulness of the projected budgets and statements. Techniques and principles are described, and a master general
forecasting template that can be used to detail line items
is included. This template will also help you to assemble
data for your company, so that our example can be
adapted for use in your business planning.*

Introduction

Computers don't decide; managers decide. Computers (so far) don't have feelings or form opinions; people do. But computers are such effective decision support tools because of their remarkable ability to process information for managers. With speed and accuracy, computers can store, sort, summarize, manipulate, and print out information.

Because a computer can handle information in so many ways, it is a general-purpose machine. That distinguishes a computer from a single-purpose machine, such as a typewriter. The computer as a data processor has many capabilities, and you determine its specific function by the software you use.

Software is the set of directions called a *program* that tells a computer what to do through specially coded instructions. If you want a computer to perform business functions, you can use prepackaged business software, such as the VisiCalc program which is used with this book. That software converts a personal computer into a "business computer," quickly and completely. And you don't have to know much about computers, or anything about programming languages, to use it effectively.

But software is only part of the complete computer system you will need.

A system is composed of interacting or interdependent parts that work together to form a whole, such as a stereo system or an accounting system. In a computer system, it is important that each part work both on its own *and* in conjunction with other parts. Otherwise, the system is nonoperational. With the rapid growth of computer technology, a variety of competing and sometimes incompatible products are on the market. They don't all work together and even when they should, there are few people who can explain how to make them do so. This situation is called the "compatibility problem."

If you have a computer system, you may have already encountered the compatibility problem. For instance, a computer company representative can tell you everything you want to know about the computer; the software company spokesman can explain everything about the software; and a person at the printer company can give advice about its printer. But there are only a few people who can tell you how the software running on your computer works with your printer. Obviously, you can't resolve a compatibility problem on your own. Your only option is to avoid the problem.

The best way to do that is to select and use brand products with proven customer support. Unless you are an experimenter or a hobbyist with a great deal of time to spare, always follow the crowd in choosing equipment and software. Let others do your testing, and only buy products that have passed a threshold of consumer acceptance. Also, work with a reliable dealer. Though the computer field is growing too rapidly for anyone to comprehend it completely, a knowledgeable dealer is a useful guide.

The computer system you need for using this book is composed of reliable products that have passed the consumer test and that work together. We've selected the essentials, the bare minimum you need to form a functioning system. We've also suggested some additional accessories that expand the capabilities of a system, but they are optional. For further advice on accessories, consult your dealer.

There are six essential parts to the computer system you need (see diagram next page). Each part is discussed briefly here, and the major ones are covered in more detail later in this chapter.

1 An IBM PC: You will need an IBM PC with a minimum of 64K of memory to run the VisiCalc program, and a minimum of 128K to run the VisiCalc Advanced Version program. In either case there will be sufficient memory to enter the example described in Chapters 3, 4, and 5, and the templates described in Chapter 7. If you expand the templates described in Chapter 7 to use in your own business, you may find that you need more memory.

2 VisiCalc or VisiCalc Advanced Version program: The VisiCalc program is business software that comes in the form of a program diskette (two diskettes for the Advanced Version) with an accompanying instruction manual. It is available for all IBM PC's that have at least 64K. But, to run the Advanced Version, the IBM PC must have a memory capacity of 128K. If your IBM PC has less memory than you need, your dealer can upgrade it to the necessary 128K.

3 Floppy disks, disk drive, and disk operating system: A floppy disk (diskette) is a round, flat, rotating sheet of plastic coated with a magnetic surface that records and stores information. You need two blank 5 1/4-inch diskettes, one for saving the example to be entered in Chapters 3, 4, and 5, and another to use for a backup copy of the information.

You also need at least one disk drive. This drive is operated by the computer, and allows the computer to record or pick up information from the disk, or diskette. The diskette spins in the disk drive while a head on the disk drive records and reads bits of information on the disk surface.

To make backup copies, format disks, print catalogs of files, and for other "housekeeping" chores you need a

The parts of the computer system you need

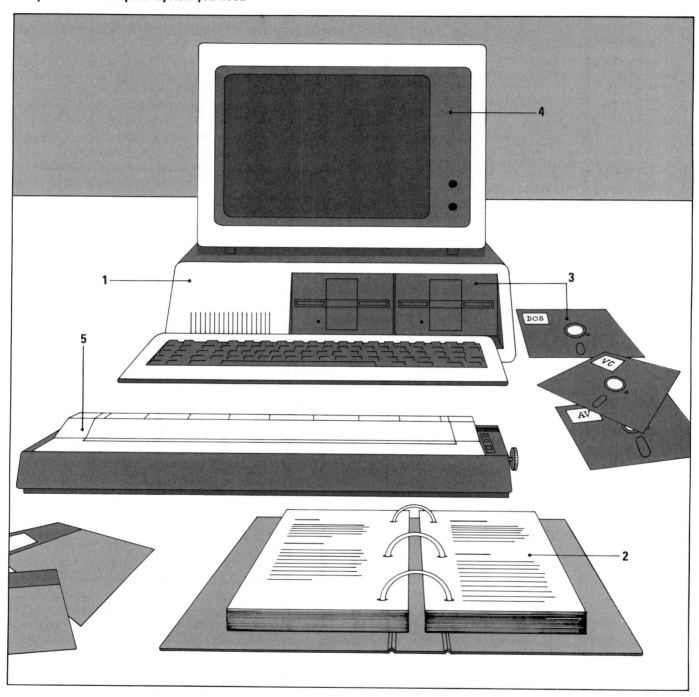

disk operating system, software that comes with the computer in a diskette, or floppy, form. When loaded into the computer's memory, a disk operating system tells the disk drive what to do and, in general, manages the computer's memory and files.

4 Monitor: A monitor displays information stored in the computer's memory. You can choose among different styles. For the purposes of this book, a black-and-white monitor is sufficient. However, the IBM PC green-and-white monitor is easier on the eyes and not much more expensive. Color monitors are expensive, and some models give poor resolution when used for financial models with many numbers. Television sets have even worse resolution, and although they can be used eye strain may result if much time is spent using one.

5 Printer: A printer is a typewriter-like machine that prints out reports just as they appear on the VisiCalc screen display. Although a printer isn't absolutely necessary, it is extremely helpful for sharing information with others or troubleshooting potential problems. It can print out an entire VisiCalc worksheet, while the screen may display only a part of the worksheet at any one time.

Printers come in two standard forms: 80 or 132 characters wide. The 80-character model uses standard 8-1/2-inch-wide paper. The 132-character model is more popular for business purposes and is sometimes called the standard business printer. You can use either an 80- or 132-character printer with this book. Many high-quality printers are available at a cost of a few hundred to a few thousand dollars. We suggest that you discuss these options with a dealer and actually take your computer in to have the dealer install the printer to make sure it does work with your system.

6 Reference books: Although books aren't a part of a computer system per se, they are so helpful in setting up d operating a system that we have included them here. In fact, we assume that you have already gone through the computer user's guide and VisiCalc manual that go with your IBM PC and the VisiCalc version you plan to use (or are using). It is impossible to duplicate in this book all the instructional material found in these manuals. However, throughout this book, we have presented those procedures that you really need to know and use as you progress through the steps.

A note on setting up the system

You may already have your computer system set up and running, but if you don't, we advise that you follow this rule: Work with a reliable dealer. You already know, perhaps from a frustrating or expensive mistake, that the parts of your system must be compatible. We advise that you have a dealer assemble the system for you and show you how to operate it. The same advice applies to optional accessories. You may have to pay a little more up front for this type of service, but it is well worth the extra cost. Your time is worth money and a dealer can help assure that it isn't wasted back in your office as you try to figure out how the parts are supposed to fit together.

A special Business User's Guide diskette to accompany **Planning and Budgeting** is available from the publishers. The diskette is not essential but it will save you much time, since it contains the cash budget, pro forma income statement, and pro forma balance sheet, as well as a general forecasting template which you can adapt for use with the cash budget and pro formas. If you did not purchase the Disk Edition of this book, and you want to order the diskette, use the Order Form on page 138.

The IBM Personal Computer

The IBM Personal Computers, the IBM PC and IBM XT, are ideal for use in a business environment. With their 16-bit microprocessor, they are extremely fast and capable of being expanded to give you access to a large amount of internal memory.

When purchasing your first computer, or upgrading your current computer, you should seriously consider certain key features before making your choice. The most important ones are features that affect memory and storage, features that affect data input, and features that affect the screen display.

Memory and storage

Memory capacity (called RAM for *Random Access Memory* and measured in K's for *Kilobytes*) determines how much data can be stored in the computer. The IBM PC comes with a minimum of 64K of memory but can easily be expanded up to 512K. When the computer is used with the VisiCalc program, a minimum of 64K is required. When used with the VisiCalc Advanced Version program a minimum of 128K is needed. The amount of memory your computer has determines how large a worksheet you can work on. The VisiCalc program is stored in memory along with any text you enter. For instance, if your IBM PC has 64K of memory and you load the VisiCalc program, the program will take up 42K leaving you with 22K of memory to work with. All memory above 64K is available for the worksheet. As you enter a worksheet, more and more memory is used. The Memory indicator in the upper right-hand corner of the screen display gives you a running count of the unused memory remaining. When you run out of internal memory (i.e., RAM), an **M** will flash in the memory indicator.

Disk storage capacity, like the computer's internal memory, is measured in Kilobytes (thousands of characters) or Megabytes (millions of characters). The larger the number of kilobytes or megabytes available, the more files can be stored on a disk. Having a large amount of disk storage capacity is helpful for a number of reasons: it reduces the number of disks and disk storage space you need; it reduces problems about keeping track of disks; and it reduces the chances of encountering **Disk Full** messages when you try to save a worksheet (see TIPS on "How to overcome a Disk Full message" on page 49).

The IBM system unit has room for up to two disk drives, either floppy disk or hard disk drives. You can choose between floppy disk drives that use single-sided disks capable of storing 160K of worksheet (equivalent to about 80 double-spaced, typewritten pages), or double-sided disks capable of storing 320K (about 160 typewritten pages). The XT model will store almost 11 megabytes (about 5500 double-spaced, typewritten pages).

The XT expansion unit that can be added to the IBM PC will store the same amount of data.

Operating systems generally aren't important to the user since the system itself is relatively invisible. They mostly affect what software you can run on your IBM PC and with what other computers you can interchange disks. The IBM personal computer DOS system is the operating system most IBM PC buyers have and it is also the one used to run the VisiCalc program. For those who want access to other programs, CP/M-86 and UCSD-p-System operating systems are also available.

Data input

This group of features includes any functions that make it easier, or faster, to enter data into the computer.

Function keys on the IBM PC can be "programmed" to perform functions that you find repetitive. When programmed, they will store and execute a series of keystrokes when pressed (in conjunction with the control key). This reduces the number of keystrokes you have to enter to execute frequently used commands, such as saving files, entering ruled lines, and replicating formulas.

Arrow keys are used to move the cursor around on the screen. The IBM PC has four arrow keys which move the cursor up, down, left, or right.

The HOME key moves you instantly to the top left corner of the worksheet.

The monochrome display

This standard IBM PC display has very sharp resolution and a nonglare surface for easy viewing.

The number of columns displayed on the screen at one time determines how much of the VisiCalc screen display you can see without having to scroll the screen. The IBM PC displays 80 characters across by 25 lines down.

Upper and lower case letters give you a choice when entering labels.

Graphics cannot be displayed on the IBM PC monochrome display. However, a separate adapter can be added to connect the computer to a monitor capable of displaying graphics.

VisiCalc: Your electronic worksheet

The VisiCalc program, an electronic worksheet, takes the work out of working with numbers. Using its automatic calculation feature, you can instantly see the results of changing a number. You don't have to sit down with pen and paper or a calculator to figure out possible results; the VisiCalc program does it for you. That shortens the time between "cause" and "effect": you can analyze the financial effect of decisions before you make them, on your electronic worksheet. Put the VisiCalc program to work for you and its capabilities expand your capabilities: you can work faster, more efficiently, more effectively.

The VisiCalc program is widely acknowledged to be the software that made the personal computer a business tool. It is designed to perform a variety of business functions for business people, most of whom don't have the time, desire, or skill to write their own computer programs. And because the VisiCalc software exists, they don't have to. In this book, you'll be using the VisiCalc program to build financial statements, calculate ratios, and explore changes on the statements. Later, you'll be

shown how to adapt or customize your own plans and budgets using the VisiCalc program.

You can use either the VisiCalc or the VisiCalc Advanced Version program with this book, which includes instructions for both. Instructions for the regular version are given first, and if different instructions are needed for the Advanced Version, these are indicated by the symbol $\boxed{\text{AV}}$. The Advanced Version has features that speed data entry, improve data output, and help protect your work. Throughout the book, the right time to use those features is pointed out, and you are shown how to use them.

Both versions of the VisiCalc program can store and manipulate a lot of information in their 63 columns and 254 rows. The number of rows and columns you can actually use depends upon the amount of memory your computer has. In this book, you'll use up to 16 columns and 93 rows for the cash budget and pro formas.

As you work at the computer, a VisiCalc screen like the one illustrated below will appear on the computer monitor.

The VisiCalc screen display

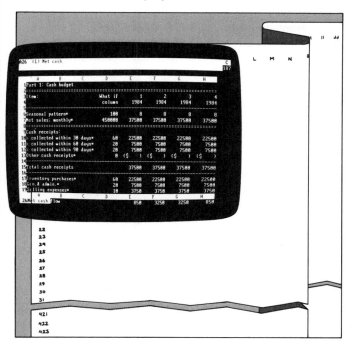

The screen provides a "window" on your worksheet by constantly displaying the information you have entered on the computer. However, the screen only displays part of your electronic worksheet at a time. To reveal the rest of the worksheet, you have to "scroll" it by using the arrow keys $\rightarrow$ or the Go To command (>).

Photos of VisiCalc screens or printouts throughout the book show you what your worksheet should look like at each step. Screen photos and printouts provide constant visual checks that help you see whether you are correctly entering the data. All screen photos show the VisiCalc screen. The screen display for the Advanced Version will look the same except column A will be wider (to speed the process of entering labels) and the dollar signs ($), commas separating thousands, negative values in parentheses, and percent signs (%) can be integrated (to make the reading of values easier).

If you have a printer, you can get a copy of your worksheet at any point. See your VisiCalc manual for detailed instructions on how to print a worksheet.

Let's now examine more closely the VisiCalc screen display and the worksheets you will be building.

The VisiCalc screen display in detail

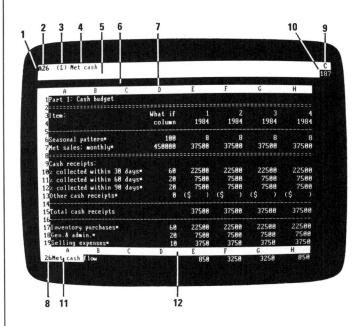

The VisiCalc screen display that appears when you load the program is packed with information. Here is a brief review of what appears on the screen and an explanation of how this information is used throughout this book.

1 Cell contents line: This line shows the contents of the cell in which the cursor is positioned. If you want to check formulas that don't normally appear on the screen display (only their calculated value does), just move the cursor to the cell in question and look at the cell contents line where the formula will appear.

2 Cell coordinate: A cell is located at the intersection of a row and column. When the cursor is placed in a cell, the coordinates of that cell will appear on the cell contents line with the column letter followed by the row number.

3 Entry type: This indicates the type of entry in the cell in which the cursor is positioned. There are three types of entries: labels (indicated by (L)), values and formulas (indicated by (V)), and repeating labels (indicated by /-).

4 Cell contents: This part of the cell contents line displays the actual contents of the cell in which the cursor is placed. There will be times when you see more on this line than you will see in the cell itself (see page 30).

5 Prompt line: This line is used by the VisiCalc program to "prompt" you to make certain choices. You will see choices presented here whenever using VisiCalc commands, such as those used when saving, loading, or replicating.

6 Edit line: Most VisiCalc commands are typed on the keyboard and then entered by pressing the enter key. Until those commands are entered with the enter key, they can be seen on this line. If you use the Edit command (/**E**) to revise a label or formula, the contents of the cell in which the cursor was positioned at the time the edit command was entered will also appear on this line.

7 Column letters: These letters indicate the columns into which the VisiCalc program divides the worksheet. They are always given first when identifying the position of a cell's coordinate, for instance, D7.

8 Row numbers: Numbers identify the rows into which the VisiCalc program divides the worksheet.

9 Recalculation order indicator: This letter indicates if the worksheet will calculate by columns (C) or by rows (R). The worksheet is always recalculated from the upper left-hand corner down, but if recalculation is by rows it will calculate all of the formulas on row 1 then move to row 2. If it is set to calculate by columns it will first calculate all formulas in column A from the top down, then calculate column B. The example and templates in this book calculate correctly when set to either recalculation order.

10 Memory indicator: This acts like the fuel gauge in an automobile, except that it tells you how much memory is available to work with. As you load the VisiCalc program you can watch the number get smaller as the program loads. As you begin building a worksheet it will continue to get smaller and smaller. If you approach the limits of memory, it will first read 0; then, a flashing M indicates you have no memory left.

11 Cursor: This is moved around the worksheet using the arrow keys or the Go To command. You can make entries only in the cell in which the cursor is placed. When using the Replicate, DIF,™ and Print commands, you can also "point" with the cursor to indicate the top left and lower right cells in the range desired.

12 Window: When the worksheet is larger than the display screen you can see different sections at the same time by using windows in the display. Windows can be vertical or horizontal and one side can be used to display one section of the worksheet while the other side displays an entirely different section.

The VisiCalc worksheet

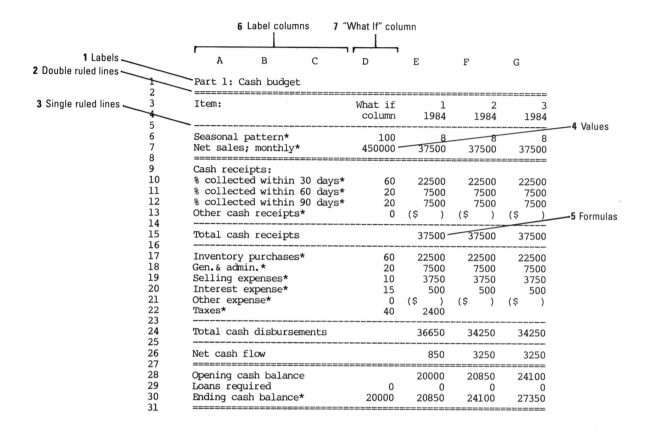

Your worksheet will build as you progress through Chapters 3, 4, and 5. As you enter the example, you will encounter expressions that are explained here.

1 Labels: Labels identify the worksheet and individual parts of it.

2 Double ruled lines: These divide worksheets into major sections to make them easier to read. The lines are made by using the equal (=) key.

3 Single ruled lines: These also separate major sections of the worksheet. They are entered using the minus (−) key.

4 Values: Values are numbers entered either directly from the keyboard, e.g., 1000, or by entering a formula, e.g., 10*100.

5 Formulas: Formulas can either be self-contained, e.g., 10*100, or used to manipulate the contents of other cells, e.g., 10*D9.

6 Label columns: These are the first three columns; they identify the contents of rows on the worksheet.

7 "What If" column (and row 6): These are used to enter changed data as the worksheet is explored by asking "What If" questions. Whenever a change is made, the entire worksheet will automatically recalculate every value so that you immediately see the results of your change.

The VisiCalc Advanced Version worksheet

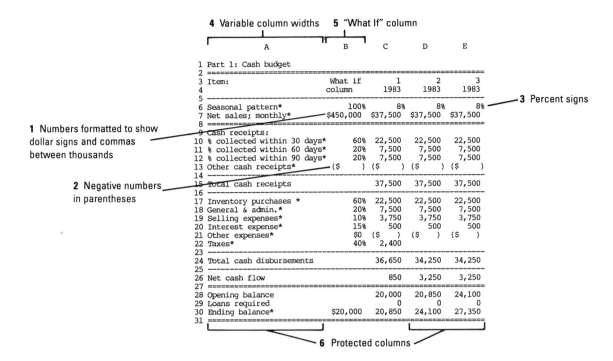

The anatomy of an Advanced Version worksheet is different from the regular VisiCalc worksheet. For instance, since the Advanced Version allows you to change column widths, we have set column A wider than other columns throughout this book. Since columns A through C for VisiCalc users are just column A for Advanced Version users, column letters will be different for the two versions. Therefore, in the instructions given throughout this book, the VisiCalc column is given first and the corresponding VisiCalc Advanced Version column is included in parentheses — for example, D(B). Also, when you use the optional features of the Advanced Version, they change the look of the worksheet. The diagram above illustrates how the Advanced Version worksheet will look if you use the optional features suggested in this book.

1 Numbers formatted to show dollar signs and commas between thousands: You can use this feature to label some or all values on the worksheet with a $ sign. Commas can make large numbers easier to read. With this feature, you can have "one million dollars" presented as $1,000,000 (also using the floating $ feature) instead of 1000000.

2 Negative numbers in parentheses: This is another cosmetic feature. It allows you to show a negative value, such as −1,000, in parentheses so that it stands out more: (1,000).

3 Percent signs: This option allows you to label some or all values with a % sign. It also automatically multiplies the result by 100 to display the percent as a whole number. When a cell is formatted using this feature, the percentage is entered by typing it as a decimal (.2), but it is displayed as a whole number (20) followed by a percent sign.

4 Variable column widths: This feature allows you to choose the width of each column individually. Therefore, you can select narrow columns for small numbers or percentages and wider columns for larger labels.

5 "What If" column: This column works the same as the "What If" column described earlier. The only difference in the Advanced Version is that they fall in column B rather than column D. This is because the first three columns in the regular version have been set so that they are only one column for Advanced Version.

6 Protected columns: This valuable feature acts like a lock on a cell (data entry space). It prevents new data from being entered into a cell that already contains data. Thus it helps protect against accidental erasures of information. It is recommended that you use this feature to protect those parts of the worksheet where you won't want to enter data. Instructions on how to do so are given in each chapter where worksheets are entered.

How your example will work

The worksheet you will build in Chapters 3, 4, and 5 contains a cash budget, pro forma income statement, and pro forma balance sheet. These three statements are linked by the formulas you enter as the example is built. A change in any of the major items on the cash budget is automatically and instantly reflected by changes on the pro forma income statement and balance sheet. This instant recalculation allows you to see immediately the effect of decisions you might make on your business. The example is an excellent learning tool, since you will be guided through a series of "What If" questions; you can instantly see the overall impact of decisions you might make and how to evaluate these results. Here is how the completed example will work:

1 You begin by entering a change in one or more cells in the What If column of the example, or in the row reflecting seasonal sales patterns. In addition to changing seasonal sales patterns, you can also change total sales, collection patterns, cost of inventory, or operating expenses.

Typical questions you could ask include:

- What if sales patterns change?
- What if sales are above or below budget?
- What if collections slow down or speed up?
- What if operating expenses increase or decrease?

2 The effects of any change you make — such as on monthly net cash flow, loans required, or ending monthly cash balances — will be shown throughout the cash budget. You can ask questions like the preceding and see how changes affect the cash you have on hand and how much you would need to borrow from the bank.

3 Changes entered in step 1 above are also instantly reflected in the pro forma income statement. You will see the effect of changes on your cash position and profitability.

4 The pro forma balance sheet also recalculates automatically when changes are entered on the cash budget. You can see the effect of changes on assets, liabilities, and retained earnings of the firm.

Part 1: Cash budget

Item:	What if column	1 1984	2 1984	3 1984	19
Seasonal pattern*	100	8	8	8	
Net sales; monthly*	450000	37500	37500	37500	3750
Cash receipts:					
% collected within 30 days*	60	22500	22500	22500	225
% collected within 60 days*	20	7500	7500	7500	750
% collected within 90 days*	20	7500	7500	7500	750
Other cash receipts*	0	($)	($)	($)	($
Total cash receipts		37500	37500	37500	375
Inventory purchases*	60	22500	22500	22500	225
Gen. & admin.*	20	7500	7500	7500	750
Selling expenses*	10	3750	3750	3750	37
Interest expense*	15	500	500	500	5
Other expense*	0	($)	($)	($)	($
Taxes*	40	2400			24
Total cash disbursements		36650	34250	34250	366
Net cash flow		850	3250	3250	8
Opening cash balance		20000	20850	24100	2735
Loans required	0	0	0	0	
Ending cash balance*	20000	20850	24100	27350	2820

Part 2: Pro forma income statement

Net sales	450000	37500	37500	37500	3750
Cost of goods sold	270000	22500	22500	22500	225
Gross profit	180000	15000	15000	15000	1500
General & administrative	90000	7500	7500	7500	750
Selling expenses	45000	3750	3750	3750	37
Depreciation	15000	1250	1250	1250	125
Operating income	30000	2500	2500	2500	250
Interest expense	6000	500	500	500	5
Other income/expense*	0	($)	($)	($)	($
Income before taxes	24000	2000	2000	2000	20
Taxes	9600	800	800	800	80
Net income	14400	1200	1200	1200	120

Part 3: Pro forma balance sheet

Assets:

<Current assets>					
Cash	20000	20850	24100	27350	2820
Accounts receivable	60000	60000	60000	60000	6000
Inventory	30000	30000	30000	30000	3000
Prepaid expenses	2000	2000	2000	2000	200
Total current assets	112000	112850	116100	119350	12020
<Fixed assets>					
Buildings & equipment	50000	50000	50000	50000	500
Less accum. depreciation	30000	31250	32500	33750	3500
Land	10000	10000	10000	10000	100
Net fixed assets	30000	28750	27500	26250	2500
Total assets	142000	141600	143600	145600	14520

Liabilities:

<Current liabilities>					
Accounts payable	22500	22500	22500	22500	225
Accrued wages & taxes	5500	3900	4700	5500	390
Other current liabilities	4000	4000	4000	4000	400
Total current liabilities	32000	30400	31200	32000	3040
Long term debt	40000	40000	40000	40000	4000
Total liabilities	72000	70400	71200	72000	7040
<Owner equity>					
Common stock	50000	50000	50000	50000	5000
Retained earnings	20000	21200	22400	23600	248
Total owner equity	70000	71200	72400	73600	748
Total liab. & owner equity	142000	141600	143600	145600	1452

Disks: Anatomy and care

Disk anatomy

Although a diskette can perform amazing functions, its anatomy is quite simple. Since reference is made in this book to parts of a diskette, a brief review of diskette anatomy is included here. With this book, you'll be using two forms of diskettes: data or storage diskettes, and a VisiCalc Program (and, for the Advanced Version, a Loader) diskette. The anatomy of a storage diskette is illustrated at right. A VisiCalc Program diskette has the same anatomy as a storage diskette except it does not have a write-protect cutout (#10 on diagram).

1 STORAGE ENVELOPE. This envelope protects the diskette from scratches, dust, and fingerprints. With better diskettes, the envelope is also treated to eliminate the static buildup that attracts abrasive grit. Always store a diskette in its storage envelope.

2 OUTER COVER. The black plastic outer cover protects the diskette while allowing it to spin smoothly. The cover is permanently sealed for safety, and contains lubricants and cleaning agents that prolong the life of the diskette. Always grasp a diskette only by this outer cover.

3 LABELS. A diskette comes with a manufacter's label on it. A user's label can be added to identify and number the diskette for easy reference.

4 OVAL OPENING. This is a space where an operating disk drive head picks up and records information on the diskette. There is an oval opening on both the top and bottom sides.

5 TOP SIDE. On a single-sided diskette, the top side is the one with the manufacturer's label on it. A diskette is inserted into the machine top-side-up, with the oval opening directed toward the machine.

6 THE ACTUAL DISKETTE. The round, flexible plastic diskette has a magnetic surface that stores information in a manner somewhat analogous to that of a tape recorder. This actual, or inner, diskette can be seen through three openings in the disk's outer cover.

7 ALIGNMENT NOTCHES. These two notches align the diskette squarely over the disk drive head when the diskette is inserted into the machine.

8 CENTRAL HOLE. The disk drive unit fits into the central hole to engage and rotate the diskette.

9 HUB RING. This plastic, protective ring, normally not on a diskette, can be glued on to the rim of a diskette's central hole to prevent the hole from deteriorating as the drive unit repeatedly rotates the diskette.

10 WRITE-PROTECT CUTOUT. This notch cues the disk drive whether or not to store a file on the diskette. When the cutout is left open, the disk drive "senses" this and will store a file (on command) on the diskette. If you cover the cutout with tape, the disk drive will not accept new files on the diskette until the tape is removed. That protects — or write-protects — the diskette. (A VisiCalc Program diskette does not have a write-protect cutout and is therefore permanently write-protected.)

11 RECORDING AND READING HEAD. This area is used by the disk drive head to locate disk sectors on which information is stored.

Anatomy of a storage disk

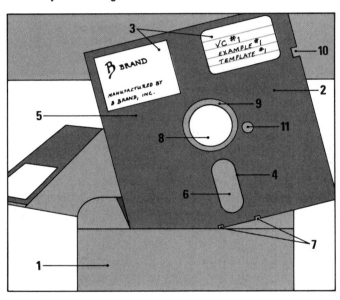

IBM PC TIPS Cleaning the disk drive

This is one of those "housekeeping chores" it is easy to overlook. But you shouldn't overlook it forever or errors can occur as a result. The disk drive head operates like a tape recorder head. It picks up magnetic signals from the magnetic recording material (in this case the diskette), and in the process it also picks up debris. If this debris isn't removed, it can begin to reduce the sensitivity of the head and its effectiveness in accurately recording and picking up data on or from the disk.

The easiest way to clean the head is with a special cleaning diskette. When it is inserted into the drive (just like a regular diskette) and the drive is operated for a while, this diskette cleans the head as it spins.

Diskette care and handling

Diskettes are relatively durable under ordinary conditions and have a useful life of about 40 hours spinning time. That life, however, can be shortened or abruptly ended by improper handling, while proper care assures that diskettes will accurately store and play back the data you need. Here are some useful tips on how to care for diskettes and assure them a useful, productive life.

Disk do's and don'ts

DO . . . Keep diskettes in their protective storage envelopes. The envelope reduces static buildup, which can attract dust that can scratch the diskette.

DO . . . Keep diskettes dry, away from sneezes, coffee, or anything wet. A wet diskette is a ruined diskette.

DO . . . Prevent diskettes from getting too hot or too cold. They should be stored at temperatures of 10–52° C (50–125° F). Temperature extremes can destroy a diskette's sensitivity, so treat them the same way you treat photographic film, i.e., keep them out of direct sunlight, don't leave them in a car exposed to temperature extremes, and so forth.

DO . . . Keep diskettes away from magnets. The magnets found in radio or stereo speakers, televisions, electric motors, air conditioners, novelty items, or even some cabinet latches can ruin diskettes' sensitivity. How far is "away"? A safe distance is at least two feet.

DO . . . Always make backup copies of important diskettes and store them a safe distance from your working area. Make sure that the same accident can't happen to both the diskette and its copy. Often the information on the diskette is worth much more than the diskette itself.

DO . . . Load the diskette into the drive unit gently. Otherwise, it may bend, center improperly, or rotate in an elliptical orbit that misses data.

DON'T . . . Touch a diskette's recording surface. Handle it only by its protective cover.

DON'T . . . Use a hard pen to write on a diskette label. Use only a felt-tip pen and light pressure.

DON'T . . . Leave a diskette in a nonoperating disk drive for more than an hour. Open the drive door and lift the drive head from the surface of the diskette.

DON'T . . . Insert or remove a diskette when the disk drive is running (when the red light is on).

DON'T . . . Bend, fold, or crimp diskettes.

One more note: Even with the best of care, diskettes can only last so long. Close to the end of their expected functional life, they show their own form of senility, by losing information or giving invalid commands. These are indications that it's time to replace the diskette which, ideally, you've already copied.

IBM PC TIPS Housekeeping

When you first begin to use a personal computer, keeping track of your diskettes isn't a problem because you have so few of them. After a very short period, however, they can begin to overrun your desk, and you need a method for filing and storing them. Here are some tips for organizing your files so that you can find what you want . . . when you want it.

1 Label each diskette with the same volume number, for instance, VC #1, VC #2, etc., for VisiCalc diskettes.

2 Periodically print out the directory, or list of files on each disk, and save the printout with the diskette. Some filing systems such as binders have a place for the directory to be kept. You can easily keep things straight by matching the number on the disk label with a label on each printout. To avoid confusion, print out directories of the diskettes one at a time, in sequential order, then number the printed-out directory listings to match the diskettes.

3 The cash budget

Introduction

The cash budget is your most useful day-to-day tool for financial planning and control. It focuses attention on your firm's cash position by showing all cash inflows and outflows, and allows you to plan for periods of cash shortages.

For most small-business owners and some managers of larger firms, cash and liquidity management are even more important than profits. Many profitable companies have gone bankrupt because they did not have enough cash at the right time to meet financial obligations. An unprofitable business with a solid cash flow and cash balance position is more likely to be around in five years than a profitable firm with a weak cash position.

In small firms, there is another reason for directing attention to the cash flow and cash budget. Many small firms are undercapitalized. Often they will try to operate at a level of sales that cannot be supported by the assets owned by the company. Usually, working capital is most affected; without sufficient initial investment in the firm (capitalization), something must be sacrificed. Since all working capital flows through the cash account, there will probably be a liquidity or cash squeeze at some point early in the firm's life. The cash budget can help identify that point, and show how tight the squeeze will be.

Small firms should also use cash budgets and cash flows to plan financial growth and sales. Most small firms are capable of rapid growth. All it takes is one good contract or selling season. But such rapid growth places a high demand on the firm's cash to finance that growth. This is caused by the lag between outflows and inflows. For example, getting ready for a peak selling season requires a firm to purchase inventory prior to the actual selling period. If the inventory is paid for before the cash from selling it is received, there is a disruption in cash flow, or a cash flow lag. That lag has to be covered by some form of cash or an adjustment in operations. The cash budget will show the amount of cash needed and when it's needed. Often, the cash difference is made up through outside financing.

This leads to another reason for using a cash budget regularly: It can increase your credibility with people outside the firm. Bankers, lenders, and investors all expect to see a firm's management provide sound cash budgets and plans. And they're more receptive to financing requests when budgets are provided. Budgets illustrate that management is anticipating rather than just reacting to cash needs.

The cash budget: Cooperation and control

Obviously, cash is a vital (and sometimes scarce) resource. There may not be sufficient cash to cover all the proposed or projected activities of a firm, so priorities must be established. These priorities will be reflected on the cash budget by the allocation of cash or other resources. The preparation of the cash budget can become a source of conflict or cooperation. People may have different ideas about the priorities that form the basis of the budget. But in the end, a budget forces making decisions on the priority of activities. It can become a means of achieving agreement.

Also, the cash budget can be a control document. It provides a basis for comparing what actually happened with what you expected to happen. Reviewing and comparing actual against forecasted results are important aspects of planning and controlling a company. For example, if sales are below forecast, comparison not only highlights this fact but also forces you to ask why this occurred. Was the reason something within or outside of your control? Once the cause (or causes) of the variation is determined, you can take action to correct the situation. And that action may include revising your cash budget.

Cash flow

If you start out with $10,000 cash at the beginning of the year, and wind up with $1.50 at the end of the year, you would like to know where it went before pronouncing the business year a disaster. It might not be a disaster at all. Granted, there was a major cash drain — but why? If the cash was used to invest in a major project that will be completed shortly after year end, the large reduction in cash may not be nearly as disastrous as it appears.

Cash flow describes how cash moves from the collection on sales through the various assets and expenses during a period of time. Analysis of cash flow can be based on what happened in the past or on what you expect to happen in the future. Generally, you want to keep your cash working for the company to produce profits. One useful way of looking at this goal is called the *cash cycle* or *cash wheel*.

The cash wheel starts at *cash*. Cash is used either to buy goods for sale (inventory in a retail business) or to make goods for sale (finished goods, converted from raw materials, in a manufacturing firm). Either way, some cash becomes invested in inventory, the goods to be sold. When those goods are sold on credit to a customer, an account receivable is created. Cash is due back into the company, and when the receivable is collected, that cash (preferably including a profit) is put back into the cash

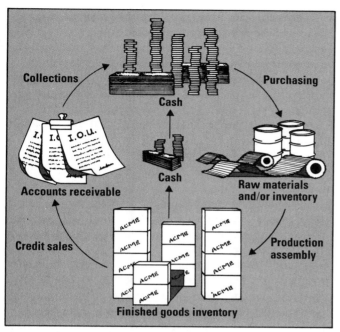

One useful way of looking at your cash flow is called the cash wheel.

wheel. The cash is ready to be used again, and if there is a profit, more cash is fed into the cycle.

The objective is to speed up the spinning of the cash wheel, thus managing assets efficiently. This can be done by increasing sales while maintaining the same level of inventory and receivables, or by reducing inventory and receivables while maintaining a constant level of sales. Either approach keeps the cash wheel moving and working. Note that cash is held up in inventory and receivables. The longer it stays in these forms, the slower the wheel turns. When inventory and receivables become too much of a drag on the wheel, management action should be taken to reduce that effect. For example, you could stop selling to slow-paying customers (thus reducing receivables time) or stop carrying slow-moving items (thus reducing inventory).

The cash budget captures on paper (or on your computer worksheet) the expected cash movements through the cash wheel.

When to construct a cash budget

When to construct a cash budget and the length of the forecast period are dependent on the nature of your business, the regularity of your firm's cash inflows and outflows, and your cash balance. In general, the more seasonal your sales are, or the greater the difference between inflows and outflows for each period, the more

frequently you should prepare and monitor a cash budget. You should also prepare a more detailed budget in this case. If your firm has a strong cash position (a consistently large and stable cash balance), you can use a longer budget period.

How to construct a cash budget

There are three basic parts to a cash budget. *Cash inflows* is the first and shows the source, amount, and timing of expected cash coming into the company. Usually, most of this cash is generated from sales and takes the form of sales receipts. The second part, *cash outflows*, outlines all the expected cash disbursements from the company over the projected period. The third is what we call the *cash position*. This shows the expected result of all the inflows and outflows. It includes the net cash flow (difference between inflows and outflows), an opening and ending balance, and a line for financing, which may be required so the company can meet its upcoming obligations.

The groundwork for preparing a cash budget consists of estimating all cash receipts (inflows) and cash payments (outflows) expected during the budget period. Separate budgets must be carefully made for cash sales (including discounts and sales returns), collections of accounts receivable, and any other expected cash income. The same kind of planning must be done for each type of expense that will go to make up the expected cash expenditures, or outflows. These budgets are based on experience and on the goals you have set for your business.

If cash receipts are greater than expenditures, you have a positive cash flow for the period. Your expected cash balance, or cash position, at the end of the period is then your cash on hand at the beginning of the period plus net cash flow (receipts minus expenditures). If you have a negative cash flow (expenditures greater than receipts), your cash balance at the period's end is your original cash on hand minus the difference between expenditures and receipts. Either way, your cash balance (plus any financing obtained) will be carried over to the next period as the opening balance.

The cash balance — how much is enough? You must decide what size cash balance you need to maintain. This, too, is based on experience. You might, for instance, decide that cash equivalent to a certain number of days' sales is a desirable level. If the cash balance at the end of the budgeted period is less than this amount, some short-term borrowing or changes in plans may be necessary. The cash budget, by bringing this to your attention early, gives you time to consider fully all the possible courses of action.

If, on the other hand, the cash balance is larger than you need, the excess can be temporarily invested in, for example, marketable securities. Remember that cash is known as a "nonearning" asset. Too much cash can reduce profits. Excess cash should be put to work for the business — that is, invested in assets that will improve the profitability of your firm.

If you need funds — what kind? Cash budgets can help you decide whether you need short-term or long-term capital. A series of twelve monthly cash budgets will show your estimated monthly cash balances for a year. Each of these balances can then be compared with the cash level you have established as desirable for your business. Perhaps your cash balance is ample at the beginning and end of the 12-month period but low at times during the year. This suggests a need for short-term funds. The need will be self-liquidating over the 12-month period.

If, however, cash budgets are developed over longer periods of time and the cash balance is consistently low, the business needs intermediate or long-term capital — intermediate if the need persists for periods lasting from 12 to 30 months, and long-term or permanent capital if it persists for a longer period.

The cash budget is your best estimate of the future cash flows of your company. Most managers find that the longer they prepare and use cash budgets as part of planning, the better they get. Initially, their cash budgets may be too optimistic, with forecasts of high sales and low expenses. They may be more accurate in general categories than in specific ones. For instance, a forecast for total expenses is likely to be better than a forecast for each individual expense. And estimates for longer periods of time are often more accurate than those for shorter periods. As managers gain experience, however, the overall budget becomes more realistic, and, therefore, more useful.

The computer can help speed up the process of learning to prepare and use a cash budget, since it does most of the "number crunching." Calculations are made more efficiently and are less prone to error. And, of course, it's easy to update the information on the budget. Because the machine takes some of the work out of working with numbers, managers are free to spend more time learning the principles behind those numbers, exploring changes in them on the computer, and, most importantly, managing the business.

BUSINESS TIPS Raising cash

Most small businesses occasionally run short of money. In the cash flow of many firms, disbursements are at times higher than receipts; for example, many retailers achieve 20 to 30 percent of annual sales during the Christmas season. When a business needs capital to get sales, buy inventory, pay employees, purchase assets, pay taxes, or expand or purchase cost-saving equipment, the owner has several options to consider. The business owner may:

- generate the capital internally;
- find capital available from trade creditors;
- borrow the money;
- sell assets; or
- sell an ownership interest in the business to equity investors.

Capital needs can be classified as either short-term, generally those of less than one year, or long-term, those of more than one year. Short-term financing is most common for assets that turn quickly, such as accounts receivable or inventories. Long-term financing more often is used for fixed assets, such as property, plant expansion, or equipment purchases. Short-term borrowing generally is cheaper than other kinds of borrowing, as well as more flexible.

Getting ready

First, let's get your computer ready to enter the example. Follow these six steps, and you'll be ready to start building the sample cash budget. Be sure to follow the steps and instructions carefully, since skipping a step could cause problems later. (*Note:* If you are using the publisher's data disk described on page 138, format only one blank diskette for a backup copy in Step 1, then follow Steps 2–6).

Materials You Need:

1 VisiCalc Program diskette

2 1 or 2 blank diskettes (not used until you save data in Step Seven under Entering the Example)

3 Adhesive disk labels

4 DOS System Master diskette for the IBM PC

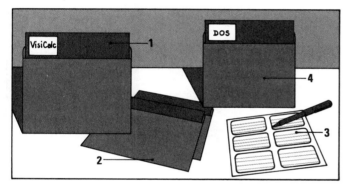

Reminder: If you stop work and turn the computer off, all data will be erased from the computer's memory. Your worksheet will be lost, unless you have saved the data on a diskette. Since saving your work is not described or recommended until you have partially entered the example on the computer (Step Seven under Entering the Example on page 47), leave your computer on as you proceed through the steps in the Getting Ready and Entering the Example sections in this and subsequent chapters.

Notation used in this book

Before you start the steps, take a moment to review the notation system used throughout this book. To simplify instructions describing keystrokes used with the IBM PC and the VisiCalc program, we use the following symbols.

Entry spaces, or cells, are indicated by column letters and row numbers. A cell is the space where a column and row intersect. For example, A23 is the entry space at the intersection of column A and row 23.

All items appearing in boldface, such as >**A23** or **Name**, are to be entered by typing each character exactly as it appears, including spaces and punctuation. Exact

typing isn't critical when you enter labels but it is critical when you enter data and formulas.

All items appearing in light typeface, Such as this, are instructions you will see on the VisiCalc prompt and edit lines. Use these prompts as a guide to your next step.

(S) is the symbol for the space bar. These (S) spaces are indicated only when they wouldn't otherwise be obvious. For instance, (S)s are indicated when the quotation (") key is to followed by a space (or spaces) to shift the first character entered in a label one or more spaces to the right. Thus the instruction "**(S)(S)(S)(S)%** tells you to press the shift and quotation keys to indicate that a label is to be typed, and then type four spaces and the percent sign.

⏎ is the symbol for the enter key on the IBM PC. It is used for a variety of functions, including the replication of data. The : (colon) key can be used whenever the ⏎ key is indicated.

→ indicates the arrow keys. They are used to move the cursor up or down a column or along a row. The IBM PC has four arrow keys.

> indicates the Go To command used to move the cursor to a specific cell. When you depress the shift key and the key with the period and > symbol, the prompt line will read Go To: Coordinate. Then you type a cell coordinate, such as A1, followed by ⏎. The cursor will immediately go to the cell specified, that is, A1. You can also move the cursor to the same position by using the arrow keys.

Remember that column identification letters are different (except for column A) for the VisiCalc and VisiCalc Advanced Version programs, since the Advanced Version has the variable column width feature. For example, in D(B)32, **D** indicates the column for VisiCalc users and **(B)** indicates the column for VisiCalc Advanced Version users who have widened column A so labels can be entered on each row without having to move the cursor. 32 is the row number.

As a check that you understand the notation system, see if you can translate the following type instructions:

>**E**(C)**5** and type "**(S)(S)(S)(S)(S)%** ⏎

Translated, the instructions read: Go to cell E (or C for Advanced Version) 5 (the intersection of column E(C) and row 5) and type a quotation mark, 5 space bars, the percentage key, and then press the enter key.

AV is the symbol used to highlight a special VisiCalc Advanced Version feature. Unless this symbol is used, the instructions given should be followed by both VisiCalc and VisiCalc Advanced Version users. Features indicated with this symbol are available only to Advanced Version users.

STEP 1   **Label and format two blank diskettes.** This is a quick but necessary step. Labeling helps you keep track of your diskettes, and formatting is required before you can store information on the diskette.

Begin by labeling the diskettes. Write an identifying code on an adhesive label; then peel the label off the backing and attach it to the top side of the diskette. We suggest that you code the diskettes using the software package and a number such as VC #1, VC #2, and so forth, for the VisiCalc diskettes. You could also use a more descriptive title, such as Example (see TIP on page 49).

The actual procedure for formatting diskettes is given in your IBM DOS manual.

STEP 2   **Load the VisiCalc program** into the computer. The Program diskette (and, in the case of the Advanced Version, the Loader diskette) should be inserted into or removed from the disk drive only when the drive isn't working (when it isn't humming and the helpful red light is off). To load the VisiCalc or VisiCalc Advanced Version program into the computer's memory, start with the IBM PC turned off and follow these steps:

For the VisiCalc program:

1 Touching only the protective cover, hold the VisiCalc Program diskette with its label-side up facing you (if the diskette is in your right hand and your thumb is on the label, you are holding it correctly). Point the end of the diskette with the oblong opening toward disk drive A, and insert the diskette into the door of disk drive A (see illustration). Gently push the diskette forward until you feel resistance. (Never push hard because the diskette will buckle if it gets caught on an obstruction.) Carefully jiggle the diskette to make sure it is fully inserted.

2 Gently close the drive door. As you slowly lower the door, make sure that the two metal fingers just clear the front end of the diskette. If they hit the top of the diskette, it isn't inserted far enough into the drive.

3 Turn the computer on. In about 40 seconds the disk drive will start and the red light will come on. When the drive stops the program is loaded into memory, and the characteristic VisiCalc display — with column letters across the top and row numbers down the side — should appear on the screen. (See illustration opposite.) You should now remove the program diskette and refile it, in its protective sleeve, in a safe place.

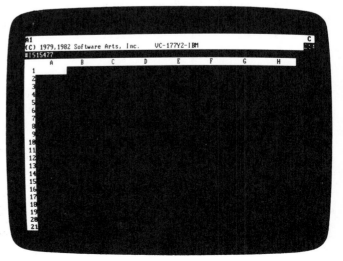

Note: If you haven't transferred part of the IBM DOS system to your VisiCalc diskette as explained in the VisiCalc manual, you will have to first "boot" the IBM DOS diskette, remove it from the disk drive, and insert the VisiCalc diskette. You then type VC80 to load the VisiCalc program.

For the VisiCalc Advanced Version program:

1 The Advanced Version is loaded into memory using two disks: the Loader and the Program diskettes.

2 Insert the VisiCalc Loader diskette into disk drive A and close the door. Turn the computer on, and the drive will begin to spin in about 40 seconds. When the drive stops you will see a VisiCalc copyright notice, and then the prompt line will read Program file missing.

3 Remove the Loader diskette and insert the VisiCalc Program diskette into disk drive A, then type ⏎. The Program diskette remains in the disk drive while you are using the program. Replace the Loader diskette in its protective sleeve, and store it in a safe place.

···

STEP 3 **Clear the screen.** Data, labels, formulas, or formats could be on the VisiCalc worksheet and not appear on the screen display. To be sure the computer's memory and the spreadsheet are clear of data before you begin work, always clear the screen.

To enter
a command to clear the screen

Type /C
The prompt line will read Clear: Type Y to Confirm
Type **Y**

AV To enter
a command to clear the screen

Type /C
The prompt line will read Clear: A or S
Type **A**
The prompt line will read Clear: Type Y to Confirm
Type **Y**

Result If the screen was already clear, you won't see any change. Whenever you start a new worksheet, however, it is wise to use this command to be sure the screen is clear of all previously entered data.

···

STEP 4 **Set column widths.** Column widths on the worksheet must be wide enough to hold the largest numbers you'll be entering in the example. The example requires a column width of 9 characters for the various numbers and formula values. If you are using the regular VisiCalc program, you'll set all columns to that width; but with the Advanced Version, you can set variable column widths by using a special command. That command makes the entering of labels easier and improves the overall appearance of the worksheet. For instance, label columns can be set wide, percent columns narrow, and dollar columns as wide as necessary. Therefore, we suggest (and assume) use of the variable column width feature with the Advanced Version for column A only.

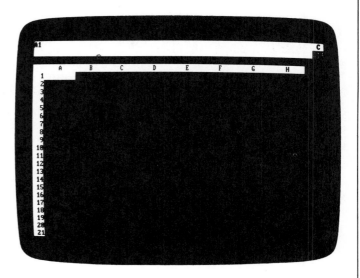

To enter
a command to set column width(s)

Type /GC9 ⏎ (The position of the cursor is unimportant.)

AV To enter
a variable column width for easier entry of labels

Type >A1 and type **/GCC27** ⏎

Result With the regular VisiCalc program you should see eight columns, A–H, displayed on the screen. The VisiCalc Advanced Version 80-column display should show six columns, A–F, with column A 27 characters wide and all other columns 9 characters wide.

Important: Because the column widths are now different for the regular VisiCalc program and the Advanced Version, a dual notation system is used throughout this book for column references. Instructions contained in the "Type" sections list the VisiCalc column first, in boldface (darker type), followed by the corresponding VisiCalc Advanced Version column in parentheses and regular typeface, as in >**D**(B)**21**. With the VisiCalc program, you would move the cursor to column D, row 21; with the Advanced Version, you would move the cursor to column B, row 21. Note that the row numbers are the same for both versions; only the column changes. However, column A, since it is the first column in both versions, will always be the same, as in >**A16**.

VISICALC TIPS Variable column widths

Using the variable column width feature of the Advanced Version will give you greater flexibility. Position the cursor in a column, and type /**GCC** followed by the number of characters wanted in that column, then ⏎. You can format a worksheet, column by column, setting label rows wide, percent columns narrow, and data columns to any width required. This format speeds the entry of labels and allows you to maximize the number of columns you can get on your monitor or printer. No extra characters are wasted, as they are with the regular version, because every column is set to the maximum width needed for that column.

In this book, our notation assumes Advanced Version users will use this feature to set the first column wide enough to accommodate the longest label (so there is no need to move the cursor when entering). All VisiCalc columns are indicated by letters (rows are indicated by numbers). Using the Advanced Version, you'll set the first column to the equivalent width of three regular VisiCalc columns, then all subsequent column references will change. What would be the fourth column in the VisiCalc sequence A-B-C-D is now the second column in the Advanced Version sequence A-A-A-B. In the typing instructions used in this book, the regular VisiCalc column label is given first, in a bold typeface. The Advanced Version column letter follows in parentheses and a regular typeface; for example, **Type** >**C**(A). The following chart lists the column notations.

VisiCalc Column Letter	VisiCalc Advanced Version Column Letter	Column Notation Used in Book
A	A	**A**
B	A	**B**(A)
C	A	**C**(A)
D	B	**D**(B)
E	C	**E**(C)
F	D	**F**(D)
G	E	**G**(E)
H	F	**H**(F)
I	G	**I**(G)
J	H	**J**(H)
K	I	**K**(I)

STEP
5

Simplify the screen display. The VisiCalc program provides a number of formats to display data on the screen and in printouts. One command drops from the display all numbers to the right of the decimal point. We will use this command to show dollar figures rounded off to the nearest dollar.

The VisiCalc Advanced Version program has several commands that can format the screen display and printouts. Since these can be entered after the example has been completed, we will not enter most of them with each individual step. They will be described at the end of each section, just before the completed example is saved for the last time.

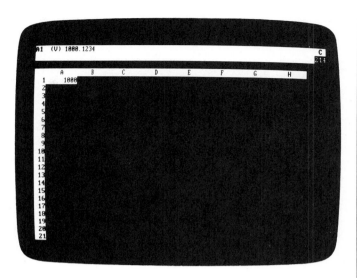

To enter

a command to simplify the screen display

Type /GFI

Result No change is apparent on the screen. To check that the command has been entered, type a number such as 1000.1234 ⏎ into cell A1. The complete number, 1000.1234, should then appear on the cell contents line at the top of the worksheet, and the rounded-off number, 1000, should appear in the entry space A1. To remove the entry you just made in cell A1, type /**B** ⏎.

···

STEP
6

Enter a command to speed up data entry. Normally, the VisiCalc program automatically recalculates the entire worksheet whenever an entry is made. As worksheets increase in size, this recalculation can take a few seconds, and will slow down the entering of data. To speed up data entry, you can change the recalculation feature from automatic to manual. On manual, it recalculates only when you press the **SHIFT** and **!** keys simultaneously.

To enter

a command to change recalculation from automatic to manual

Type /GR
    Prompt line will read Recalc: A M
    Type **M**

Result Although no change appears on the screen, the recalculation feature should now work only at your command. This means that you can enter data more quickly as you build the example on the computer. To return the program at any time to automatic recalculation, type /**GRA**. But we suggest that you leave recalculation on manual while you build the example.

VISICALC TIPS Speeding entries by avoiding continual recalculations

When you build a template, every time you enter a new formula or a new value the entire sheet will be automatically recalculated. The larger the model you are building, the longer this takes. Initially this isn't a problem, but when you find yourself waiting longer and longer for the sheet to recalculate before you can enter the next information, you will want a quicker way. All you have to do is type /**GRM** to switch the sheet to manual recalculation. Now when you want to recalculate, just type **!** (the **SHIFT** and exclamation keys pressed together). Until you press these keys, the worksheet won't be recalculated; and the data you enter won't be used by formulas that reference the cell into which those data are placed. You can switch back to automatic recalculation by typing /**GRA.**

Getting ready, Continued

VISICALC TIPS Getting around the spreadsheet

The simplest way to move short distances on the electronic spreadsheet is to move the cursor with the arrow ⟶ keys.

A faster way to move around the spreadsheet, especially when the distances involved are large, is to use the Go To command; just type >, then the coordinates of the cell you want to go to, followed by ⏎, or >**A1**⏎ for example. If you don't know the exact coordinates of the cell you want to go, enter a rough approximation of the coordinates and make your final moves with the arrow keys. You'll still save time.

To return to the upper left hand corner of the worksheet type **HOME.**

VISICALC TIPS Getting around with the Advanced Version

In addition to the arrow keys or the Go To command, the Advanced Version has two other entry features which can dramatically speed template building or data entry into a completed template.

■ **Keystroke memory**, like a function key, can be used to substitute a single character for a long string of characters. When the /**K**= command is used, up to 125 separate keystrokes can be saved in memory and assigned a single keystroke name. Type Control **K**, then the keystroke and the entire sequence of up to 125 keystrokes will be performed. Whenever you encounter a situation where the same series of keystrokes is used repetitively, this feature can save a lot of time. Typical applications might include the dating of cash flow statements or entering ruled lines on financial worksheets.

■ **The tab command**, /**AT**, can be used to specify a sequence of cell coordinates. It operates in a way similar to the tab set key on a typewriter. You type /**AT** followed by the desired cell coordinates, then type the **TAB** or the Control **B** key, and the cursor will automatically move to the next position. This command can be very useful when you enter data into templates where the same data-entry positions are used repeatedly.

A special Business User's Guide diskette to accompany **Planning and Budgeting** is available from the publishers. The diskette is not essential but it will save you much time, since it contains the cash budget, pro forma income statement, and pro forma balance sheet, as well as a general forecasting template which you can adapt for use with the cash budget and pro formas. If you did not purchase the Disk Edition of this book, and you want to order the diskette, use the Order Form on page 138.

Entering the example

You are now ready to begin building the sample cash budget on the computer. Before you actually begin putting information into the computer, take a few minutes to read below how the steps are organized and described in the instructions. The same organization is used in other "Entering the Example" sections in later chapters.

Each step has a number and title, such as "Step One. Enter headings and labels," or "Step Four. Save your work." Under each step, you'll be entering data or using computer procedures to transform or save data as you build the sample budget. Follow the steps in sequence, unless you are using the data diskette from the publisher (see page 138). In that case, see the special instructions that come with the diskette.

Each step is broken down into smaller units, or substeps. For most of the steps, the smaller units are row-by-row instructions that follow this outline:

Row number: For example, "Row 9."

Row title: For example, "Enter cash receipts."

Row description: Explanation of label or term to be entered. All business terms used, such as *opening cash balance*, are explained.

To enter: Tells you what you will be entering on the computer. You could be entering labels, values, formulas, or special commands to the computer, such as replication, saving files, loading files, etc. Most of the data you'll be entering will be in the form of labels (such as *opening cash balance*), values (numeric entries such as 5, 12, or .09), or formulas. Formulas are used to manipulate the data contents of various entry spaces. A formula could be a simple one, such as 2*10 (which uses the VisiCalc program as a calculator), or more powerful, such as 2*D2, which would make the values in the entry space containing the formula twice as large as the value in D2.

Type: Tells you what to type on the computer keyboard. For example, you might see >**D**(B)**5** and type **2000** ⏎, which reads: Go to cell D5 (B5 for users of the Advanced Version) and type 2000 and then the ENTER key.

When *type* instructions are different for the regular VisiCalc program and the Advanced Version, the Advanced Version instructions are given separately and identified by the symbol [AV]. With the Advanced Version, type the regular instructions first and *then* the Advanced Version unless instructed otherwise. The commands available to Advanced Version users that are most useful for the topics covered in this book are formatting and protecting the worksheet. Since these can be used after the labels, data, and formulas have been entered, they will not be entered until just before the completed example is saved. Remember that column widths are different if you use the variable column width feature with the Advanced Version, so those columns are listed in parentheses after the column for the regular version.

Result: This describes what should happen if you have entered the data correctly. Occasionally, photos of the screen display appear to illustrate the result. Except in the earliest sections, results are not given for entering labels or values into entry spaces on a row, since the expected result is so obvious. You should, however, always check the Results section after entering a formula.

Illustrations, such as the one below, show what data you'll be entering as you follow the instructions beginning on page 28. Note that the illustration has shaded areas. The *unshaded* area shows what you will be entering. For example, this illustration tells you that you'd be entering all data on the rows appearing in the white space.

Part 1: Cash budget													
Item:	What if column	1 1984	2 1984	3 1984	4 1984	5 1984	6 1984	7 1984	8 1984	9 1984	10 1984	11 1984	12 1984
Seasonal pattern*	100	8	8	8	8	8	8	8	8	8	8	8	8
Net sales; monthly*	450000	37500	37500	37500	37500	37500	37500	37500	37500	37500	37500	37500	37500
Cash receipts:													
% collected within 30 days*	60	22500	22500	22500	22500	22500	22500	22500	22500	22500	22500	22500	22500
% collected within 60 days*	20	7500	7500	7500	7500	7500	7500	7500	7500	7500	7500	7500	7500
% collected within 90 days*	20	7500	7500	7500	7500	7500	7500	7500	7500	7500	7500	7500	7500
Other cash receipts*	0	($)	($)	($)	($)	($)	($)	($)	($)	($)	($)	($)	($)
Total cash receipts		37500	37500	37500	37500	37500	37500	37500	37500	37500	37500	37500	37500
Inventory purchases*	60	22500	22500	22500	22500	22500	22500	22500	22500	22500	22500	22500	22500
Gen.& admin.*	20	7500	7500	7500	7500	7500	7500	7500	7500	7500	7500	7500	7500
Selling expenses*	10	3750	3750	3750	3750	3750	3750	3750	3750	3750	3750	3750	3750
Interest expense*	15	0	0	0	0	0	0	0	0	0	0	0	0
Other expense*	0	($)	($)	($)	($)	($)	($)	($)	($)	($)	($)	($)	($)
Taxes*	40	2400			0			0			0		
Total cash disbursements		36150	33750	33750	33750	33750	33750	33750	33750	33750	33750	33750	33750
Net cash flow		1350	3750	3750	3750	3750	3750	3750	3750	3750	3750	3750	3750
Opening cash balance		20000	21350	25100	28850	32600	36350	40100	43850	47600	51350	55100	58850
Loans required	0	0	0	0	0	0	0	0	0	0	0	0	0
Ending cash balance*	20000	21350	25100	28850	32600	36350	40100	43850	47600	51350	55100	58850	62600

Entering the example, Continued

Note to the reader

The example you are about to enter has several "forward references." This means that some of the formulas you enter now will reference cells in other parts of the example that have not yet been entered. This leads to some calculated results that appear strange, but they will change as the example is expanded. If, for instance, a formula on row 10 requires an entry on row 50 to work, it will not give the correct result until row 50 is entered. When the example is finished all of the cells should work together to give you the final results shown in the printouts in Chapter 6. Until then we provide results that show what you should get until the example is completed. If you get the same results, your final results should also match our final results. If your

results don't match those given as you enter formulas, be sure to recalculate the worksheet a number of times using the **SHIFT** and **!** keys before you check for problems. If your results still don't match (some formulas require you to recalculate up to five times) then see "Troubleshooting the example" on page 125.

The sample cash budget which you'll build on your computer is a condensed one modeled on a retail operation. The exact format or organization needed for your business may be different from that of our model. We suggest that you enter the sample cash budget first, and customize it or add details for your business later. You can also use the General Forecasting Template, described in Chapter 7.

Step One

Enter headings and ruled lines.

	A	B(A)	C(A)	D(B)	E(C)	F(D)	G(E)	H(F)	I(G)	J(H)	K(I)	L(J)	M(K)	N(L)	O(M)	P(N)
1	Part 1: Cash budget															
2	==
3	Item:			What if	1	2	3	4	5	6	7	8	9	10	11	12
4				column	1984	1984	1984	1984	1984	1984	1984	1984	1984	1984	1984	1984

(rows 5–31 contain ruled lines only)

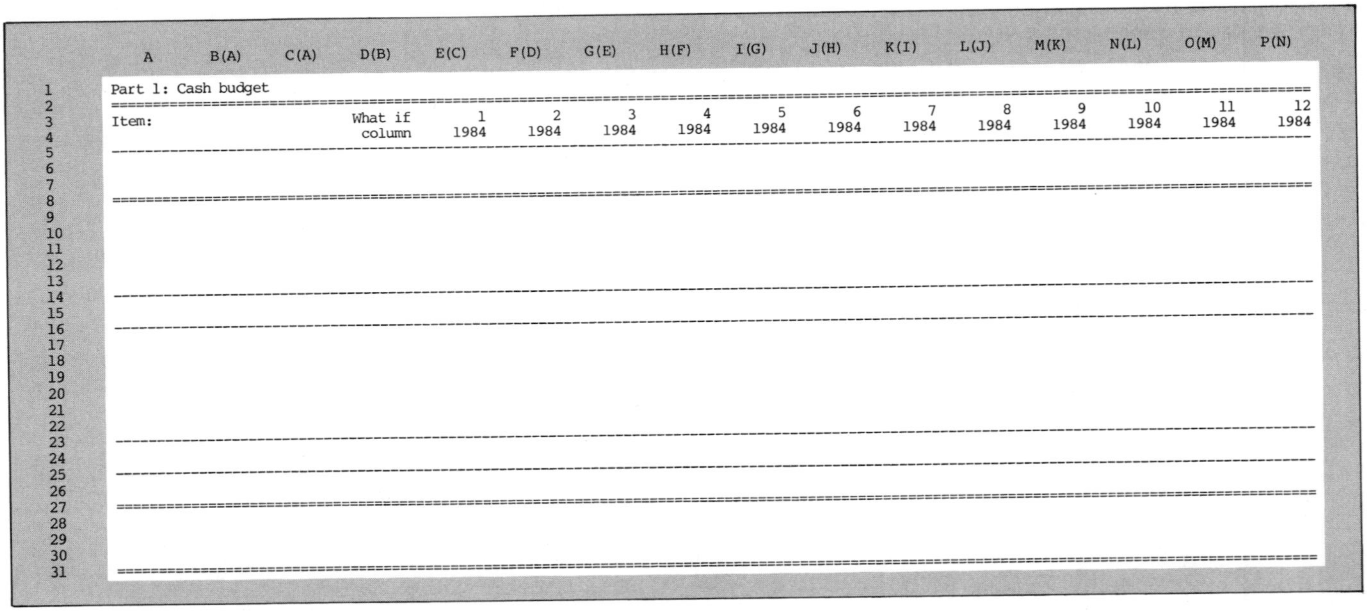

ROW 1 **Headings and ruled lines** identify this section of the example as Part I — The cash budget. The ruled lines divide major segments of the budget. These make the example more attractive and easier to read, both on the screen and in printouts. You'll also enter a phantom prompt to indicate the lower right-hand corner of the finished example. (A phantom prompt can be seen only when the cursor is placed in the cell containing it and will not appear on printouts. The phantom

prompt will be used when you print out the example. See TIPS on "Phantom prompts," page 30, for further description.)

To enter

a label to identify this section as Part I of the example, the cash budget

double ruled lines from column A to column P(N)

phantom instructions that can't be seen unless the cursor is positioned in the cell containing them (If you are using the Advanced Version, you will have to enter 18 spaces before the *P* in PRINT to push it out to the right edge of the cell. Then it can only be seen when the cursor is positioned in the cell and it appears on the cell contents line.)

Type >**A1** and type **Part 1: C:Print to P**(N)**93** →
  >**B**(A)**1** and type **ash budge** →
  >**C**(A)**1** and type **t** ⏎
  >**A2** and type **/-=** ⏎

To replicate

from one cell to a range

Type >**A2** and type **/R** ⏎ **B2.P**(N)**2** ⏎

from one range to another range

Type >**A2** and type **/R.P**(N)**2** ⏎ **A8** ⏎
  >**A2** and type **/R.P**(N)**2** ⏎ **A27** ⏎
  >**A2** and type **/R.P**(N)**2** ⏎ **A31** ⏎

Result The first command, **/-=**, should have put a double ruled line in cell A2. The first replication should have extended this ruled line across to column P(N). The subsequent replications should have copied this ruled line to rows 8, 27, and 31. You should use the arrow keys → to scroll around the screen to see that the lines were entered correctly.

. . . .

Column headings are entered next. Columns A through C (column A for Advanced Version) are used for labels describing line items on the cash budget. The heading Item is used to label the column. Column D(B) on the cash budget section of the example is the "What If" column, used to make changes and explore the outcomes. Columns E(C) through P(N) are the monthly periods covered by the cash budget. Since planning isn't always done for a January-to-December period, you will enter formulas that automatically change the column dates when the first month is changed. These formulas are long, but all you have to do is enter them exactly as in the instructions. Once they are entered, adjustments are simple.

To enter

a label to identify columns A through C (column A on the Advanced Version) as items, and the first part of the label for the "What If" column, D(B)

VISICALC TIPS Entering ruled lines

There are several ways to enter ruled lines on a worksheet. The three fastest and most frequently used methods (for either regular or Advanced Version) are as follows:

■ One of the fastest ways is to type /--⏎, or /-=⏎. The first series of keystrokes will fill a cell with a single dashed line (-----), and the second a double dashed line (=====). You can replicate these lines across the worksheet as needed. Lines made in this way will not be saved and reloaded when the DIF command is used. When you reload the DIF file, the ruled lines will appear in each cell just as they were entered, i.e., /-- or /-= instead of as ruled lines.

■ To enter ruled lines that will be saved and reloaded when the DIF command is used, enter the ruled line in the original cell by typing "---- (quotation marks followed by enough strokes to fill the cell) ⏎, or "===== ⏎. This cell can then be replicated as needed, and will appear as a complete line when the saved DIF file is reloaded.

■ The fastest way of all is to use function keys if your computer has them. With the Advanced Version, you can also use keystroke memory. Program one key to enter and replicate a double ruled line and another to do the same with a single ruled line. Refer to your owner's manual if you want to use these methods.

VISICALC TIPS Entering labels

When you enter labels, you can frequently make good use of the **SHIFT (")** (shift and quotation keys depressed together) command. When you type this command first, before typing anything else, you can:

■ Enter numbers, commas, periods, or other nonalphabetic characters such as −, +, =, %, $, #, ", *, and they will be treated as labels rather than as numbers or commands.

■ Indent a label by using the space bar to shift the first letter, number, or character to the right. After you type the command, the first character to be entered will be shifted to the right one character space for each time the space bar is pressed. Throughout this book we use this command frequently, and when it is used to shift characters to the right each strike of the space bar key is indicated by **(S)**. For instance, indenting the first letter of a word, such as Cost, four spaces would be shown as **"(S)(S)(S)(S)Cost** ⏎.

The cash budget   **29**

a local format to align the label in cell D(B)3 with the right margin of the column

a value of 1 in cell E(C)3 to indicate the month of January

a formula in cell F(D)3 that will automatically calculate the month based on the entry you make in cell E(C)3

Type >**A3** and type **Item:** ⟶ ⟶ ⟶
>**D(B)3** and type **/FR What If** ⟶
>**E(C)3** and type **1** ⟶
>**F(D)3** and type **@IF(E(C)3 = 12,1,E(C)3 + 1** ⏎

To replicate
from one cell to a range

Type >**F(D)3** and type **/R** ⏎ **G(E)3.P(N)3** ⏎
Prompt line will read N = No change
R = Relative
Type **RR**

Result The monthly columns should be numbered 1 to 12. Try changing the number in cell D(B)3. If you enter a new number, all the others should change automatically. (You will have to use the **SHIFT** and **!** keys if you are in manual recalculation.) When the number 12 (for December) is reached, the next number on the row will become 1 (for January). When you adapt the example to your own business (Chapter 7), you can budget from any month and the labels for the other months will change automatically.

. . . .

R O W 4   **Column headings** continue on this row. You will complete the label for the "What If" column and add formulas to automatically change the year, if you either change the beginning year or cover more than one year in your budget.

To enter
a local format that will align the label in cell D(B)4 with the right edge of the column

a value in cell D(B)4 to identify the year covered by the budget

a formula in cell F(D)4 that will change the year if the period covered by the budget is other than January through December

Type >**D(B)4** and type **/FR Column** ⟶
>**E(C)4** and type **1984** ⟶
>**F(D)4** and type **@IF(E(C)3 = 12,E(C)4 + 1,E(C)4** ⏎

To replicate
from one cell to a range

Type >**F(D)4** and type **/R** ⏎ **G(E)4.P(N)4** ⏎
Prompt line will read N = No change
R = Relative
Type **RRR**

Result The columns should all be dated 1984, since the period covered is January through December, 1984. If you change the beginning month in D(B)4 to any other month, the year will also change in the appropriate column. Try entering 11 (for November) in D(B)4 and press the **SHIFT** and **!** keys to recalculate. Column F(D) should now be dated 1 (for January 1985). Be sure to restore the original form before proceeding.

VISICALC TIPS Phantom prompts

Phantom prompts are what we call the abbreviated instructions that appear on the entry contents line but that don't show on the normal screen display or on printouts of the worksheet (hence the name *phantom*). These prompts act as guides for entering information; throughout the book we have suggested times for you to enter phantom instructions on the computer.

To enter phantom prompts, you overtype the desired prompt into an entry space. It works like this: with either the regular or the Advanced Version, the number of letters you can type into an entry space is determined by the column width used. In our example, that column width is seven characters; in our template it is nine (column A for Advanced Version users is 21 and 27 characters respectively). When you type beyond that number of characters, the additional (or overtyped) characters will not appear on the worksheet but they will appear as phantom prompts. Type ⏎ and you'll see the overtyped characters appear on the entry contents line, as a phantom prompt. To see the prompt, you must position the cursor in the cell where you overtyped the characters. Phantom prompts are especially helpful for:

■ **Printing out a worksheet.** Enter a phantom prompt to identify the lower right-hand corner of your worksheet.

■ **Saving or loading with the DIF command.** You can enter a phantom prompt to specify the place to position the cursor when you save or load a DIF file. Or, you can specify the lower right-hand corner.

<table>
<tr><td><u>R O W</u>
5</td><td>Single ruled lines will be entered with the same replication techniques used previously to enter double ruled lines.</td></tr>
</table>

To enter

single ruled lines from column A to column P(N) on rows 5, 14, 16, 23, and 25

Type >**A5** and type /-- ⏎

To replicate

from one cell to a range

Type >**A5** and type /**R** ⏎ **B5.P(N)5** ⏎

from one range to another range

Type >**A5** and type /**R.P**(N)**5** ⏎ **A14** ⏎
>**A5** and type /**R.P**(N)**5** ⏎ **A16** ⏎
>**A5** and type /**R.P**(N)**5** ⏎ **A23** ⏎
>**A5** and type /**R.P**(N)**5** ⏎ **A25** ⏎

Result The first step should have put a single ruled line into cell A5. The first replication should have replicated it across to column P(N). The next series of replications should have copied the ruled line to rows 14, 16, 23, and 25.

Step Two

Enter seasonal patterns and net sales.

	A	B(A)	C(A)	D(B)	E(C)	F(D)	G(E)	H(F)	I(G)	J(H)	K(I)	L(J)	M(K)	N(L)	O(M)	P(N)
1	Part 1: Cash budget															
2																
3	Item:			What if	1	2	3	4	5	6	7	8	9	10	11	12
4/5				column	1984	1984	1984	1984	1984	1984	1984	1984	1984	1984	1984	1984
6	Seasonal pattern*			100	8	8	8	8	8	8	8	8	8	8	8	8
7	Net sales; monthly*			450000	37500	37500	37500	37500	37500	37500	37500	37500	37500	37500	37500	37500

<table>
<tr><td><u>R O W</u>
6</td><td>Seasonal patterns occur in many businesses. There can be fluctuations in sales with either sales or the resulting collection of receivables unevenly distributed throughout the year. When fixed expenses are evenly distributed and sales aren't, cash flow problems can arise, making access to short-term outside financing essential. At this point in the example, we assume an even distribution of sales throughout the year. Later when you explore "What Ifs," the sales patterns can easily be changed by changing the percentages on this row.</td></tr>
</table>

To enter

a label to identify this row as having the seasonal sales pattern percentages (An asterisk (*) is added to indicate that this line can be changed when you explore "What If" questions.)
a formula in cell D(B)6 that will total up the monthly seasonal percentages. This formula is entered so that any changes you make when exploring "What Ifs" can be checked to be sure the total is exactly 100%.
formulas in each of the monthly columns that calculate the monthly percentage if sales are divided equally throughout the year, i.e., 100/12

Entering the example, Continued

VISICALC TIPS Formatting percentages

If you are using the VisiCalc Advanced Version program, you can format percentages to display them as whole numbers followed by a percent sign, such as 25%. The command to do this (**/AV%**) is suggested for Advanced Version users throughout this book. If you use this command keep the following in mind.

■ If you use a division formula to calculate percentages and normally multiply the result by 100 to display the calculated percentage as a whole number, you won't have to do this when using the Advanced Version percent format; it will multiply by 100 for you.

■ If you are entering a percentage figure directly in a cell formatted using this command, it has to be entered as a decimal, such as .25. The command used to format the cell will automatically multiply your entered figure by 100 and add a percent sign to display it as 25%.

The /AV% command is suggested for Advanced Version users on rows 6, 7, 10, 11, 12, 17, 18, 19, 20, and 22 on the cash budget, rows 35 and 48 on the income statement, and for all "What Ifs" in Chapter 6.

VISICALC TIPS Using the @SUM command

When using the **@SUM** command (or many other commands beginning with the prefix @) it is best if you establish the range of the formula between two ruled lines rather than two data entry points. This allows rows to be added or deleted, and as long as this is done between the ruled lines, the formula will continue to work. If this isn't done and the formula adds a column of figures, when you delete or add to the top or bottom figures in the range of the formula, the VisiCalc program will give an ERROR message.

Type >**A6** and type **Seasonal** (→)
>**B(A)6** and type **pattern*** (→)(→)
>**D(B)6** and type **@SUM(E(C)6.P(N)6)** (→)
>**E(C)6** and type **100/12** (↵)

[AV] **Type** >**C6** and type **/AV%** (↵) (↵) **1/12** (↵)

To replicate
from one cell to a range

Type >**E(C)6** and type **/R** (↵) **F(D)6.P(N)6** (↵)

Result Each monthly column should have the number 8 for 8%. Actually the amount is 8.3333%, as you can see by positioning the cursor in one of the cells containing the formula. Setting the display to "integer" as you did earlier rounds off all decimals so that only whole numbers are displayed. If you use the **SHIFT** and ! to recalculate, the total of the monthly sales percentages should appear as 100 in cell D(B)6.

VISICALC TIPS Entering data: The final (key) stroke

Although the **ENTER** key, (↵), is often the final keystroke when you enter information, it isn't the only one you can use. When making entries across a row or down a column, it's often faster to use the arrow (→) key, since it completes the entry just as the return key does, but it also moves the cursor to the next entry position, saving you a keystroke each time. When replicating, the : (colon) key can be used instead of the (↵) key.

Net sales represent gross sales minus discounts and returns. Gross sales is total sales (unit or selling price times the number of units sold) expected during the forecast period. It is expected sales before any deductions. When the accrual system of accounting is used, all sales, both cash and credit, are entered at the time they are expected to occur. In a cash system, sales are entered only when payment is expected.

Discounts and returns are the adjustments made to gross sales. They represent any deductions that account for the difference between gross sales and net sales. Discounts are the cash reductions in price offered by a company to customers who pay early or buy in large quantities. Discounts are often treated as an adjustment and separated from the selling price, because management wants to evaluate the effectiveness of offering such discounts. If, instead, discounts are included within gross sales (netted out), it is difficult and costly to go back and reconstruct the information needed to determine their effect. Returns are the goods or services that are either returned to the company (in the case of goods) or not accepted (in the case of services) because they don't meet the company's and/or the customer's standards. Defective merchandise is an example.

Our example assumes the adjustment from gross sales to net sales has been made already. In the example, the total net annual sales are entered into cell D(B)7. The figure entered in this cell is distributed to the months by the formulas in cells E(C)7 through P(N)7 and the seasonal percentages on row 6. When you explore "What Ifs," a change in total sales (cell D(B)7) causes changes in all monthly sales. A change in the percentages on the seasonal pattern line will also cause a change in the monthly sales for each month.

To enter

a label to identify this line item as net sales (An asterisk is added to indicate that this line can be changed when you explore "What If" questions.)
a value of $450,000 in cell D(B)7
formulas to calculate monthly sales, based on the seasonal distribution percentages, in cells E(C)7 through P(N)7 and total sales entered in cell D(B)7 (See TIPS on "Formatting percentages" on page 32.)

Type >**A7** and type **Net sales** ⟶
>**B(A)7** and type **";(S)Monthly** ⟶
>**C(A)7** and type **"*** ⟶
>**D(B)7** and type **450000** ⟶
>**E(C)7** and type **(E(C)6*D(B)7)/100** ⏎

[AV] **Type** >**C7** and type **/AV%** ⏎ ⏎ **+C6*D7** ⏎

VISICALC TIPS Speeding up replication of formulas

When you replicate long columns or rows containing numerous formulas, the need to type **N** (for No change) or **R** (for Relative) for each reference to other cells can become tedious. Sometimes the references are either all Rs or all Ns. In such situations you can dramatically speed up the replication process. Type the appropriate key (either **N** or **R**), and hold it down so it automatically repeats. You can watch the flashing formulas on the prompt line to get a rough idea of which formulas on the worksheet are being replicated. When the column replication is completed, the cell containing the cursor will begin to fill with Rs or Ns. At this point, release the N or R key and use the backspace key to back over and erase all of the Rs or Ns appearing in the cell containing the cursor. When the last is erased, the original cell contents will reappear in the cell occupied by the cursor and the replication is complete.

VISICALC TIPS Entering formulas that begin with letters

The VisiCalc program automatically interprets the first character you type at any entry position. If the first character is a letter, the VisiCalc program assumes the entry will be a label. When entering formulas, however, you must specify the entry position of the data to be used in the formula. Since each entry position begins with a letter, e.g., **D12**, the VisiCalc program will assume the entry is a label unless the + command is used before entering the coordinate of the entry position. Rather than type **D12**, for instance, type **+D12**.

The + isn't the only command that will tell VisiCalc a formula is coming. Other keys that can be used to indicate a formula include @, (, and other mathematical symbols.

To replicate

from one cell to a range

Type >**E(C)7** and type **/R** ⏎ **F(D)7.P(N)7** ⏎
Prompt line will read N=No change
R=Relative
Type **RN**

Result If all of the formulas were entered correctly, monthly sales on row 7 should all be $37,500. If you want to check that the formulas work, change the

$450,000 net sales total to a larger or smaller number. You should see all the monthly figures increase or decrease by the same amount. You can also change the seasonal percentages on row 6. If you do, the monthly numbers will also change. If you try

these changes, remember to restore total annual net sales in cell D(B)7 to 450000 and the seasonal pattern on row 6 by re-entering and replicating the formulas described above.

Step Three

Enter cash receipts.

	A	B(A)	C(A)	D(B)	E(C)	F(D)	G(E)	H(F)	I(G)	J(H)	K(I)	L(J)	M(K)	N(L)	O(M)	P(N)
1	Part 1: Cash budget															
2																
3	Item:			What if	1	2	3	4	5	6	7	8	9	10	11	12
4				column	1984	1984	1984	1984	1984	1984	1984	1984	1984	1984	1984	1984
5																
6	Seasonal pattern*			100	8	8	8	8	8	8	8	8	8	8	8	8
7	Net sales; monthly*			450000	37500	37500	37500	37500	37500	37500	37500	37500	37500	37500	37500	37500
8																
9	Cash receipts:															
10	% collected within 30 days*			60	22500	22500	22500	22500	22500	22500	22500	22500	22500	22500	22500	22500
11	% collected within 60 days*			20	7500	7500	7500	7500	7500	7500	7500	7500	7500	7500	7500	7500
12	% collected within 90 days*			20	7500	7500	7500	7500	7500	7500	7500	7500	7500	7500	7500	7500
13	Other cash receipts*			0	($)	($)	($)	($)	($)	($)	($)	($)	($)	($)	($)	($)
14																
15	Total cash receipts				37500	37500	37500	37500	37500	37500	37500	37500	37500	37500	37500	37500
16																
17																
18																
19																
20																
21																
22																
23																
24																
25																
26																
27																
28																
29																
30																
31																

ROW 9 **Cash receipts** — receipt or collection of payment for sales — are essential to the successful operation of any business. Until payment is collected, your money is in someone else's hands. Sales that haven't been collected on can be just as expensive to you as maintaining inventory and perhaps even more so, since credit sales have hidden costs in terms of paperwork and collection. If the sales cannot be collected on, the cost is even higher, since it includes all the expense incurred in producing the good or service plus the profit you didn't earn, as well as collection costs.

Not only is payment required to keep your company operating, but payments must be timely. The longer the period between the sale and the collection, the more expensive the transaction becomes. The money you have tied up could be invested elsewhere, perhaps for a higher return. This loss of potential income from other possible investments is called the *opportunity cost.*

In our sample budget, you'll break down receipts into the percentage collected within 30, 60, and 90 days. There is also a line for other sales collections, such as cash sales. With these breakdowns, you can explore

changes in collection patterns when you get to the "What Ifs" in Chapter 6.

In the next three steps, you will be entering the formulas for the collections. Collection pattern estimates should be as accurate as possible since they influence when you will turn sales into cash. The best approach for obtaining this estimate is to start with the historical collection pattern for your company. Next decide whether anything may happen to change the pattern. For example, if the economy is in trouble, you would expect customers to take longer to pay you. So you might adjust your expected collection pattern to reflect this. You can also influence the pattern by dropping poor-paying customers or offering trade discounts to encourage earlier payment. In both of these cases, the pattern changes and more of each sales dollar would be collected earlier.

To enter

a label to identify this section as cash receipts

Type >**A9** and type **Cash rece** (→)
>**B**(A)**9** and type **ipts:** (↵)

Slow-paying customers drain cash from a company and can even make borrowing necessary to keep the company going. Further, a business that allows these accounts to become overextended runs the risk of losing money from bad debts. Excessive bad debt losses plague many small companies by sapping cash needed to pay expenses. Small business losses on bad debts range from a fraction of a percent of sales to percentages large enough to topple a company. An efficient collection system that converts accounts receivable quickly to cash is vital to the health of the business.

One business consultant recommends that firms speed up collection by: invoicing promptly; keeping credit terms tight within federal and state credit laws and local trade practices; and maintaining effective collection follow-up practices.

Prompt invoicing can forestall delays in payment. Customers seldom pay before receiving a bill. Therefore, the longer a company delays in invoicing, the longer the delay in payment. Even a one-day delay can be costly.

Billing methods vary from handwritten notices on preprinted forms to printouts from in-house computers. Seeking to eliminate tedious paperwork and cut personnel costs, small retailers and other small business people often buy computerized billing services offered by some financial institutions or commercial service bureaus.

Operators with a great need for cash on the first of the month arrange billing cycles to encourage customers to pay at that time. Manufacturers often offer discounts of one, two, or even five percent to customers who pay during a specified period.

Collection efforts should be made promptly once an account becomes overdue. "One of the worst errors is to postpone collection efforts in order to hold a past-due customer's goodwill," says one business consultant. "If the account has paid well in the past but is in a difficult situation temporarily, give it extra time or a partial payment schedule. But watch it closely. If it is a habitual 'slow-pay,' that goodwill may not be worth the time spent in collection efforts, the loss of interest on your money — and the possibility of total loss."

This expert recommends that business owners use the "tickler method," which involves calling the delinquent customer and obtaining a definite date of promised payment. Then, if the customer's check hasn't arrived within a reasonable time after the promised date, another call may be placed to tickle the customer's memory. While letters are not as effective as direct phone calls, written reminders are sometimes a sufficient nudge.

Maintaining the inflow of cash from accounts receivable is a continuous task. One month's aggressive efforts may yield adequate working capital for that period, but without a systematic procedure to be followed on a regular basis, collection efforts will lapse and a cash shortage is likely to surface again.

If a small business cannot afford to hire a full-time credit manager, it may find it advisable to hire one part-time during collection periods to ensure efficiency in bill collecting. In addition, many small businesses pay bill collection agencies to round up money owed to them. An attorney also can help by sending collection letters or even arranging legal action.

R O W
10

Collections within 30 days are the first receipt item. All cash sales are collected immediately, and in many industries it is common for payment terms to be net 30 days. But there are a variety of ways to date payment terms, and the method used can affect the length of the period between the sale and the collection. (See TIPS on "Credit collection," above.)

In the example, we assume that 60 percent of sales are either cash or credit sales collected within 30 days.

To enter

a label to identify row 10 as collections made within 30 days of the date of the sale (The asterisk indicates that this line can be changed when you explore "What If" questions.)

a value of 60% in cell D(B)10 to show the percentage collected in this period and to use in the formulas that calculate receipts on this row

a value of $22,500 in cell E(C)10. Since most credit sales collected within the last thirty days were actually made in the previous month, this figure has to be entered directly and not calculated. The assumption is that sales in the last month of the previous forecasting period were identical to those projected for the first month of the new period.

formulas in cell F(D)10 through P(N)10 that will multiply the percentage of sales collected within 30 days (cell D(B)10) times the sales made in the previous month

(See TIPS on "Formatting percentages" on page 32.)

Type >**A10** and type **"% Collect** →
>**B(A)10** and type **ed within** →
>**C(A)10** and type **"(S)30 days*** →
>**D(B)10** and type **60** →
>**E(C)10** and type **22500** →
>**F(D)10** and type **(D(B)10/100)*E(C)7** ↵

AV **Type** >**B10** and type **/AV%** ↵ ↵ **.60** ↵
>**D10** and type **+B10*C7** ↵

To replicate

from one cell to a range

Type >**F(D)10** and type **/R** ↵ **G(E)10.P(N)10** ↵
Prompt line will read N=No change
R=Relative
Type **NR**

Result All monthly columns for row 10 should show $22,500. If you change the figure in D(B)10 from 60 to any other percent, and press the **SHIFT** and **!** keys together, you will see the monthly values change, as they are recalculated by the computer. (Remember to restore the original form before proceeding.)

. . . .

ROW 11 **Collections within 60 days,** or receipts collected between 30 and 60 days of the date of sale, are entered next. We assume that you collect 20 percent of receipts during that period. You'll enter a formula to calculate the percentage of sales and then replicate the formula to other monthly columns.

To enter

a label to identify row 11 as collections made within 60 days of the date of the sale (The asterisk indicates that this line can be changed when you explore "What If" questions.)
a value of 20% in cell D(B)11 to show the percentage collected in this period and to use in the formulas that calculate receipts on this row
a value of $7,500 in cells E(C)11 and F(D)11. Since most credit sales collected within the last sixty days were actually made in the previous two months, these figures have to be entered directly and not calculated. The assumption is that sales in the last two months of the previous period were identical to those projected for the first two months of the new period.
formulas in cells G(E)11 through P(N)11 that will multiply the percentage of sales collected within 60 days (cell D(B)11) (after dividing it by 100 to convert

it to a decimal) times the net sales made two months previously
(See TIPS on "Formatting percentages" on page 32.)

Type >**A11** and type **"% Collect** →
>**B(A)11** and type **ed within** →
>**C(A)11** and type **"(S)60 days*** →
>**D(B)11** and type **20** →
>**E(C)11** and type **7500** →
>**F(D)11** and type **7500** →
>**G(E)11** and type **(D(B)11/100)*E(C)7** ↵

AV **Type** >**B11** and type **/AV%** ↵ ↵ **.20** ↵
>**E11** and type **+B11*C7** ↵

To replicate

from one cell to a range

Type >**G(E)11** and type **/R** ↵ **H(F)11.P(N)11** ↵
Prompt line will read N=No change
R=Relative
Type **NR**

Result All monthly columns for row 11 should show $7,500. If you change the figure in D(B)11 from 20% to any other percent, and press the **SHIFT** and **!** keys together, you will see the monthly values change as the computer recalculates them.

. . . .

ROW 12 **Collections within 90 days,** or receipts collected between 60 and 90 days of the date of sale, are entered last. We assume that you collect 20 percent, or the remainder, of receipts during this period.

To enter

a label to identify row 12 as collections made between 60 and 90 days after the date of the sale
a value of 20% in cell D(B)12 to show the percentage collected in this period and to use in the formulas that calculate receipts on this row
a value of $7,500 in cells E(C)12, F(D)12, and G(E)12. Since most credit sales collected within the last ninety days were actually made prior to the forecast period, these figures have to be entered directly and not calculated. The assumption is that sales in the last month of the previous period were identical to those projected for the first two months of the new period.
formulas in cell H(D)12 through P(N)12 that will multiply the percentage of sales collected within 90

days (cell D(B)12) times the sales made three months previously (cell E(C)7)
(See TIPS on "Formatting percentages" on page 32.)

Type >**A12** and type **"% Collect** →
>**B(A)12** and type **ed within** →
>**C(A)12** and type **"(S)90 days*** →
>**D(B)12** and type **20** →
>**E(C)12** and type **7500** →
>**F(D)12** and type **7500** →
>**G(E)12** and type **7500** →
>**H(F)12** and type **(D(B)12/100)*E(C)7** ⏎

[AV] **Type** >**B12** and type **/AV%** ⏎ ⏎ **.20** ⏎
>**F12** and type **+B12*C7** ⏎

To replicate

from one cell to a range

Type >**H(F)12** and type **/R** ⏎ **I(G)12.P(N)12** ⏎
Prompt line will read N=No change
R=Relative
Type **NR**

Result All monthly columns for row 12 should show $7,500. To recalculate, you can change the figure in D(B)12 from 20% to any other percentage, and press the **SHIFT** and **!** keys together. The monthly values will change.

Note: Whenever you change the percentage of credit sales collected in one period (say within 60 days), the percentages in the other two must be adjusted. The collection pattern percentages must always add up to 100% in our example because they are based on net sales. For example, if the percentage collected within 30 days is decreased from 60% to 50%, the difference must be accounted for in either the 60 day or 90 day collection percentage.

....

ROW 13 **Other cash receipts** include cash received from sources other than sales. These could include tax refunds, proceeds from selling an asset, income from an investment, and so forth.

To enter

a label to identify this row as other cash receipts
a data entry space ($), in cell E(C)13 that can be used to enter information on the screen or on a printed-out blank template
a local format to align the data entry space with the right edge of the column

VISICALC TIPS Displaying dollar values

The VisiCalc Advanced Version program has attribute commands that improve the way dollar values are displayed. You can choose to use any or all of the following attributes:

- All values over 1000 can be displayed with a comma at the thousand position, million position, etc. For example, with this command, a value of 100000 is displayed as 100,000. To activate the command, type **/AV,**

- Dollar signs ($) can be added to numbers so they are immediately recognizable as dollar figures. The value of 100000 is then displayed as $100000. Type **/AV$**

- Parentheses can be automatically displayed to highlight negative values. This is especially valuable when used with accounting or financial applications. A value of −1000, for instance, is displayed as (1000). Type **/AV(**

- The number of decimal places can be precisely controlled. A value of 100 can be displayed as 100.0 (**/AV1F**), 100.00 (**/AV2F**), 100.000 (**/AV3F**) and so on. Type **/AV** followed by the desired number of decimal places, then **F**.

You can use any combination of these commands to display numbers such as −100000 as (100000), ($100000), (100,000.00), or many other ways. Try several possibilities and pick the format you like best.

These attributes can be used locally or globally, and can be added before data are being entered, while data are being entered, or later. The format can be replicated to other cells, columns, rows, or blocks, along with other cell contents or by itself.

Type >**A13** and type **Other cas** →
>**B(A)13** and type **h receipt** →
>**C(A)13** and type **s*** →
>**D(B)13** and type **@SUM(E(C)13.P(N)13)** →
>**E(C)13** and type **/FR "($)** ⏎

To replicate

from one cell to a range

Type >**E(C)13** and type **/R** ⏎ **F(D)13.P(N)13** ⏎

Result A row of data entry spaces should extend from column E(C) to column P(N) on row 13. The formula in cell D(B)13 that adds entries made on the row should be 0 since no entries have been made.

Entering the example, Continued

<table>
<tr><td>R O W
15</td><td>**Total cash receipts** shows the totals for all monthly receipts, which are calculated by the computer.</td></tr>
</table>

To enter

> *a label* to identify row 15 as containing total cash receipts
>
> *a formula* in cell E(C)15 that adds the receipts entered or calculated in the receipt rows (rows 10 through 13). The range of the formula will be the ruled lines above and below the cash receipts line. Entering the SUM command this way allows you to add or delete rows between the ruled lines without affecting the formula.

Type >**A15** and type **Total cas** →
> >**B(A)15** and type **h receipt** →
> >**C(A)15** and type **s** → →
> >**E(C)15** and type **@SUM(E(C)8.E(C)14)** ⏎

To replicate

> *from one cell to a range*

Type >**E(C)15** and type **/R** ⏎ **F(D)15.P(N)15** ⏎
> Prompt line will read N=No change
> R=Relative
> Type **RR**

Result The total for each month's receipts should be $37,500.

Step Four

Enter cash disbursements.

	A	B(A)	C(A)	D(B)	E(C)	F(D)	G(E)	H(F)	I(G)	J(H)	K(I)	L(J)	M(K)	N(L)	O(M)	P(N)
1	Part 1: Cash budget															
2	=====															
3	Item:			What if	1	2	3	4	5	6	7	8	9	10	11	12
4				column	1984	1984	1984	1984	1984	1984	1984	1984	1984	1984	1984	1984
5																
6	Seasonal pattern*			100	8	8	8	8	8	8	8	8	8	8	8	8
7	Net sales; monthly*			450000	37500	37500	37500	37500	37500	37500	37500	37500	37500	37500	37500	37500
8																
9	Cash receipts:															
10	% collected within 30 days*			60	22500	22500	22500	22500	22500	22500	22500	22500	22500	22500	22500	22500
11	% collected within 60 days*			20	7500	7500	7500	7500	7500	7500	7500	7500	7500	7500	7500	7500
12	% collected within 90 days*			20	7500	7500	7500	7500	7500	7500	7500	7500	7500	7500	7500	7500
13	Other cash receipts*			0	($)	($)	($)	($)	($)	($)	($)	($)	($)	($)	($)	($)
14																
15	Total cash receipts				37500	37500	37500	37500	37500	37500	37500	37500	37500	37500	37500	37500
16																
17	Inventory purchases*			60	22500	22500	22500	22500	22500	22500	22500	22500	22500	22500	22500	22500
18	Gen.& admin.*			20	7500	7500	7500	7500	7500	7500	7500	7500	7500	7500	7500	7500
19	Selling expenses*			10	3750	3750	3750	3750	3750	3750	3750	3750	3750	3750	3750	3750
20	Interest expense*			15	0	0	0	0	0	0	0	0	0	0	0	0
21	Other expense*			0	($)	($)	($)	($)	($)	($)	($)	($)	($)	($)	($)	($)
22	Taxes*			40	2400			0			0			0		
23																
24	Total cash disbursements				36150	33750	33750	33750	33750	33750	33750	33750	33750	33750	33750	33750
25																
26																
27	=====															
28																
29																
30																
31	=====															

<table>
<tr><td>R O W
17</td><td>**Inventory purchases** are actual or expected cash payments made for inventory. In a wholesale or retail firm the inventory will be resold. In a manufacturing business the inventory purchased will be used to produce goods to be sold. Estimates for inventory purchases are usually made by reviewing the company's past experience. In Chapter 7 a separate template is described that can forecast your own expenses in this area. In this example, the formulas entered to calculate inventory purchases for each month are set to multiply 60% times the next month's sales. This assumes the firm in the</td></tr>
</table>

example orders inventory two months prior to its sales and pays for it one month prior to its sale. For more details on how this row works in relation to the rest of the example, see TIPS on "Assumptions about inventory purchases," page 123.

To enter

> *a label* to identify this row as inventory purchases (An asterisk is added to identify this as a "What If" line.)

a value of 60% as a starting inventory figure in cell D(B)17 (This cell will be used by the formulas in the monthly columns entered on this row to calculate payments for each month's inventory purchases. A change in the percentage value will automatically change the monthly figures.)

formulas in cells E(C)17 through O(M)17 that multiply the percentage in D(B)17 times the next month's sales

a formula in cell P(N)17 to make the inventory figure in that cell refer back to the first month's sales to calculate inventory purchases (Since each of the previous formulas referenced the next month, this final entry on the cash budget has no "next month" to refer to. The assumption in the example is that sales in the first month after the period covered by the budget will be the same as the opening month covered by the budget.)

(See TIPS on "Formatting percentages" on page 32.)

Type >**A17** and type **Inventory** →
   >**B(A)17** and type **"(S)purchase** →
   >**C(A)17** and type **s*** →
   >**D(B)17** and type **60** →
   >**E(C)17** and type **(D(B)17/100)*F(D)7** ⏎
   >**P(N)17** and type **(D(B)17/100)*E(C)7** ⏎

[AV] **Type** >**B17** and type **/AV%** ⏎ ⏎ **.60** ⏎
   >**C17** and type **+B17*D7** ⏎
   >**N17** and type **+B17*E7** ⏎

To replicate
from one cell to a range

Type >**E(C)17** and type **/R** ⏎ **F(D)17.O(M)17** ⏎
   Prompt line will read N=No change
   R=Relative
   Type **NR**

Result The inventory purchases amount in each of the monthly columns should be $22,500. Try changing the inventory percentage figure in cell D(B)17 from 60% to some other figure. Use the **SHIFT** and ! keys to recalculate and watch the monthly inventory figures change. Be sure to put 60% back into cell D(B)17 and recalculate before you proceed to the next row. If you don't, your results may not match the ones given.

ROW 18 **General and administrative expenses** (G&A) include general salaries and wages, supplies, and other operating costs necessary to the overall running of the business. Examples are officers' salaries, office overhead, light, heat, communication expense, salaries of general office and clerical help, cost of legal and accounting services, "fringe" taxes payable on administrative personnel, various types of franchise and similar fees, and other expenses. G&A expenses are estimated based on past experience, adjusted for any anticipated changes, or by preparing a detailed forecast as explained in Chapter 7. Our starting assumption in the example is that these costs average 20 percent of net sales and are paid for in equal monthly amounts.

To enter
a label to identify this row as general and administrative expenses (The asterisk indicates that this line can be changed when you explore "What If" questions.)

a value of 20% in cell D(B)18 which is the starting value (20% of the original sales figure of $450,000)

formulas in cells E(C)18 and F(D)18 that will multiply the 20 percent figure entered as the starting assumption (after dividing it by 100) times total net sales (which is divided by 12 to give a monthly sales figure). The percentage could be multiplied times monthly sales instead of the total sales divided by twelve but G&A expenses usually don't vary with monthly sales changes. These costs are normally quite even, except for seasonal businesses.

(See TIPS on "Formatting percentages" on page 32.)

Type >**A18** and type **Gen.& adm** →
   >**B(A)18** and type **in.*** → →
   >**D(B)18** and type **20** →
   >**E(C)18** and type **(D(B)18/100)*(D(B)7/12)** ⏎

[AV] **Type** >**B18** and type **/AV%** ⏎ ⏎ **.20** ⏎
   >**C18** and type **+B18*(B7/100)** ⏎

To replicate
from one cell to a range

Type >**E(C)18** and type **/R** ⏎ **F(D)18.P(N)18** ⏎
   Prompt line will read N=No change
   R=Relative
   Type **NN**

Result The monthly G&A expenses shown in each column should be $7,500 ($450,000 x .20 divided by 12 months = $7,500). Try changing the percentage figure in cell D(B)18, and then recalculate. The com-

Entering the example, Continued

puter will instantly recalculate the monthly figures. If you do this be sure to reenter the original 20% and recalculate, otherwise your results may not match those given for subsequent steps.

....

ROW 19
Selling expenses are the actual cash payments you expect to make which are directly or indirectly related to sales. These include such items as salaries of salespeople and sales executives, wages of other sales employees, commissions, travel expenses, entertainment expenses, and advertising. Freight-out is included if the selling firm pays freight or shipping expense. A share of the company's rent, heat, light, power, supplies, and other expenses may also be charged to selling expense, since they were used to support the company's sales activities. However, in many small businesses, these expenses are charged to general and administrative expense. How to estimate selling expense is covered in more detail in Chapter 7.

To enter

a label to identify this row as selling expenses (In our example, we assume that these costs average 10 percent of net sales and are paid for in equal monthly payments.) (The asterisk indicates that this line item can be changed during "What If" questions.)
a value of 10% in cell D(B)19 for total selling expenses (10% of the original sales figure of $450,000)
formulas in cells E(C)19 through P(N)19 that will multiply the 10 percent figure in cell D(B)19 times total net sales. The percentage figure is divided by 100 to convert it to a decimal and total net sales is divided by 12 to give a monthly figure.
(See TIPS on "Formatting percentages" on page 32.)

Type >A19 and type **Selling e** →
>B(A)19 and type **xpenses*** → →
>D(B)19 and type **10** →
>E(C)19 and type **(D(B)19/100)*(D(B)7/12)** ↵

[AV] Type >B19 and type **/AV%** ↵ ↵ **.10** ↵
>C19 and type **(B19/100)*(B7/12)** ↵

To replicate
from one cell to a range

Type >E(C)19 and type **/R** ↵ **F(D)19.P(N)19** ↵
Prompt line will read N=No change
R=Relative
Type **NN**

Result The monthly selling expenses shown in each column should be $3,750 ($45,000 divided by 12). Try changing the total in cell D(B)17 by pressing the **SHIFT** and ! keys to recalculate. The monthly totals will change.

If you do this be sure to restore the selling expenses percentage figure in cell D(B)19 to 10% and recalculate a few times to restore the example before proceeding.

....

ROW 20
Interest expense includes all cash payments for interest made by the company on loans used to finance the business during the period covered by the cash budget.

To enter

a label to identify this row as interest expense (The example assumes that these costs average 15 percent of loans. The loans included will be entered later on row 29 of the cash budget and row 82, long-term debt, on the balance sheet.) (The asterisk identifies this as a "What If" row.)
a value of 15% in cell D(B)20 that is the example's starting assumption for interest rates
formulas in each of the monthly columns to calculate the interest payable on loans entered on row 29 of the cash budget and row 82 of the balance sheet. The formula is embedded in an @IF statement using a VisiCalc function with which you may not be familiar. Since row 20 references row 29 and row 29 references row 20 (indirectly) we have a circular reference built into the model. It will work fine until saved or reloaded, at which point both rows will have ERRORs appear in their cells that can not be cleared. The @IF statement with the @ISERROR(E29) = @TRUE function tells the VisiCalc program that when it calculates row 20 and finds an error in row 29, to calculate 0. This allows the ERRORs to be cleared by pressing the **SHIFT** and ! keys to recalculate when the example is saved and reloaded.
(See TIPS on "Formatting percentages" on page 32.)

Type >A20 and type **Interest** →
>B(A)20 and type **expense*** → →
>D(B)20 and type **15** →
>E(C)20 and type **@IF(@ISERROR(E(C)29)= @TRUE,0,((D(B)20/100)*(@SUM(E(C)29.E(C)29) + E(C)82))/12** ↵

AV Type >**B20** and type **/AV%** (⏎) (⏎) **.15** (⏎)
>**C20** and type **@IF (@ISERROR (C29) = @TRUE,
0,(B20*@SUM (C29.C29) + C82)/12** (⏎)

To replicate
from one cell to a range

Type >**E(C)20** and type **/R** (⏎) **F(D)20.P(N)20** (⏎)
Prompt line will read N=No change
R=Relative
Type **RNNR**

Result Since no loans on long-term debts have been entered to this point, all monthly interest expenses
should be 0.

. . . .

<u>R O W</u>   **Other expense** includes a variety of miscella-
21   neous expenses such as the amount of cash
paid to lenders to reduce the loan balance (the principal
on existing debt) or to equipment suppliers for new fixed
assets.

To enter
a label to identify this row as other expense (The asterisk identifies this is a "What If" row.)
a formula in cell D(B)21 that will total any entries in
the monthly columns on this row
data entry spaces that can be used to enter other expenses

Type >**A21** and type **Other exp** (→)
>**B(A)21** and type **ense*** (→)(→)
>**D(B)21** and type **@SUM(E(C)21.P(N)21)** (→)
>**E(C)21** and type **/FR "($)** (⏎)

To replicate
from one cell to a range

Type >**E(C)21** and type **/R** (⏎) **F(D)21. P(N)21** (⏎)

Result Since the original example contains no other expenses, the formula in cell D(B)21 should show 0,
and the monthly columns should each show a blank
data entry space.

<u>R O W</u>   **Taxes** are the actual cash amounts paid dur-
22   ing a month to meet federal, state, and local
tax obligations. In the example we assume that the starting tax rate is 40% of income before taxes (these will be
calculated on the income statement entered in Chapter 4)
and are paid quarterly.

To enter
a label to identify this row as taxes (The asterisk
identifies this as a "What If" row.)
a value of 40% for the starting tax rate (Taxes, in
this example, are 40% of income before taxes; in the
next chapter this will be entered on row 47 of the pro
forma income statement.)
a value in cell D(B)22 of $2,400 representing the
total taxes due in January based on income earned in
the period previous to the start of this budget
formulas in cells H(F)22 (April), K(I)22 (July), and
N(L)22 (October) that add the monthly taxes calculated on row 48 of the income statement (Each formula adds the taxes calculated for the previous quarter (three months) and enters the results into the
month when payment is due.)
(See TIPS on "Formatting percentages" on page 32.)

Type >**A22** and type **Taxes*** (→)(→)(→)
>**D(B)22** and type **40** (→)
>**E(C)22** and type **2400** (→)(→)(→)
>**H(F)22** and type **@SUM(E(C)48.G(E)48)** (⏎)

AV Type >**B22** and type **/AV%** (⏎) (⏎) **.40** (⏎)

To replicate
from one cell to another

Type >**H(F)22** and type **/R** (⏎) **K(I)22** (⏎)
Prompt line will read N=No change
R=Relative
Type **RR**

from one cell to another

Type >**H(F)22** and type **/R** (⏎) **N(L)22** (⏎)
Prompt line will read N=No change
R=Relative
Type **RR**

Result Since no income before taxes has yet been entered,
all quarterly tax payments on this row should be 0
with the exception of January which has been entered as a value, not a formula.
When you explore "What Ifs" in Chapter 6,
this line may occasionally show negative figures.

ROW 24

Total cash disbursements are the totals of all cash outlays for all months.

To enter

a label to identify this line as total cash disbursements
a formula in cell E(C)24 that will total all of the operating expenses entered between the ruled lines on rows 16 and 23

Type >**A24** and type **Total cas** →
>**B(A)24** and type **h disburs** →
>**C(A)24** and type **ements** → →
>**E(C)24** and type **@SUM(E(C)16.E(C)23)** ⏎

To replicate

from one cell to a range

Type >**E(C)24** and type **/R** ⏎ **F(D)24.P(N)24** ⏎
Prompt line will read N=No change
R=Relative
Type **RR**

Result All the monthly columns on the total cash disbursements line will be $36,150 in January (column E(C)) and the rest of the months should all be $33,750.

Step Five

Enter net cash flow.

	A	B(A)	C(A)	D(B)	E(C)	F(D)	G(E)	H(F)	I(G)	J(H)	K(I)	L(J)	M(K)	N(L)	O(M)	P(N)
1	Part 1: Cash budget															
2																
3	Item:				What if	1	2	3	4	5	6	7	8	9	10	11	12
4					column	1984	1984	1984	1984	1984	1984	1984	1984	1984	1984	1984	1984
5																
6	Seasonal pattern*			100	8	8	8	8	8	8	8	8	8	8	8	8
7	Net sales; monthly*			450000	37500	37500	37500	37500	37500	37500	37500	37500	37500	37500	37500	37500
8																
9	Cash receipts:															
10	% collected within 30 days*			60	22500	22500	22500	22500	22500	22500	22500	22500	22500	22500	22500	22500
11	% collected within 60 days*			20	7500	7500	7500	7500	7500	7500	7500	7500	7500	7500	7500	7500
12	% collected within 90 days*			20	7500	7500	7500	7500	7500	7500	7500	7500	7500	7500	7500	7500
13	Other cash receipts*			0	($)	($)	($)	($)	($)	($)	($)	($)	($)	($)	($)	($)
14																
15	Total cash receipts				37500	37500	37500	37500	37500	37500	37500	37500	37500	37500	37500	37500
16																
17	Inventory purchases*			60	22500	22500	22500	22500	22500	22500	22500	22500	22500	22500	22500	22500
18	Gen. & admin.*			20	7500	7500	7500	7500	7500	7500	7500	7500	7500	7500	7500	7500
19	Selling expenses*			10	3750	3750	3750	3750	3750	3750	3750	3750	3750	3750	3750	3750
20	Interest expense*			15	0	0	0	0	0	0	0	0	0	0	0	0
21	Other expense*			0	($)	($)	($)	($)	($)	($)	($)	($)	($)	($)	($)	($)
22	Taxes*			40	2400			0			0			0		
23																
24	Total cash disbursements				36150	33750	33750	33750	33750	33750	33750	33750	33750	33750	33750	33750
25																
26	Net cash flow				1350	3750	3750	3750	3750	3750	3750	3750	3750	3750	3750	3750
27																
28																
29																
30																
31																

ROW 26

Net cash flow is the difference between all cash received and all cash spent. This figure is extremely important for most small businesses. It basically determines whether or not you will be in business in the future. Operating with negative net cash flow for too long a period of time means financial failure unless there is some other source of cash that you can draw upon.

To enter

a label to identify this line as net cash flow (In our example, net cash flow is determined by subtracting total cash disbursements from total receipts.)
a formula in cell E(C)26 that will subtract total cash disbursements on row 24 from total cash receipts on row 15

Type >**A26** and type **Net cash** →
>**B(A)26** and type **flow** → → →
>**E(C)26** and type **+E(C)15-E(C)24** ⏎

To replicate

from one cell to a range

Type >**E(C)26** and type **/R** ⏎ **F(D)26.P(N)26** ⏎
Prompt line will read N=No change
R=Relative
Type **RR**

Result The monthly columns on the net cash flow row will read $1,350 in January (column E(C)) and $3,750 in each of the other monthly columns.

Enter cash position.

	A	B(A)	C(A)	D(B)	E(C)	F(D)	G(E)	H(F)	I(G)	J(H)	K(I)	L(J)	M(K)	N(L)	O(M)	P(N)
1	Part 1: Cash budget															
2	===
3	Item:			What if	1	2	3	4	5	6	7	8	9	10	11	12
4				column	1984	1984	1984	1984	1984	1984	1984	1984	1984	1984	1984	1984
5	===
6	Seasonal pattern*			100	8	8	8	8	8	8	8	8	8	8	8	8
7	Net sales; monthly*			450000	37500	37500	37500	37500	37500	37500	37500	37500	37500	37500	37500	37500
8	===
9	Cash receipts:															
10	% collected within 30 days*			60	22500	22500	22500	22500	22500	22500	22500	22500	22500	22500	22500	22500
11	% collected within 60 days*			20	7500	7500	7500	7500	7500	7500	7500	7500	7500	7500	7500	7500
12	% collected within 90 days*			20	7500	7500	7500	7500	7500	7500	7500	7500	7500	7500	7500	7500
13	Other cash receipts*			0	($)	($)	($)	($)	($)	($)	($)	($)	($)	($)	($)	($)
14																
15	Total cash receipts				37500	37500	37500	37500	37500	37500	37500	37500	37500	37500	37500
16																
17	Inventory purchases*			60	22500	22500	22500	22500	22500	22500	22500	22500	22500	22500	22500	22500
18	Gen. & admin.*			20	7500	7500	7500	7500	7500	7500	7500	7500	7500	7500	7500	7500
19	Selling expenses*			10	3750	3750	3750	3750	3750	3750	3750	3750	3750	3750	3750	3750
20	Interest expense*			15	0	0	0	0	0	0	0	0	0	0	0	0
21	Other expense*			0	($)	($)	($)	($)	($)	($)	($)	($)	($)	($)	($)	($)
22	Taxes*			40	2400			0			0			0		
23	===
24	Total cash disbursements				36150	33750	33750	33750	33750	33750	33750	33750	33750	33750	33750
25																
26	Net cash flow				1350	3750	3750	3750	3750	3750	3750	3750	3750	3750	3750
27	===
28	Opening cash balance				20000	21350	25100	28850	32600	36350	40100	43850	47600	51350	55100	58850
29	Loans required			0	0	0	0	0	0	0	0	0	0	0	0	0
30	Ending cash balance*			20000	21350	25100	28850	32600	36350	40100	43850	47600	51350	55100	58850	62600
31	===

ROW 28 **Opening cash balance** shows the cash on hand at the beginning of each month. It is the same figure as the ending cash balance from the previous month.

To enter

a label to identify this line as the opening balance
formulas in cells E(C)28 through P(N)28 that carry the ending cash balance forward from the previous month to be entered on row 30

Type >**A28** and type **Opening c** →
    >**B**(A)**28** and type **ash balan** →
    >**C**(A)**28** and type **ce*** → →
    >**E**(C)**28** and type **+D**(B)**30** ↵

To replicate

from one cell to a range

Type >**E**(C)**28** and type **/R** ↵ **F**(D)**28.P**(N)**28** ↵
    Prompt line will read N=No change
    R=Relative
    Type **R**

Result Since this row picks up the values from a row that is not yet entered (row 30, ending cash balance) all monthly values should be 0.

ROW 29 **Loans required** represent the amount of cash you need to borrow to insure that the ending balance (to be entered on row 30) is positive; that is, to make sure you don't run out of cash.

To enter

a label to identify this line of the budget as loans required
a formula that will automatically calculate the loans you require based on the month's opening cash balance (row 28) and the monthly net cash flow on row 26
(If the month's net cash flow plus opening balance is less than zero the formula converts the minus value to a positive figure with the @ABS command and enters it on the loan line.)

Type >**A29** and type **Loans req** →
    >**B**(A)**29** and type **uired** → →
    >**D**(B)**29** and type **@SUM(E**(C)**29.P**(N)**29)** →
    >**E**(C)**29** and type **@IF((E**(C)**26 + E**(C)**28)<0,
    @ABS(E**(C)**26 + E**(C)**28),0)** ↵

Entering the example, Continued

To replicate
from one cell to a range

Type >**E**(C)**29** and type **/R** ⏎ **F**(D)**29.P**(N)**29** ⏎
Prompt line will read N=No change
R=Relative
Type **RRRR**

Result Since the ending cash balance row has not yet been entered, you should again have a row of zeros in the monthly columns. Even after row 30 is entered, all entries on this row will remain 0 because the beginning example is designed to require no loans. Values will appear on this row during some of the "What Ifs" we will explore later.

BUSINESS TIPS Borrowing funds

Loans play a critical role in cash management. Commercial banks are a primary source of financing for small-business working capital needs and provide many services to help small businesses achieve financial stability. Other sources of loan money are the Small Business Administration, insurance companies, commercial finance companies, savings and loan companies, and small business investment companies.

When determining the most practical source of raising money, the business manager should consider these factors:

- cost
- risk
- flexibility
- control
- availability

Two common sources of funds for small businesses are:

Line of credit. A line of credit is a commitment by a lending institution to lend a company a negotiated amount of money for a specified period of time, usually one year. The line of credit provides assurance that the firm will be able to get funds when needed, although the company is under no obligation to borrow the full amount negotiated. Usually secured by accounts receivable and/or inventory, credit lines are used most commonly by businesses associated with seasonal financing of inventories and receivables. Such businesses might include garden supply stores and toy stores.

Once a year, the lender may expect the unsecured borrower to "clear the line" by paying off the open line entirely. The ability to pay off the line completely, even for a short period, is proof to the lender that the borrower has not "locked" the line of credit into the company's cash flow system. The line usually is cleared at the period when the debt is at its lowest level, typically immediately following a seasonal sales peak.

Credit agreements. Usually written for one year, credit agreements are of two types. Under a *revolving* agreement, the company may borrow, repay, and reborrow up to a certain limit, at a variable interest rate, any time funds are needed. A *nonrevolving* agreement contracts the lending institution to lend a maximum amount, all at once or in portions. Agreements may be canceled if the borrower fails to live up to the loan agreement terms. For these contracts, lending institutions may require a commitment fee.

Frequently, a combination of funding sources will provide the best solution to a company's capital needs. A firm might find it wise to take these steps:

- Use available internal sources by retaining the maximum earnings, managing assets carefully, and controlling costs.

- Take advantage of available trade credit, while avoiding unnecessary costs that might be incurred through delinquency penalties or forfeiture of cash discounts.

- Use short-term debt capital to meet short-term needs, avoiding the higher interest expense and restrictive conditions of long-term borrowing. (The availability of short-term loans is likely to be increased if the business presents quality collateral as security for the loans.)

- Combine debt and equity as needed to meet the longer-term capital requirements of the business.

- Obtain funds from an outside source, such as the refinancing of the owner's residence or a home equity loan.

BUSINESS TIPS A checklist for cash management

General cash management

- Study cash-flow cycle to determine the working cash needs of the company.

- Prepare a monthly (or quarterly) budget forecast against which to measure performance.

- Determine break-even point, based on fixed and variable costs and sales needs.

Banking

- Make deposits at least daily.

- Use night deposit facilities for remittances received after regular banking hours.

- Keep bank account balances at levels sufficient to avoid bank service charges.

- Put cash to work in appropriate interest-bearing accounts.

- Make arrangements for concentration banking if several businesses and banking locations are used.

- Use cash management services whenever advantageous.

Accounts receivable

- Bill all regular sales and services promptly.

- Check customer credit standing promptly and adequately.

- Maintain realistic credit policies.

- Offer incentives, such as cash discounts, for early payment.

- Develop and enforce penalties for consistently late payments.

- Prepare receivables aging reports regularly and use them for following up delays in collections.

- Use COD terms for chronic slow payers or customer shipments above credit limits.

- Use progressive billing for partial shipments of customer orders.

- To avoid delayed collection of balances, process customers' claims (for short shipments, defective merchandise, losses in transit, etc.) immediately.

- Turn over delinquent customer account balances to collection agencies or attorneys as soon as warranted.

- Beware of extending significant credit balances to customers whose businesses may be in precarious financial condition.

Inventory

- Limit purchases to materials needed for business.

- When making repeated volume purchases from the same supplier, seek price guarantees for a definite time.

- Secure all possible cash discounts for purchases.

- Periodically review stock-movement figures.

- As soon as market changes become evident, dispose of slow-moving goods on the best possible terms.

- Provide inventory with physical safeguards and controls to minimize risk of unauthorized withdrawals.

Expenses

- Pay insurance premiums and other large bills in installments.

- Consider leasing equipment or other large items, in order to avoid large cash outlays.

- Arrange advertising schedules to take advantage of media rate reductions for multiple insertions or spots.

- Develop barter arrangements for goods and services.

- Use a WATS (Wide Area Telephone Service) line if volume of long distance telephone calls warrants it.

- Use services of freight-rate and routing consultants to keep down the cost of outbound freight.

- Use outside professionals only for work that they alone can do, but use free-lance or temporary workers if they can do the job to keep down full-time payroll.

- Use computerized billing and payroll services offered by service bureaus and financial institutions.

- Evaluate periodically the cost-effectiveness of the sales personnel.

Revenues

- Reevaluate the profitability of product lines frequently.

- Use by-products, scrap, waste, and so-called "seconds" to realize additional income.

ROW 30

Ending cash balance shows the cash on hand at the end of each month. It is equal to what you start the month with (the opening cash balance) plus the month's net cash flow and any necessary loans.

To enter

a label to identify this line as ending cash balance (The asterisk identifies this as a "What If" row.)

a value of $20,000 which is the example's ending balance from the previous month (not on this budget)

a formula in cell E(C)30 that adds net cash flow, opening balance, and loans borrowed for each month

Type >**A30** and type **Ending ca** →
>**B(A)30** and type **sh balanc** →
>**C(A)30** and type **e*** →
>**D(B)30** and type **20000** →
>**E(C)30** and type **+E(C)26+E(C)28+E(C)29** ⏎

To replicate

from one cell to a range

Type >**E(C)30** and type **/R** ⏎ **F(D)30.P(N)30** ⏎
Prompt line will read N=No change
R=Relative
Type **RRR**

Result Use the **SHIFT** and **!** keys to recalculate the worksheet. The values on the ending cash balance row should read as follows:

Cell	Month	Value	Cell	Month	Value
E(C)30	1	$21350	K(I)30	7	$43850
F(D)30	2	$25100	L(J)30	8	$47600
G(E)30	3	$28850	M(K)30	9	$51350
H(F)30	4	$32600	N(L)30	10	$55100
I(G)30	5	$36350	O(M)30	11	$58850
J(H)30	6	$40100	P(N)30	12	$62600

Note that you now also have values for each month's opening balance. As you will see when we explore "What Ifs," should the ending balance for any previous month be negative, or so small that a negative net cash flow in the current month results, values will be calculated on the loans required line so that the monthly closing balance is 0. This automatic calculation shows how much money has to be borrowed to make sure the firm does not run out of cash. Normally most businesses will never want an ending cash balance of zero. They establish a minimum cash balance. If necessary they will borrow cash to meet the minimum cash balance.

Step Seven

Formatting, protecting, and saving.

Formatting the cash budget. If you are using the Advanced Version you can format a worksheet after it has been finished. This allows you to experiment with a number of different formats without having to replicate formulas and data as you would with the regular VisiCalc program. In our example we are going to format all numbers so that they have commas separating thousands, and so negative numbers appear in parentheses.

[AV] To format
the cash budget

Type >**B7** and type **/AV,(** ⏎ ⏎

To replicate

from one cell to a range

Type >**B7** and type **/R**
The prompt line will read Replicate: (, Source range or ENTER
Type **(**
The prompt line will read Replicate:Limit: ACNR)
Type **A) B8.B30** ⏎

from one range to another

Type >**B7** and type **/R**
The prompt line will read Replicate: (, Source range or ENTER
Type **(**
The prompt line will read Replicate:Limit: ACNR)
Type **A).B30** ⏎ **C7.N7** ⏎

Result The cash budget is now formatted. All dollar values $1,000 or larger should appear with commas separating thousands and negative numbers should be in parentheses.

Protecting the cash budget. If you are using the Advanced Version all of the cells in the cash budget that won't be changed when you explore "What Ifs" can be protected. You will do this by first protecting the entire worksheet, and then go back to "unprotect" those few cells where changes will be made.

[AV] To protect
the cash budget

Type >**A1** and type **/AMP** ⏎ ⏎

The best time to format a worksheet, so it will be easy to read and will provide the precision you need, is after it has been completed and data entered. At this point, you can try different options and choose the best. This is easy to do with general formats, but local formats can be a problem. Local formats can't be replicated into cells, rows, or columns without affecting cell contents. Formulas and data are erased unless they are replicated along with the format. Formats can be changed, but large worksheets can often require a great deal of formatting and replicating.

The Advanced Version solves this problem. When you use the *replicate* command you can choose from several options.

You can replicate just the attributes (a number of decimal places, numbers displayed with commas and dollar signs, negative values displayed in parentheses) by replicating with the **/R(A)** command. (Look up this command in your owner's manual if you need instruction on how to use it.) Or you can choose to replicate just the contents of a cell and not the attributes. The command **/R(C)** replicates just cell contents (formulas, data, labels).

To replicate
from one cell to a range

Type >**A1** and type **/R**
The prompt line will read Replicate: (, Source range or ENTER
Type (
The prompt line will read Replicate:Limit: ACNR)
Type **A)** ⏎ **A2.A31** ⏎

from one range to another

Type >**A1** and type **/R**
The prompt line will read Replicate: (, Source range or ENTER
Type (
The prompt line will read Replicate:Limit: ACNR)
Type **A).A31** ⏎ **B31.N31** ⏎

AV To unprotect
those cells you'll use to explore "What Ifs"

Type >**C6** and type **/AMU** ⏎ ⏎

To replicate
from one cell to a range

Type >**C6** and type **/R**

The prompt line will read Replicate: (, Source range or ENTER
Type (
The prompt line will read Replicate:Limit: ACNR)
Type **A)** ⏎ **D6.N6** ⏎

>**B7** and type **/AMU** ⏎ ⏎

from one cell to a range

Type >**B7** and type **/R**
The prompt line will read Replicate: (, Source range or ENTER
Type (
The prompt line will read Replicate:Limit: ACNR)
Type **A)** ⏎ **B8.B22** ⏎

>**B30** and type **/AMU** ⏎ ⏎

Result The entire cash budget is now protected except those cells where new data will be entered when exploring "What Ifs." To check that it is, go to any cell and try entering a value, label, or formula. In those cells you unprotected (indicated with an * following the label) you should be able to do so. In all other cells the new entry shouldn't be accepted and you should get a message telling you the cell is protected. If you do make any changes be sure to reenter the original value and recalculate the worksheet a few times, otherwise your results may not match those given in the instructions that follow.

Save your work. You will often want to save a VisiCalc worksheet even when it isn't complete (a worksheet is any combination of labels, data, or formulas entered into the VisiCalc program when working out a problem). This protects your work when you want to take a break and prevents its loss if a mistake is made or if something goes wrong.

Entering the example, Continued

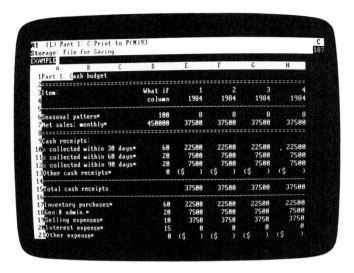

Step by step with the IBM PC and the regular VisiCalc program:

1 Insert a formatted diskette into drive A and close the drive door. *Note:* If you are using two drives and want to save the worksheet on drive B, insert the blank diskette into that drive.

2 Move the cursor to the upper left corner of the worksheet by typing >**A1** ⏎ or the HOME key. When a file is reloaded from the diskette into memory, the screen display will come up exactly as it was when saved. Since file titles can be conveniently placed in the upper left-hand corner, it helps always to reload the files with the top left-hand corner visible on the screen.

3 To save the file onto the diskette, type **/SS**. The prompt line will read **Storage: File for Saving**. Since this is the first time this file has been saved, it needs a file name.

Type **Example** ⏎

Note: If you are saving the worksheet on drive B, type **/SS**. The prompt line will read **Storage: File for Saving**. When you type in the file name you have to first indicate that you want it saved on drive B, so type **B:Example** ⏎.

Result The disk drive will spin, the red light will come on, and the diskette will record the worksheet so that it can be reloaded when needed. The display on the screen is unchanged, as is the data in memory. You can choose to continue or to turn the computer off. Everything that was in memory is now safely stored on the diskette, from which it can easily be reloaded back into memory (see "Reload your example," page 51). To be even safer, make a backup copy of the disk so that you have two of them. Store them separately so the same accident can't happen to both.

VISICALC TIPS Protecting your templates

When a template is finished and saved, it is normally reloaded and filled in with data when needed. Problems can arise at this point. You, or others asked to use the template, can inadvertently erase or change formulas, delete rows or columns, or cause an unending list of difficulties. There are several ways to prevent this situation. You can write-protect diskettes so the master and other files can't be inadvertently overwritten by storing another VisiCalc file on top of them. In addition, the Advanced Version has an option that can protect the contents of individual or groups of cells in a worksheet. The new option works in the following way:

1 Complete protection of a cell is obtained by typing the **/AMP** command, which prevents anything from being entered until the cell is unprotected by typing **/AMU**

2 Partial, or selective, protection is obtained with these commands:

■ You can prevent labels from being overtyped (except with other labels) by typing **/AML**

■ You can prevent numbers from being overtyped and erased by typing **/AM#**

■ You can protect numbers and formulas from being overwritten with labels by typing **/AMV**

These formats can be entered either locally or globally, and can be added before data are entered, while they are being entered, or after they are entered. These formats can be replicated by themselves or along with other contents of a cell.

With the VisiCalc or VisiCalc Advanced Version pro-grams, you can save information in three ways: as text files, DIF files, or print files. Because different com-mands load and save each of these three types of files, it helps to know how each was saved. The IBM PC adds a suffix to every file you save to tell you what kind of file it is.

■ **.VC** used as a suffix after a file name indicates that the file is a regular VisiCalc text file saved using the **/SS** command, which can be reloaded using the **/SL** command.

■ **.DIF** following a file name indicates that the file is in the disk interchange format used to move files from one file to another, or from one program to another. DIF files are saved using the **/S#S** command, and can be reloaded using the **/S#L** command.

■ **.PF** as a suffix indicates that the file is a print file saved using the **/PF** command. Print files cannot be reloaded into the VisiCalc worksheet, but with the ap-propriate program these files can be transferred to a word processing program.

VisiCalc file names on the IBM PC:

■ Can be up to 8 characters long.

■ Must start with a letter.

■ Remaining characters can be letters or numbers. A file name cannot include periods (except before a suffix which is assigned automatically) or spaces.

If you try to save a file with an improper file name, you may receive an ERROR message and must try again.

Be sure not to overwrite. When you save a file, there is no automatic file name checking. For instance you can load the example, explore "What Ifs" on it, and then store it back on the disk over the original example by mistake. If you do this, the file you stored over will be erased. To protect valuable files against this possibil-ity, you can keep the master file on a separate diskette that is write-protected.

To write-protect an entire diskette, place a piece of tape (usually included with newly purchased disks) over the write-protect cutout on the side of the disk-ette. If you want to change the file at some point, just remove the tape before trying to save a file to the diskette.

When you try to store a file and there isn't sufficient room left on the diskette, the prompt line will read Storage:File for Saving File Name Error:Disk Full, fol-lowed by a blinking cursor. To save the file, you can simply insert another formatted diskette (if it isn't formatted, you can still do so without affecting the data in memory or on the screen) and save the file. If you don't have any other diskettes handy, you will have to make a choice whether to lose this file or to erase another one on the same diskette to make room for it. To see if there is another file you can erase, just type **/SD** and the edit line will read Storage:File to Delete. Use the ⟶ key to scroll through the disk directory. If you find a file you can live without, type ⏎. The edit line will read Delete File:Type Y to Confirm. If you type **Y**, the file will be erased and you'll have room on the diskette to save the new file. Type any key other than Y and the command will be cancelled. If you don't find a file you can spare, scroll right on through the directory to take you back to the starting point without deleting any files.

4 · The pro forma income statement

Introduction

Projected financial statements

Projected financial statements are called *pro forma*, as in a pro forma income statement or pro forma balance sheet. *Pro forma* derives from the Latin words *pro*, meaning before or in place of, and *forma*, which means form, figure, or appearance. Thus, when you construct pro forma statements, you are estimating figures, or the state or appearance of your company before the fact. You are recording what you expect the company to look like financially a month, six months, or a year from now.

By providing a look into the future of your business, projected financial statements enable you to judge what the financial needs of your business will be at the end of the forecast period. You can then plan ahead of time for whatever steps may be needed to strengthen the business or to prepare for future growth. If you wait until the need actually arises, it will be more difficult and may even be too late.

Regardless of when you prepare a pro forma, always bear in mind two characteristics of projected financial statements. First, these statements can be built up in a number of ways. The best approach is to rely on whatever information is fairly easy to get together and enables you to make the most accurate estimates for the various accounts. Second, remember that these statements are based on estimates and assumptions. They provide only a rough sketch of what may happen.

If actual performance differs widely from the estimates at any point, however, the reason should be sought. Was the estimate unrealistic, or were there weaknesses in your company's performance at that point? Whichever proves to be the case, the trouble spot should be attended to.

The pro forma income statement

While the cash budget projects cash flows and cash balances, the pro forma income statement projects performance of the business in terms of profit (based on an estimated level of sales or other income) over a certain period of time. It is the primary document used to project profits, so it brings together a lot of assumptions and forecasts about the firm's future operations and activities, including sales, cost of goods sold, and operating expenses.

Structurally, a pro forma income statement looks like a regular income statement, but the figures, or values of the line items, are projected. If you use the accrual method of accounting, the income statement records sales when goods are shipped or services are performed.

All expenses that are directly the result of producing those goods or services are also recorded at the time the sale is declared. If you are on a cash basis, sales are recorded when payment is received and expenses are entered on your books when they are actually paid. You follow the same basic procedure with a pro forma, but you record projected instead of actual sales and costs.

The purpose of preparing or using a pro forma is plain: It is part of planning for profit. It can help set targets for profits, estimate financing requirements, and identify asset management needs. It can also be used in performance assessment, particularly over short periods, by comparing it to actual performance. In short, the pro forma can help management anticipate the future and plan for it. To be effective, the statement must be prepared carefully and realistically. Optimism needs to be balanced with shrewd analysis to achieve a useful, working document. The income statement must also be consistent with the pro forma balance sheet and the cash budget; these three planning tools should work together.

When to construct a pro forma income statement

A pro forma income statement should be drawn up at least quarterly; and if your business is short of funds, you would be wise to prepare one more often. The pro forma can help you avoid unforeseen peak-period needs that might prove embarrassing. Most small firms find monthly statements the best for planning and control.

How to construct a pro forma income statement

The value of the projected income statement as a guide depends largely on your estimate of sales during the period for which the projection is made. It is therefore worth your time to develop this estimate as accurately as possible. (Forecasting sales is covered in more detail in Chapter 7 of this book.) To get that estimate, you use the past experience of your firm, figures provided by salespeople, other managers' projections, and information such as trade or market trends.

Next, you estimate the cost of goods sold. The first step is to analyze past operating data to find out the percentage of cost of goods sold relative to sales in previous periods. This percentage can then be adjusted for expected variations in costs, such as labor, prices of raw materials or supplies, and efficiency of operations. (A more detailed method estimates each cost item separately and totals the results. Experience will dictate the better method for you.)

Finally, estimate other expenses, other income, and taxes. Remember that all estimates based on past experience must be updated to accommodate cost increases.

Getting ready

Reload your example. If you proceeded directly to this chapter without turning off the computer, you can continue with this chapter without any preparation. If, however, you turned the computer off after saving the example, you will have to reload it to resume working. To reload the example follow these steps.

1 Load the VisiCalc Program diskette into the computer. If you can't remember how to do this refer to Step 2, "Load the VisiCalc program," on page 22.

2 When the characteristic VisiCalc display appears on the screen, remove the VisiCalc Program diskette (or in the case of the Advanced Version the Loader diskette) from the drive and file it carefully in a safe place.

3 Insert the data diskette on which you saved the example into drive A.

> Type **/SL**
> The prompt line reads Storage: File to Load
> Type **Example** ⏎ (Or you could use the →
> key to scroll through the files until Example
> appears on the screen and then type ⏎.)

The drive will begin to spin and its red light will come on. In a few seconds the drive will stop and your example should appear on the screen exactly as it appeared when last saved.

When the example is reloaded, some cells may have ERROR messages appear in them. To remove these ERROR messages, just press the **SHIFT** and **!** keys simultaneously twice to recalculate the worksheet.

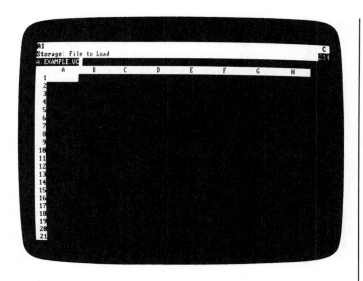

Entering the example

You'll build a pro forma income statement on the computer by following step-by-step, row-by-row instructions as in the previous chapter. Remember that this sample statement, like the cash budget and the balance sheet (Chapters 3 and 5), represents that of a typical small retail operation. You may want your pro formas and cash budget set up in a slightly different manner, but changes can be made after the model is built. We advise you to follow our model first, and adapt it later. Otherwise, you could get out of step with the instructions, which will make your work unnecessarily difficult. With either VisiCalc version, you should follow Steps One through Five.

Only users of VisiCalc Advanced Version should follow the formatting and protecting sections in Step Six. Since the entire statement will be protected, these features are used after the example is completed. All users should follow the instuctions for saving your work (the last section of Step Six).

Once the pro forma income statement is built, it will be possible to automatically and instantly recalculate the data. The statement will use information entered under the cash budget so the worksheets are linked and consistent.

Part 2: Pro forma income statement

Net sales	450000	37500	37500	37500	37500	37500	37500	37500	37500	37500	37500	37500	37500
Cost of goods sold	270000	22500	22500	22500	22500	22500	22500	22500	22500	22500	22500	22500	22500
Gross profit	180000	15000	15000	15000	15000	15000	15000	15000	15000	15000	15000	15000	15000
General & administrative	90000	7500	7500	7500	7500	7500	7500	7500	7500	7500	7500	7500	7500
Selling expenses	45000	3750	3750	3750	3750	3750	3750	3750	3750	3750	3750	3750	3750
Depreciation	15000	1250	1250	1250	1250	1250	1250	1250	1250	1250	1250	1250	1250
Operating income	30000	2500	2500	2500	2500	2500	2500	2500	2500	2500	2500	2500	2500
Interest expense	0	0	0	0	0	0	0	0	0	0	0	0	0
Other income/expense*	0	($)	($)	($)	($)	($)	($)	($)	($)	($)	($)	($)	($)
Income before taxes	30000	2500	2500	2500	2500	2500	2500	2500	2500	2500	2500	2500	2500
Taxes	12000	1000	1000	1000	1000	1000	1000	1000	1000	1000	1000	1000	1000
Net income	18000	1500	1500	1500	1500	1500	1500	1500	1500	1500	1500	1500	1500

Enter headings and ruled lines.

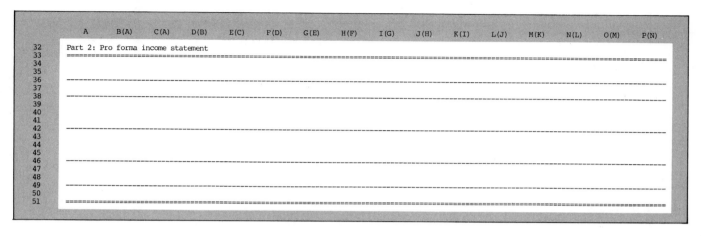

<table>
<tr><th></th><th>A</th><th>B(A)</th><th>C(A)</th><th>D(B)</th><th>E(C)</th><th>F(D)</th><th>G(E)</th><th>H(F)</th><th>I(G)</th><th>J(H)</th><th>K(I)</th><th>L(J)</th><th>M(K)</th><th>N(L)</th><th>O(M)</th><th>P(N)</th></tr>
</table>

```
32   Part 2: Pro forma income statement
33   ================================================================================================
34
35   -------------------------------------------------------------------------------------------------
36
37
38   -------------------------------------------------------------------------------------------------
39
40
41
42   -------------------------------------------------------------------------------------------------
43
44
45
46   -------------------------------------------------------------------------------------------------
47
48
49   -------------------------------------------------------------------------------------------------
50
51   ================================================================================================
```

ROW 32

Headings and ruled lines for the pro forma income statement identify the statement and make it easier to read.

To enter

a label to identify Part 2 of the example as the pro forma income statement
double ruled lines across the worksheet
a single ruled line from column A to column P(N)

Type >**A32** and type **Part 2: P** →
   >**B**(A)**32** and type **ro forma** →
   >**C**(A)**32** and type **income st** →
   >**D**(B)**32** and type **atement** ⏎

   >**A33** and type **/-=**

   >**A36** and type **/--**⏎

To replicate

from one cell to a range

Type >**A33** and type **/R** ⏎ **B33.P**(N)**33** ⏎
   >**A36** and type **/R** ⏎ **B36.P**(N)**36** ⏎

from one range to another range

Type >**A33** and type **/R.P**(N)**33** ⏎ **A51** ⏎
   >**A36** and type **/R.P**(N)**36** ⏎ **A38** ⏎
   >**A36** and type **/R.P**(N)**36** ⏎ **A42** ⏎
   >**A36** and type **/R.P**(N)**36** ⏎ **A46** ⏎
   >**A36** and type **/R.P**(N)**36** ⏎ **A49** ⏎

Result A label now is entered for the statement. The command, /-=, should have put a double ruled line in cell A33. The first replication should have extended this ruled line across to column P(N). The subsequent replication should have copied this ruled line onto row 51. The command, /--, should have put a single ruled line in cell A36. The first replication should have replicated it across to column P(N). The next series of replications should have copied the ruled line to rows 38, 42, 46, and 49.

Step Two

Enter net sales, cost of goods sold, and gross profit.

	A	B(A)	C(A)	D(B)	E(C)	F(D)	G(E)	H(F)	I(G)	J(H)	K(I)	L(J)	M(K)	N(L)	O(M)	P(N)
32	Part 2: Pro forma income statement															
33																
34	Net sales			450000	37500	37500	37500	37500	37500	37500	37500	37500	37500	37500	37500
35	Cost of goods sold			270000	22500	22500	22500	22500	22500	22500	22500	22500	22500	22500	22500
36																
37	Gross profit			180000	15000	15000	15000	15000	15000	15000	15000	15000	15000	15000	15000
38																
39																
40																
41																
42																
43																
44																
45																
46																
47																
48																
49																
50																
51																

ROW 34 **Net sales** on this row are the same sales figures as on row 7 of the cash budget. If any changes occur on that row, this row will change automatically. (How to estimate sales was covered briefly under row 7 and is discussed more fully in Chapter 7.)

To enter
> *a label* to identify this row as the net sales line
> *a formula* in cell D(B)34 that will bring down the total net sales entered in cell D(B)7 of the cash budget

> **Type** >**A34** and type **Net sales** (→)(→)(→)
> >**D**(B)**34** and type **+D**(B)**7** (⏎)

To replicate
> *from one cell to a range*

> **Type** >**D**(B)**34** and type **/R** (⏎) **E**(C)**34.P**(N)**34** (⏎)
> Prompt line will read N=No change
> R=Relative
> Type **R**

Result You should see the same net sales figures on this line as are on row 7 of the cash budget. The total net sales should be $450,000 and all monthly net sales should be $37,500.

ROW 35 **Cost of goods sold** (also known as cost of goods, cost of sales, cost of goods manufactured) is the total cost paid for the products sold during the accounting period, plus any freight-in costs. (Freight-out is usually shown as a separate expense under another section of the income statement.)

Most small retail and wholesale businesses compute cost of goods sold by adding the value of the goods purchased during the accounting period to the value of the beginning inventory, and then subtracting from that figure the value of the inventory on hand at the end of the accounting period.

For manufacturers, cost of goods sold includes, in addition to raw materials, the direct cost of manufacturing labor (including social security and unemployment taxes on factory employees), and overhead charges such as depreciation on assets used in production, supervision, power, and supplies. Cost of goods sold is a variable cost which is usually estimated as a percentage of sales. The historical cost of goods as a percent of sales is the best starting point. It should be adjusted upwards or downwards based on any foreseen changes. The formulas in this row will calculate cost of goods sold by multiplying the percentage used to determine inventory costs (60 percent) in cell D(B)17 of the cash budget times this month's net sales.

To enter
> *a label* to identify this row as cost of goods sold
> *a formula* in cell D(B)35 that will total the monthly entries on this row

formulas in cells E(C)35 through P(N)35 that will multiply the "inventory purchases" percentage in cell D(B)17 times this month's sales
(*Note:* If you are using the Advanced Version and you formatted the percentage in cell B17 (on page 39) to display it as a whole number followed by a percent sign, the formula entered into cell C35 will have to be entered differently. To use this command, follow the instructions given in the section marked [AV] for this cell. All other instructions are the same for both versions.)

Type >**A35** and type **Cost of g** (→)
>**B**(A)**35** and type **oods sold** (→)(→)
>**D**(B)**35** and type **@SUM(E(C)35.P(N)35)** (→)
>**E**(C)**35** and type **(D(B)17/100)*E(C)34** (⏎)

[AV] **Type** >**C35** and type **+B17*C34** (⏎)

To replicate
from one cell to a range

Type >**E**(C)**35** and type **/R** (⏎) **F(D)35.P(N)35** (⏎)
Prompt line will read N=No change
R=Relative
Type **NR**

Result Press the **SHIFT** and **!** keys together once to recalculate the sheet. You should get a total cost of goods figure of $270,000 and monthly figures of $22,500.

....

ROW 37 **Gross profit** is net sales minus cost of goods sold. It represents the profit of the business before other expenses are met. Gross profit, when expressed as a percentage of net sales, is known as the gross margin. Your estimated gross profit is based on your sales and cost of goods sold estimates, since it is the difference between the two.

To enter
a label to identify this row as the gross profit line
formulas in cells D(B)37 through P(N)37 that will calculate gross profit by subtracting cost of goods sold from net sales

Type >**A37** and type **Gross pro** (→)
>**B**(A)**37** and type **fit** (→)(→)
>**D**(B)**37** and type **+D(B)34-D(B)35** (⏎)

To replicate
from one cell to a range

Type >**D**(B)**37** and type **/R** (⏎) **E(C)37.P(N)37** (⏎)
Prompt line will read N=No change
R=Relative
Type **RR**

Result You should get the following gross profit figures: $180,000 (for the year) in cell D (B)37, and $15,000 for each month.

Step Three

Enter operating expenses and income.

	A	B(A)	C(A)	D(B)	E(C)	F(D)	G(E)	H(F)	I(G)	J(H)	K(I)	L(J)	M(K)	N(L)	O(M)	P(N)
32	Part 2: Pro forma income statement															
33	==															
34	Net sales			450000	37500	37500	37500	37500	37500	37500	37500	37500	37500	37500	37500	37500
35	Cost of goods sold			270000	22500	22500	22500	22500	22500	22500	22500	22500	22500	22500	22500	22500
36																	
37	Gross profit			180000	15000	15000	15000	15000	15000	15000	15000	15000	15000	15000	15000	15000
38																	
39	General & administrative			90000	7500	7500	7500	7500	7500	7500	7500	7500	7500	7500	7500	7500
40	Selling expenses			45000	3750	3750	3750	3750	3750	3750	3750	3750	3750	3750	3750	3750
41	Depreciation			15000	1250	1250	1250	1250	1250	1250	1250	1250	1250	1250	1250	1250
42																	
43	Operating income			30000	2500	2500	2500	2500	2500	2500	2500	2500	2500	2500	2500	2500
44																	
45																	
46																	
47																	
48																	
49																	
50																	
51																	

ROW 39 **General and administrative expenses** on this row will be identical to those on row 18 of the cash budget. Any changes made on that row will automatically be entered on this row. (How to estimate G&A expenses was discussed briefly under row 18 and is discussed in more detail in Chapter 7.)

To enter
a label to identify this as the general and administrative expenses row
formulas in cells D(B)39 through P(N)39 that will calculate G&A expenses based on net sales on row 34 and the G&A percentage figure entered in cell D(B)18

Type >**A39** and type **General &** →
>**B(A)39** and type **"(S)administ** →
>**C(A)39** and type **rative** →
>**D(B)39** and type **@SUM(E(C)39.P(N)39** →
>**E(C)39** and type **+E(C)18** ⏎

To replicate
from one cell to a range

Type >**E(C)39** and type **/R** ⏎ **F(D)39.P(N)39** ⏎
Prompt line will read N=No change
R=Relative
Type **R**

Result Press the **SHIFT** and **!** keys together to recalculate the worksheet. You should have the same figures on

this row as those on row 18 of the cash budget. The total should be $90,000 and the monthly figures should all be $7,500.

ROW 40 **Selling expenses** on this row will be identical to those on row 19 of the cash budget. Any changes made on that row will automatically be entered on this row also. (How to estimate selling expenses is covered in more detail in Chapter 7.)

To enter
a label to identify this as the selling expenses row
formulas in cells D(B)40 through P(N)40 that will calculate the selling expenses based on net sales on row 34 and the selling expense percentage entered in cell D(B)19

Type >**A40** and type **Selling e** →
>**B(A)40** and type **xpenses** → →
>**D(B)40** and type **@SUM(E(C)40.P(N)40** →
>**E(C)40** and type **+E(C)19** ⏎

To replicate
from one cell to a range

Type >**E(C)40** and type **/R** ⏎ **F(D)40.P(N)40** ⏎
Prompt line will read N=No change
R=Relative
Type **R**

Result Press the **SHIFT** and **!** keys together to recalculate the worksheet. You should have the same figures on this row as those on row 19 of the cash budget. The total should be $45,000 and the monthly figures should all be $3,750.

. . . .

R O W
41

Depreciation represents the estimated decline in the value of fixed assets during a period; depreciation expense charges part of the cost of large assets to the periods when they are used. There are a variety of ways to calculate depreciation. An accountant can suggest the best method to use for your company, which will depend on present tax laws and other factors. For example, many manufacturing firms include depreciation in cost of goods sold instead of in operating expenses. This is true particularly when a large percentage of depreciable assets are devoted to the actual manufacturing of products.

This expense is easily filled in on a pro forma income statement once the fixed assets and depreciation method are determined. Unless you plan to purchase new fixed assets, the amount is usually known ahead of time. (See TIPS on "Depreciation," below.)

To enter
a label to identify this as the depreciation row
a value of $15,000 annual depreciation in cell D(B)41

BUSINESS TIPS Depreciation

Depreciation is a method of matching revenue and related asset expense over a prescribed period.

The Economic Recovery Tax Act of 1981 replaced the prior concept of depreciation — based on the useful life of an asset — with a new system called the Accelerated Cost Recovery System (ACRS). Under ACRS, the entire cost of an asset is recovered over a predetermined period. The newly prescribed recovery periods are generally shorter than the useful life of the asset. By offering faster recovery of capital costs, ACRS provides greater incentives for increased capital investment.

ACRS applies to assets placed in service after 1980. Different rules apply to business assets placed in service prior to 1981. These are discussed in IRS Publication 534, "Depreciation."

Under ACRS, the cost of personal property can be recovered over a 3-, 5-, 10-, or 15-year recovery period. The recovery periods are based on the type of property. For example, autos and light-duty trucks are eligible for a 3-year write-off; however, most depreciable property (such as office furniture, equipment, and machinery) will qualify for a 5-year write-off. Depreciable real property can be written off over 15 years. Certain longer recovery periods are optional. Business owners may also use the straight-line method of depreciation over either the regular recovery period or the optional longer recovery periods.

Generally, to determine the ACRS write-off, the basis (usually the cost) of the property is multiplied by a percentage stated in the recovery tables. The percentage to be applied depends on the property's class and the number of years since the property was placed in service. The recovery percentages for property placed in service during 1981 through 1984 (with the exception of 15-year property) are shown below:

Class of property and application percentage

Recovery year	3-year property	5-year property	10-year property
1	25%	15%	8%
2	38%	22%	14%
3	37%	21%	12%
4		21%	10%
5		21%	10%
6			10%
7			9%
8			9%
9			9%
10			9%

For example, if a business purchased a piece of machinery in 1981 for $1,000, under the accelerated method the equipment would be depreciated over five years. The depreciation write-off would be $150 in the first year, $220 in the second year, and $210 in each of the following three years.

Although the purpose of ACRS is to stimulate capital investment, unless a cash reserve is funded with the amount of the depreciation expensed, a business will not necessarily have the cash to recover the cost of a purchased asset. Business owners must still use cash flow prudence in managing capital investment and growth.

formulas in cells E(C)41 through P(N)41 that will divide total depreciation by 12 to calculate the amount of depreciation for each month

Type >**A41** and type **Depreciat** →
>**B(A)41** and type **ion** → →
>**D(B)41** and type **15000** →
>**E(C)41** and type **+D(B)41/12** ↵

To replicate
from one cell to a range

Type >**E(C)41** and type **/R** ↵ **F(D)41.P(N)41** ↵
Prompt line will read N=No change
R=Relative
Type **N**

Result Each of the twelve monthly depreciation amounts should be $1,250 ($15,000 divided by 12).

· ·

R O W
43

Operating income is income that is produced by a company's normal operations. It does not include "other" income, such as royalties, interest earned, or extraordinary income (e.g., the sale of a subsidiary or other assets). Therefore, operating income is a good measure of the profitability of a company's normal business activities. When expressed as a percentage of net sales, it is known as the operating margin. You determine the estimated operating income by subtracting expenses (G&A, selling, and depreciation) from gross profit.

To enter
a label to identify this as the operating income row
formulas in cells D(B)43 through P(N)43 that will subtract the sum of G&A, selling expenses, and depreciation from gross profit

Type >**A43** and type **Operating** →
>**B(A)43** and type **"(S)income** → →
>**D(B)43** and type **+D(B)37-**
@SUM(D(B)38.D(B)42) ↵

To replicate
from one cell to a range

Type >**D(B)43** and type **/R** ↵ **E(C)43.P(N)43** ↵
Prompt line will read N=No change
R=Relative
Type **RRR**

Result You should have a total operating income of $30,000 and monthly operating incomes of $2,500.

Step Four

Enter other expenses and income before taxes.

	A	B(A)	C(A)	D(B)	E(C)	F(D)	G(E)	H(F)	I(G)	J(H)	K(I)	L(J)	M(K)	N(L)	O(M)	P(N)
32	Part 2: Pro forma income statement															
33	====															
34	Net sales			450000	37500	37500	37500	37500	37500	37500	37500	37500	37500	37500	37500	37500
35	Cost of goods sold			270000	22500	22500	22500	22500	22500	22500	22500	22500	22500	22500	22500	22500
36																	
37	Gross profit			180000	15000	15000	15000	15000	15000	15000	15000	15000	15000	15000	15000	15000
38																	
39	General & administrative			90000	7500	7500	7500	7500	7500	7500	7500	7500	7500	7500	7500	7500
40	Selling expenses			45000	3750	3750	3750	3750	3750	3750	3750	3750	3750	3750	3750	3750
41	Depreciation			15000	1250	1250	1250	1250	1250	1250	1250	1250	1250	1250	1250	1250
42																	
43	Operating income			30000	2500	2500	2500	2500	2500	2500	2500	2500	2500	2500	2500	2500
44	Interest expense			0	0	0	0	0	0	0	0	0	0	0	0	0
45	Other income/expense*			0	($)	($)	($)	($)	($)	($)	($)	($)	($)	($)	($)	($)
46																	
47	Income before taxes			30000	2500	2500	2500	2500	2500	2500	2500	2500	2500	2500	2500	2500
48																	
49																	
50																	
51	====															

Interest expense is identical to the interest expense line on the cash budget (row 20). To enter this expense here you will replicate row 20.

To enter
a label to identify this as the interest expense line
formulas to carry down interest payments from row 20 of the cash budget (This interest is calculated on loans required (row 29) in the cash budget and the long-term debt (row 82) on the pro forma balance sheet which you will construct in Chapter 5.) A formula is entered in cell D(B)44 to calculate total monthly interest payments.

Type >**A44** and type **Interest** →
>**B(A)44** and type **expense** → →
>**D(B)44** and type **@SUM(E(C)44.P(N)44)** →
>**E(C)44** and type **+E(C)20** ↵

To replicate
from one range to another range

Type >**E(C)44** and type **/R** ↵ **F(D)44.P(N)44** ↵
Prompt line will read N=No change
R=Relative
Type **R**

Result The total and monthly interest expenses should all read 0.

. . . .

Other income/expense includes income or expense from sources outside of the company's normal business activities. Sources of other income might include interest, dividends, sales of assets, rents, royalties, or capital gains. Other expenses might include losses on the sale of assets or other unusual expenses. We have combined other income and other expenses, but you may want to list them on separate lines when you build your own statement.

Often this income or expense is difficult to estimate for a pro forma statement. If you kept track of these items during the previous year, you can use those figures as a base. Then make any known adjustments for the upcoming period.

To enter
a label to identify this as the line for other income or expense (An asterisk is added to identify this as a "What If" line.)
a formula in cell D(B)45 that will give the total sum of any entries on the other income or expense line

data entry spaces in cells E(C)45 through P(N)45 that can be used to enter any other income or expenses in the month they are expected to occur

Type >**A45** and type **Other inc** →
>**B(A)45** and type **ome/expen** →
>**C(A)45** and type **se*** →
>**D(B)45** and type **@SUM(E(C)45.P(N)45)** →
>**E(C)45** and type **/FR "($)** ↵

To replicate
from one cell to a range

Type >**E(C)45** and type **/R** ↵ **F(D)45.P(N)45** ↵

Result The total for other income/expense in cell D(B)45 should read zero and a row of data entry spaces should extend from column E(C)45 to P(N)45. Any entries made in this row will be automatically calculated in the total, income before taxes, following. On this line, expenses should be entered as a positive number (e.g., 2000) and income as a negative number (e.g., −2000). This approach may seem a little confusing. Since the formula you are about to enter for income before taxes subtracts interest expense plus other income/expense from operating income, it assumes that the entry under other income/expense is actually an expense. If other income exceeds other expense, then it must be entered as a negative number on row 45.

. . . .

Income before taxes shows what the firm's profit is after all expenses except taxes have been deducted from sales. This item is often called *earnings before taxes* or *profit before taxes*. When expressed as a percentage of sales, it is known as the *before-tax profit margin*, or the *before-tax earnings margin*.

To enter
a label to identify this as the income before taxes line
formulas in cells D(B)47 through P(N)47 that will subtract interest and other income or expenses from operating income

Type >**A47** and type **Income be** →
>**B(A)47** and type **fore taxe** →
>**C(A)47** and type **s** →
>**D(B)47** and type **+D(B)43-D(B)44-D(B)45** ↵

To replicate

from one cell to a range

Type >D(B)**47** and type **/R** ⏎ **E**(C)**47.P**(N)**47** ⏎
Prompt line will read N=No change
R=Relative
Type **RRR**

Result The net income before taxes will be a total of
$30,000 and monthly figures should be $2500.

Step Five

Enter taxes and net income.

	A	B(A)	C(A)	D(B)	E(C)	F(D)	G(E)	H(F)	I(G)	J(H)	K(I)	L(J)	M(K)	N(L)	O(M)	P(N)
32	Part 2: Pro forma income statement															
33	======															
34	Net sales			450000	37500	37500	37500	37500	37500	37500	37500	37500	37500	37500	37500	37500
35	Cost of goods sold			270000	22500	22500	22500	22500	22500	22500	22500	22500	22500	22500	22500	22500
36																	
37	Gross profit			180000	15000	15000	15000	15000	15000	15000	15000	15000	15000	15000	15000	15000
38																	
39	General & administrative			90000	7500	7500	7500	7500	7500	7500	7500	7500	7500	7500	7500	7500
40	Selling expenses			45000	3750	3750	3750	3750	3750	3750	3750	3750	3750	3750	3750	3750
41	Depreciation			15000	1250	1250	1250	1250	1250	1250	1250	1250	1250	1250	1250	1250
42																	
43	Operating income			30000	2500	2500	2500	2500	2500	2500	2500	2500	2500	2500	2500	2500
44	Interest expense			0	0	0	0	0	0	0	0	0	0	0	0	0
45	Other income/expense*			0	($)	($)	($)	($)	($)	($)	($)	($)	($)	($)	($)	($)
46																	
47	Income before taxes			30000	2500	2500	2500	2500	2500	2500	2500	2500	2500	2500	2500	2500
48	Taxes			12000	1000	1000	1000	1000	1000	1000	1000	1000	1000	1000	1000	1000
49																	
50	Net income			18000	1500	1500	1500	1500	1500	1500	1500	1500	1500	1500	1500	1500
51	======															

ROW 48 **Taxes** include the federal, state, and local
taxes paid by (or in some cases refunded to)
the company. Some firms include only federal, state, and
local income taxes on this line. All other taxes such as
property taxes are expenses under cost of goods sold or
general and administrative expenses. We are assuming a
tax rate of 40 percent. In actuality you may have a different rate that should be substituted in cell D(B)48. Or you
could set up the IRS tax table for your form of
organization elsewhere on the spreadsheet and use the
VisiCalc program's LOOKUP function.

To enter

a label to identify this as the taxes line
a formula in a cell D(B)48 that will add the monthly
taxes calculated on this row
formulas in cells E(C)48 through P(N)48 that will
calculate taxes due based on the monthly income before taxes (row 47 of this statement) and the tax rate
in cell D(B)22 of the cash budget

(*Note:* If you are using the Advanced Version and
you formatted the percentage in cell B22 (on page
41) to display it as a whole number followed by a
percent sign, the formula entered into cell C48 will
have to be entered differently. To use this command,
follow the instructions given in the section marked
AV for those two cells. All other instructions are the
same for both versions.)

Type >**A48** and type **Taxes** → → →
>D(B)**48** and type **@SUM (E**(C)**48.P**(N)**48)** →
>**E**(C)**48** and type **(D**(B)**22/100)*E**(C)**47** ⏎

AV **Type** >**C48** and type **+B22*C47** ⏎

To replicate

from one cell to a range

Type >**E**(C)**48** and type **/R** ⏎ **F**(D)**48.P**(N)**48** ⏎
Prompt line will read N=No change
R=Relative
Type **NR**

Result Begin by recalculating the worksheet with the **SHIFT** and **!** keys. The total on this row should now be $12,000 and the monthly amounts should be $1000 ($12,000 divided by 12).

. . . .

R O W
50

Net income (also known as net profit, after-tax income, after-tax profit, net earnings, after-tax earnings) is the money or profits left after all expenses have been paid. The net profit is available for distribution to shareholders or for retention within the business to help finance operations or expansion. Net income is called *profit margin*, *net margin*, or *after-tax margin* when it is presented as a percentage of net sales. Net income is determined by subtracting taxes from income before taxes.

To enter

a label to identify this as the net income line
formulas in cells D(B)50 through P(N)50 that will subtract taxes from income before taxes

Type >**A50** and type **Net incom** →
>**B(A)50** and type **e** → →
>**D(B)50** and type **+ D(B)47-D(B)48** ↵

To replicate

from one cell to a range

Type >**D(B)50** and type **/R** ↵ **E(C)50.P(N)50** ↵
Prompt line will read N=No change
R=Relative
Type **RR**

Result Total net income in cell D(B)50 should be $18,000, and monthly net income figures should be $1,500.

Step Six

Formatting, protecting, and saving.

Formatting the pro forma income statement. If you are using the Advanced Version you can format a worksheet after it has been finished. This allows you to experiment with several different formats since you don't have to replicate formulas and data along with the format as you would with the VisiCalc program. In this example we suggest that you format all numbers, so that commas separate figures into thousands and negative numbers appear in parentheses.

[AV] **To format**
the income statement

Type >**B32** and type **/AV,(** ↵ ↵

To replicate
from one cell to a range

Type >**B32** and type **/R**
The prompt line will read Replicate: (, Source range or ENTER
Type **(**
The prompt line will read Replicate:Limit: ACNR)
Type **A)** ↵ **B33.B51** ↵

from one range to other ranges

Type >**B32** and type **/R**
The prompt line will read Replicate: (, Source range or ENTER
Type **(**
The prompt line will read Replicate:Limit: ACNR)
Type **A).B51** ↵ **C32.N32** ↵

Result The entire pro forma income statement is now formatted. All dollar values should appear with commas separating thousands, and negative numbers should be in parentheses.

Protecting the pro forma income statement. If you are using the Advanced Version you can protect all of the cells in the income statement so that they can't be inadvertently overwritten or erased. There is only one line on the statement where data may have to be entered (the other income/expense line), so it's faster to protect the entire statement and then unprotect that row if you need to enter data on it.

[AV] **To protect**
the income statement

Type >**A32** and type **/AMP** ↵ ↵

To replicate

from one cell to a range

Type >**A32** and type **/R**
The prompt line will read Replicate: (, Source range or ENTER
Type **(**
The prompt line will read Replicate:Limit: ACNR)
Type **A)** ⏎ **A33.A51** ⏎

from one range to other ranges

Type >**A32** and type **/R**
The prompt line will read Replicate: (, Source range or ENTER
Type **(**
The prompt line will read Replicate:Limit: ACNR)
Type **A).A51** ⏎ **B32.N32** ⏎

AV **To unprotect**

those cells you'll use to explore "What Ifs"

Type >**C45** and type **/AMU** ⏎ ⏎

To replicate

from one cell to a range

Type >**C45** and type **/R**
The prompt line will read Replicate: (, Source range or ENTER
Type **(**
The prompt line will read Replicate:Limit: ACNR)
Type **A)** ⏎ **D45.N45** ⏎

Result The entire pro forma income statement with the exception of the data entry spaces on row 45 will now be protected. To check that it is, go to any cell and try entering a value, label, or formula. The new entry shouldn't be accepted and you should get a message telling you that the cell is protected.

Save your work. Now that you have added the income statement, it's time again to save your work. Here you'll be saving the example for the second time so a file name doesn't have to be entered. You will be saving it on top of the old file on the disk. This erases the old file and replaces it with the later version. Detailed instructions for saving your work are given on page 48. Here is a summary of how to save a VisiCalc worksheet step by step (make sure you use the correct version):

A

B

C

How to save with the IBM PC and the VisiCalc program:

1 Since you have already saved Example to a diskette, insert that same diskette into drive A.

2 Move the cursor to the upper left corner of the worksheet by typing >**A1** ⏎ or the HOME key.

3 To save the file on which you are working onto the disk, type **/SS**. The prompt line will read Storage: File for Saving (see A above).

4 Since the file has already been saved once, use the → key to scroll through the diskette directory until the file name appears on the edit line (see B above), then type ⏎.

   Note: If you are saving the worksheet on drive B, type **/SS**. The prompt line will read Storage: File for Saving. To find a previously saved file on that drive you have to first indicate that you want to look at the files on drive

B, so type **B:** and then use the (→) key to scroll through the files on that drive.

5 The prompt line will read Storage: File Exists: Y to Replace (see C opposite). Stop and make sure this is the file you want to replace. The VisiCalc program does not automatically store a file back under the same title; it stores it to whatever file you have scrolled on the edit line. Make sure the edit line title and the title of the file you want to save match; otherwise you will store the new file over the old, eliminating the old file forever.

If you are sure, type **Y** and the disk drive will begin humming as the file is saved. If you want to save this file to a diskette other than the one in drive A, you will have to address that drive (see your IBM PC owner's manual).

Result The screen display and the worksheet in memory will remain unchanged, but the file is now saved to the diskette. You can turn off the computer, or you can continue. If anything goes wrong, your work won't be lost. Because saving your work is so easy to do you should get into the habit of saving frequently. It is also prudent to write-protect the diskette at this point (see TIP on page 49).

Introduction

The financial condition of a firm is revealed through an analysis of its balance sheet. The expected condition of the business, a month or year from now, is shown on its pro forma balance sheet. This statement is a summary of the results expected at the end of the period for which the projection is being made. It shows the expected effect on each balance sheet item of the activities of the firm as projected on the cash budget and pro forma income statement.

If you have a cash budget and a pro forma income statement, why bother to construct or monitor a pro forma balance sheet? There are a number of reasons, all of which are captured in two words — *balance* and *condition*. The cash budget and pro forma income statement depict what you are going to do, whereas the pro forma balance sheet shows what you have to do it with. Balance refers to the mix of assets and the mix of liabilities and equity. Condition is defined as whether the balance between assets, between liabilities and equity, and between the left side of the balance sheet (assets) and right side (liabilities and equity) is appropriate and reasonable for your type of business. Use of the pro forma balance sheets allows you to determine whether the activities portrayed by the cash budget and pro forma income statement will have a favorable or unfavorable impact on your financial condition. Managing both sides of the balance sheet is vital to effective control and performance of your business.

For example, suppose that sales are up, higher than forecasted. Collection of accounts receivable is right on target according to your cash budget. But actually customers are paying more slowly and thereby tying up too much of the firm's assets in accounts receivable. The reason that collections appear on target is that they were based on a lower level of sales. With the higher level of sales, they should be adjusted upwards. This situation wouldn't show up on the cash budget or the pro forma income statement. But it would show on the pro forma balance sheet, with accounts receivable being higher than forecast because accounts receivable, in the model, are directly determined as a percentage of sales. Knowing this, management can then try to restore the best balance of assets by improving collections.

Carrying the example to the liability side of the balance sheet we would see higher accounts payable and possibly more short-term debt (notes payable) required to finance the higher level of sales and accounts receivable. This comes about because your inventory requirements will be higher to support higher sales. The cash budget will reveal the higher purchase requirements if it has been updated to reflect the increased sales. It may also indicate the need for more short-term debt. But it will not show whether the higher level of current liabilities (accounts payable and notes payable) increases the

```
Part 3: Pro forma balance sheet
================================================================================
Assets:
--------------------------------------------------------------------------------
<Current assets>
Cash                 20000  20850  24100  27350  28200  31450  34700  35550  38800  42050  42900  46150  49400
Accounts receivable  60000  60000  60000  60000  60000  60000  60000  60000  60000  60000  60000  60000  60000
Inventory            30000  30000  30000  30000  30000  30000  30000  30000  30000  30000  30000  30000  30000
Prepaid expenses      2000   2000   2000   2000   2000   2000   2000   2000   2000   2000   2000   2000   2000
--------------------------------------------------------------------------------
Total current assets 112000 112850 116100 119350 120200 123450 126700 127550 130800 134050 134900 138150 141400

<Fixed assets>
Buildings & equipment 50000  50000  50000  50000  50000  50000  50000  50000  50000  50000  50000  50000  50000
Less accum.depreciation 30000 31250 32500 33750 35000 36250 37500 38750 40000 41250 42500 43750 45000
Land                 10000  10000  10000  10000  10000  10000  10000  10000  10000  10000  10000  10000  10000
--------------------------------------------------------------------------------
Net fixed assets     30000  28750  27500  26250  25000  23750  22500  21250  20000  18750  17500  16250  15000
--------------------------------------------------------------------------------
Total assets        142000 141600 143600 145600 145200 147200 149200 148800 150800 152800 152400 154400 156400
================================================================================
Liabilities:
--------------------------------------------------------------------------------
<Current liabilities>
Accounts payable     22500  22500  22500  22500  22500  22500  22500  22500  22500  22500  22500  22500  22500
Accrued wages & taxes  5500   3900   4700   5500   3900   4700   5500   3900   4700   5500   3900   4700   5500
Other current liabilities 4000 4000 4000  4000   4000   4000   4000   4000   4000   4000   4000   4000   4000
--------------------------------------------------------------------------------
Total current liabilities 32000 30400 31200 32000 30400 31200 32000 30400 31200 32000 30400 31200 32000

Long term debt       40000  40000  40000  40000  40000  40000  40000  40000  40000  40000  40000  40000  40000
--------------------------------------------------------------------------------
Total liabilities    72000  70400  71200  72000  70400  71200  72000  70400  71200  72000  70400  71200  72000

<Owner equity>
Common stock         50000  50000  50000  50000  50000  50000  50000  50000  50000  50000  50000  50000  50000
Retained earnings    20000  21200  22400  23600  24800  26000  27200  28400  29600  30800  32000  33200  34400
--------------------------------------------------------------------------------
Total owner equity   70000  71200  72400  73600  74800  76000  77200  78400  79600  80800  82000  83200  84400
--------------------------------------------------------------------------------
Total liab. & owner equity 142000 141600 143600 145600 145200 147200 149200 148800 150800 152800 152400 154400 156400
================================================================================
```

total debt of the company beyond an acceptable level. The pro forma balance sheet will reveal this so that appropriate action can be taken to bring the balance between current and long-term liabilities into line.

The detail needed for a projected balance sheet varies from business to business. In the example used in this book, the pro forma balance sheet is condensed to simplify the explanations. It is set up for a retail operation. This condensation does include the major asset and liability items found on most pro forma balance sheets. On a more detailed statement, these categories are broken down into smaller subdivisions. Once you have built the basic pro forma on your computer, you can easily customize it for your business.

When to construct a pro forma balance sheet

Projected balance sheets are often prepared quarterly or annually, but we advise that you construct them monthly. They should also be prepared in conjunction with your cash budget and pro forma income statement. When you have the pro forma on the computer, it is easy to update and use this statement to check the financial condition of your firm regularly and to help you manage your firm's assets and liabilities.

How to construct a pro forma balance sheet

There are a variety of techniques used to construct pro forma balance sheets. Many involve the use of "plug" items that force total assets to equal total liabilities and equity. Although these methods have the advantage of being simpler and sometimes easier to develop, they suffer one major disadvantage. The drawback is that they are not linked to the cash budget and pro forma income statement. When this is the case you are not able to directly see the impact of some event or activity in the cash budget and pro forma income statement on the pro forma balance sheet.

In this chapter you will actually link the pro forma balance sheet to your cash budget and pro forma income statement. All items on the balance sheet are calculated based on what occurs in the cash budget and pro forma income statement and your previous balance sheet. With this approach you will have a completely integrated financial forecasting tool. Any contemplated action or event that occurs will be reflected in your cash position, financial performance, and financial condition simultaneously. With this information you will be able to manage and control your firm more efficiently and more effectively.

We'll start by showing you how to construct the statement, line item by line item, and we'll describe briefly how to estimate these line items. Once you have the pro forma on your computer, and customized to your business, you can see the tremendous advantage of having it integrated with and linked to your cash budget and pro forma income statement.

....

Getting ready

<table>
<tr><td>STEP
1</td><td>**Reload your example.** If you proceeded directly to this chapter without turning off the</td></tr>
</table>

computer, you can continue with this chapter without any preparation. If, however, you turned the computer off after saving the example you will have to reload it to resume working. To reload the example follow these steps.

1 Load the VisiCalc Program diskette into the computer. If you can't remember how to do this refer to Step 2, "Load the VisiCalc program," on page 22.

2 When the characteristic VisiCalc display appears on the screen, remove the VisiCalc Program diskette (or in the case of the Advanced Version the Loader diskette) from the drive and file it carefully in a safe place.

3 Insert the data diskette on which you saved the example into drive A.

Type /SL
> The prompt line reads Storage: File to Load Type **Example** ⏎ (Or you could use the →
> key to scroll through the files until Example appears on the screen and then type ⏎.)

The drive will begin to spin and its red light will come on. In a few seconds the drive will stop and your example should appear on the screen exactly as it appeared when last saved.

When the example is reloaded, some cells may have ERROR messages appear in them. To remove these ERROR messages, just press the **SHIFT** and **!** keys simultaneously twice to recalculate the worksheet.

Entering the example

Enter headings and ruled lines for assets.

	A	B(A)	C(A)	D(B)	E(C)	F(D)	G(E)	H(F)	I(G)	J(H)	K(I)	L(J)	M(K)	N(L)	O(M)	P(N)
52	Part 3: Pro forma balance sheet															
53	===															
54	Assets:															
55	---															
56																
57																
58																
59																
60																
61	---															
62																
63	---															
64																
65																
66																
67																
68	---															
69																
70	---															
71																
72	===															

ROW 52

Headings and double ruled lines identify this section of the template as the balance sheet.

To enter

a label to identify this section as Part 3 of the example, the pro forma balance sheet

double ruled lines to separate major sections of the pro forma balance sheet

Type >**A52** and type **Part 3: P** (→)
>**B(A)52** and type **ro forma** (→)
>**C(A)52** and type **balance s** (→)
>**D(B)52** and type **heet** (↵)

>**A53** and type **/-=** (↵)

To replicate

from one cell to a range

Type >**A53** and type **/R** (↵) **B53.P(N)53** (↵)

from one range to another range

Type >**A53** and type **/R.P(N)53** (↵) **A72** (↵)

Result A label is entered for this part of the example. The next step should have put a ruled line into cell A53. The first replication should have carried it across to column P(N). The next replication should have copied the ruled line to row 72.

ROW 54

Assets are everything the business owns (that has money value). They commonly include cash, accounts receivable, notes receivable, inventories, land, buildings, machinery, equipment, and other investments. Assets are generally classified into current assets, fixed assets, and other assets.

To enter

a label to identify this section as the assets section of the pro forma balance sheet

Type >**A54** and type **Assets:** (↵)

ROW 55

Single ruled lines will be entered using the same approach as for the double ruled lines.

To enter

a single ruled line from column A to column P(N)

Type >**A55** and type **/--** (↵)

To replicate

from one cell to a range

Type >**A55** and type **/R** (↵) **B55.P(N)55** (↵)

from one range to another range

Type >**A55** and type **/R.P(N)55** ↵ **A61** ↵
>**A55** and type **/R.P(N)55** ↵ **A63** ↵
>**A55** and type **/R.P(N)55** ↵ **A68** ↵
>**A55** and type **/R.P(N)55** ↵ **A70** ↵

Result The first step should have put a single ruled line into cell A55. The first replication should have carried it across to column P(N). The next series of replications should have copied the ruled line to rows 61, 63, 68, and 70.

Step Two

Enter current assets.

	A	B(A)	C(A)	D(B)	E(C)	F(D)	G(E)	H(F)	I(G)	J(H)	K(I)	L(J)	M(K)	N(L)	O(M)	P(N)
52	Part 3: Pro forma balance sheet															
53	==============															
54	Assets:															
55	--------------															
56	<Current assets>															
57	Cash			20000	21350	25100	28850	29600	33350	37100	37850	41600	45350	46100	49850	53600
58	Accounts receivable			60000	60000	60000	60000	60000	60000	60000	60000	60000	60000	60000	60000	60000
59	Inventory			30000	30000	30000	30000	30000	30000	30000	30000	30000	30000	30000	30000	30000
60	Prepaid expenses			2000	2000	2000	2000	2000	2000	2000	2000	2000	2000	2000	2000	2000
61	--------------															
62	Total current assets			112000	113350	117100	120850	121600	125350	129100	129850	133600	137350	138100	141850	145600
63	--------------															
64																
65																
66																
67																
68	--------------															
69																
70	--------------															
71																
72	==============															

ROW 56 **Current assets** are normally expected to flow into cash in the course of the firm's operating year. Ordinarily these include cash, marketable securities with maturities of less than a year (such as Treasury bills or money market securities), accounts receivable, notes receivable, inventory, and other current assets or prepaid expenses (such as insurance payments). Although some firms may consider items such as the cash-surrender value of life insurance current assets, they should really be treated as noncurrent or other assets, since in the normal course of business they will not be converted to cash. (Current assets are sometimes called *working capital assets* or just *working capital*.)

To enter

a label to identify this section of assets on the pro forma balance sheet as current assets

Type >**A56** and type **"<Current** →
>**B(A)56** and type **assets>** ↵

ROW 57 **Cash** is the total cash in the bank or on hand. Often firms will include the value of any marketable securities (investments with maturities of less than a year, such as Treasury bills or commercial paper) in the cash account if these securities do not amount to much in dollar value.

There is no tried-and-true method of estimating cash. Some managers assume that it is proportional to sales and estimate it based on a percentage of sales, such as 2 percent. Others use a minimum cash figure determined by company managers.

In our example, the computer will give you an estimated cash figure by bringing the closing balance of the cash budget down to this line.

To enter

a label to identify this as the cash line
formulas in cells D(B)57 through P(N)57 that will carry down the closing balance of the cash budget to the cash line of the balance sheet

Type >**A57** and type **Cash** → → →
>**D(B)57** and type **+D(B)30** ↵

To replicate

from one cell to a range

Type >**D**(B)**57** and type /**R** ⏎ **E**(C)**57**.**P**(N)**57** ⏎
Prompt line will read N=No change
R=Relative
Type **R**

Result The monthly cash figures should be the same as those on the closing balance line of the cash budget. They are:

Cell	Month	Value	Cell	Month	Value
D(B)57	Beginning	$20,000	K(I)57	7	$37,850
E(C)57	1	$21,350	L(J)57	8	$41,600
F(D)57	2	$25,100	M(K)57	9	$45,350
G(E)57	3	$28,850	N(L)57	10	$46,100
H(F)57	4	$29,600	O(M)57	11	$49,850
I(G)57	5	$33,350	P(N)57	12	$53,600
J(H)57	6	$37,100			

. . . .

ROW 58 **Accounts receivable** are what people owe the company. Accounts receivable come from credit sales to customers, and are expected to be collected within the year. Some customers, however, won't pay up, so the balance in the accounts receivable account should be adjusted for the expected percent of bad debts. This is accomplished by establishing a *reserve for bad debts* account, which is subtracted from the accounts receivable. Sometimes notes receivable (loans made by the company to customers, the owner/manager, or stockholders) are also included under accounts receivable. (Accounts receivable are also called *trades receivable, trade credit due,* or *net receivables*).

To estimate accounts receivable, managers often use the average collection period ratio (see TIPS, "Monitoring credit"). You can assume that this ratio will increase and decrease, depending on your customers' payment behavior, and that sales will fluctuate. Using the most current figures, you can determine accounts receivable: the average collection period times average sales per day equals accounts receivable.

In our example, you'll start by entering a value for accounts receivable that were outstanding from a prior period. Then you'll enter a formula that will keep accounts receivable current by adjusting for net sales made and receipts collected.

BUSINESS TIPS Monitoring credit

A useful way to track credit sales is to monitor the average number of days customers take to pay. To arrive at the average days taken by customers to settle accounts, managers use the following formula: Divide the *average outstanding accounts receivable (AOAR)* by the *annual sales level (ASL)* and multiply by 365 days. For example:

$$\text{Last year: } \frac{\$520,000 \text{ (AOAR)}}{\$6,000,000 \text{ (ASL)}} \times 365 = 32 \text{ days}$$

$$\text{This year: } \frac{\$680,000 \text{ (AOAR)}}{\$6,000,000 \text{ (ASL)}} \times 365 = 41 \text{ days}$$

This year, the customers of this hypothetical company are taking an average of 9 days longer to pay their accounts, or an average of 11 days beyond the 30 allowed. The owner of this company would be advised to tighten credit controls in order to stop losing the use of the money tied up in accounts receivable.

BUSINESS TIPS Cash on hand

While the amount of cash kept on hand should be minimized, some money must be readily available. Experts urge business owners to deposit their funds in a bank account, rather than storing them in a strongbox or safe. This account should be a separate business checking and/or savings account, not the owner's personal account. "Mixing personal and business finances results in chaos," explains one business analyst. The Internal Revenue Service also requires separate records for personal and business finances.

Some corporate treasurers believe that as long as cash can earn at least some interest elsewhere, it should not sit in a cash register or checking account. Although a small-business owner's needs differ from those of a corporate treasurer, the small business operation may be able to get by with a small amount of non-interest-bearing cash in the checking account. Following a cash flow plan might release excess funds that could be put to work in a business savings account.

Even emergency funds for the unexpected expenses every business encounters can be kept in a day-of-deposit/day-of-withdrawal savings account. Such accounts compute interest daily and compound quarterly on an average minimum balance, provided the account remains open through the end of the quarter. Thus, the funds are readily available and earning interest.

BUSINESS TIPS Inventory control

For many small businesses, control of inventory costs can be a critical factor in the success or failure of the operation. Physical protection of inventory secures this valuable asset against theft, shrinkage, and deterioration. Investment control of inventory makes certain that money is not tied up unnecessarily in excessive stock. Material and product flow control ensures that delays in the movement of inventory do not cause lost sales and declining profits.

A substantial amount of cash may be trapped in a firm's own inventory — which commandeers additional dollars just for its maintenance. In determining the cost of inventory, the manager should consider not only interest, but storage space expenses, facilities, handling, insurance, deterioration, obsolescence, and taxes. The owner also must remember that, in times of inflation, the dollars invested in inventory will earn dollars with less purchasing power.

Inventory control records can be divided into three types: *physical control*, in which individual items are counted periodically; *"perpetual" or "book" records*, in which running records of merchandise sold are kept; and *dollar control*, which gives a rough idea of the dollar value of inventory from day to day. The latter is more practical when stock is made up primarily of thousands of different items, as in a variety store. Both perpetual records and dollar inventories should be verified periodically, perhaps every six months, with a physical inventory count.

The basic method for calculating the inventory level for a retail stock item is to multiply the average daily sales by the number of days one is purchasing for. For example, if a store wanted to carry 2 days' supply of an item and average daily sales of that item was 15 boxes, the manager would multiply 2 by 15 to determine a needed inventory level of 30 boxes. If the supply on hand were fewer than 30 boxes, the manager would need to purchase more.

In many businesses, determining inventory levels is a more complex process. But managers can determine the correct purchase amounts by considering the expected sales in the coming period. Often, correct levels can be based upon average monthly sales or upon the sales of an appropriate review period.

BUSINESS TIPS Monitoring inventory movement

Efficient inventory control calls for periodic reviews of stock-movement figures. Close examination may reveal products that aren't moving or that contribute minimally to profits — items that never should have been purchased in the first place or products that, once appropriate, now are obsolete. A substantial amount of cash and space can be freed for more productive use by selling at distress prices or scrapping dead-weight inventory.

A useful way to track inventory movement is to calculate inventory turnover and monitor the average number of days that inventory is on hand. Inventory turnover is the number of times inventory turns over in one accounting period. To determine the turnover rate, the business owner divides the average of inventory on hand (the average of beginning and ending inventory for an accounting period) by the cost of goods sold. For example, if a company's cost of goods sold is $35,000 and average inventory on hand is $7,000, the formula would look like this:

$$\frac{\$35,000 \text{ (Cost of goods sold)}}{\$7,000 \text{ (Average inventory on hand)}} = 5 \text{ times}$$

To arrive at the number of days that inventory is on hand, the total number of days in the accounting period (in this case, 365) is divided by the turnover rate:

$$\frac{365 \text{ days}}{5 \text{ times}} = 73 \text{ days}$$

When compared with past figures or with industry averages, inventory-movement figures can serve as rough guidelines for spotting understocking, overstocking, obsolescence, and need for merchandising improvement.

Entering the example, Continued

To enter

a label to identify this as the accounts receivable line
a value of $60,000 representing the accounts receivable outstanding at the end of the last month of the previous period (not shown on this statement)
formulas in cells E(C)58 through P(N)58 that will add accounts receivable at the end of the previous period to sales made in the current period and subtract receipts collected in the current period

Type >**A58** and type **Accounts** →
>**B(A)58** and type **receivabl** →
>**C(A)58** and type **e** →
>**D(B)58** and type **60000** →
>**E(C)58** and type **+D(B)58+E(C)7-E(C)15** ↵

To replicate

from one cell to a range

Type >**E(C)58** and type **/R** ↵ **F(D)58.P(N)58** ↵
Prompt line will read N=No change
R=Relative
Type **RRR**

Result The beginning and monthly figures should all be $60,000.

. . . .

ROW 59 **Inventory** for a manufacturer is the sum of raw materials, material in process, and finished merchandise on hand. It does not include supplies unless they are for sale. For retailers and wholesalers, inventory is the stock of salable goods on hand. Usually, inventory is valued conservatively, according to standard accounting methods. For instance, it is valued at cost or market value, whichever is lower.

Some businesses estimate inventory for a projected year using the cost of goods sold figure (a percentage of expected sales) and the inventory turnover ratio (see TIPS, "Monitoring inventory movement," page 69). Cost of goods sold divided by the inventory turnover equals inventory (in dollars). For example:

$$\frac{\text{Cost of goods sold}}{\text{Inventory turnover}} = \text{Inventory}$$

$$\frac{\$400,000}{5.0} = \$80,000$$

In our example, the computer will use the formula described below under "To enter" to calculate inventory for you.

To enter

a label to identify this as the inventory line
a value of $30,000 in cell D(B)59 to represent the closing inventory balance at the end of the last period
formulas in cells E(C)59 through O(M)59 that will add the closing inventory balance of the previous period to next month's inventory purchases and then subtract this month's inventory sales. Inventory purchases are entered on this row when they are received two months before they are sold and one month before they are paid for. The formulas on this row refer to one month out on the inventory purchases row (17) which is referring one month into the future, hence a two month "lead" in respect to sales.
a formula in cell P(N)59 to calculate inventory for December. Because there is no "one month in the future" on the inventory purchases row for this last column on the forecast, the formula refers to the January period on the inventory purchases row. The example assumes the first month of next year will have the same inventory purchases as the first month of the period covered by the budget. For more detail on how this row relates to other inventory and accounts payable rows, see TIPS, "Assumptions about inventory purchases," page 123.

Type >**A59** and type **Inventory** → → →
>**D(B)59** and type **30000** →
>**E(C)59** and type **+D(B)59+F(D)17-E(C)35** ↵
>**P(N)59** and type **+O(M)59+E(C)17-P(N)35** ↵

To replicate

from one cell to a range

Type >**E(C)59** and type **/R** ↵ **F(D)59.O(M)59** ↵
Prompt line will read N=No change
R=Relative
Type **RRR**

Result Press the **SHIFT** and **!** keys together to recalculate the worksheet. The beginning figure and all monthly figures should be $30,000.

. . . .

ROW 60 **Prepaid expenses** are expenses that are recorded before the service purchased by the expenditure is received. They might include, for example, insurance premiums, which are paid at the beginning of the period which the insurance covers. Another example is rent, if paid in advance. For new firms just starting up, deposits for electric service, telephones, and some types of equipment would be considered prepaid expenses. (Prepaid expenses are sometimes listed as other current assets.)

Many prepaid expenses are known in advance and therefore easy to estimate for a pro forma statement. They also tend to be a small percentage of overall business expenses. Basically, estimating prepaid expenses is simply a matter of collecting the necessary figures from the firm's books.

To enter

a label to identify this as the prepaid expenses line of the pro forma balance sheet
a value of $2,000 in cell D(B)60 to represent opening prepaid expenses, which would be the same as the closing balance of this item from the last period of a previous balance sheet
formulas in cells E(C)60 through P(N)60 that will carry the opening prepaid expenses across the periods covered by the statement

Type >**A60** and type **Prepaid e** (→)
>**B**(A)**60** and type **xpenses** (→)(→)
>**D**(B)**60** and type **2000** (→)
>**E**(C)**60** and type **+D**(B)**60** (↵)

To replicate

from one cell to a range

Type >**E**(C)**60** and type **/R** (↵) **F**(D)**60.P**(N)**60** (↵)
Prompt line will read N=No change
R=Relative
Type **R**

Result The monthly prepaid expenses figures should all be $2,000.

ROW 62 **Total current assets** is the sum of all cash, marketable securities, accounts receivable, inventory, and prepaid expenses. The computer will total current assets by using a formula that you'll enter.

To enter

a label to identify this as the total current assets line of the pro forma balance sheet
formulas in cells D(B)62 through P(N)62 that will add all current assets (which are between the ruled lines on rows 55 and 61)

Type >**A62** and type **Total cur** (→)
>**B**(A)**62** and type **rent asse** (→)
>**C**(A)**62** and type **ts** (→)
>**D**(B)**62** and type @**SUM(D**(B)**55.D**(B)**61)** (↵)

To replicate

from one cell to a range

Type >**D**(B)**62** and type **/R** (↵) **E**(C)**62.P**(N)**62** (↵)
Prompt line will read N=No change
R=Relative
Type **RR**

Result The figures should be as follows.

Cell	Month	Value	Cell	Month	Value
D(B)**62**	Beginning	$112,000	**K**(I)**62**	7	$129,850
E(C)**62**	1	$113,350	**L**(J)**62**	8	$133,600
F(D)**62**	2	$117,100	**M**(K)**62**	9	$137,350
G(E)**62**	3	$120,850	**N**(L)**62**	10	$138,100
H(F)**62**	4	$121,600	**O**(M)**62**	11	$141,850
I(G)**62**	5	$125,350	**P**(N)**62**	12	$145,600
J(H)**62**	6	$129,100			

If your figures don't match those in the chart, recalculate the worksheet by pressing the **SHIFT** and ! keys simultaneously four times.

Step Three

Enter fixed assets.

	A	B(A)	C(A)	D(B)	E(C)	F(D)	G(E)	H(F)	I(G)	J(H)	K(I)	L(J)	M(K)	N(L)	O(M)	P(N)
52	Part 3: Pro forma balance sheet															
53	===															
54	Assets:															
55																
56	<Current assets>															
57	Cash			20000	21350	25100	28850	29600	33350	37100	37850	41600	45350	46100	49850	53600
58	Accounts receivable			60000	60000	60000	60000	60000	60000	60000	60000	60000	60000	60000	60000	60000
59	Inventory			30000	30000	30000	30000	30000	30000	30000	30000	30000	30000	30000	30000	30000
60	Prepaid expenses			2000	2000	2000	2000	2000	2000	2000	2000	2000	2000	2000	2000	2000
61																
62	Total current assets			112000	113350	117100	120850	121600	125350	129100	129850	133600	137350	138100	141850	145600
63																
64	<Fixed assets>															
65	Buildings & equipment			50000	50000	50000	50000	50000	50000	50000	50000	50000	50000	50000	50000	50000
66	Less accum.depreciation			30000	31250	32500	33750	35000	36250	37500	38750	40000	41250	42500	43750	45000
67	Land			10000	10000	10000	10000	10000	10000	10000	10000	10000	10000	10000	10000	10000
68																
69	Net fixed assets			30000	28750	27500	26250	25000	23750	22500	21250	20000	18750	17500	16250	15000
70																
71																
72	===															

ROW 64 **Fixed assets** are those acquired for long-term use in the business, although "fixed" doesn't mean absolutely permanent. These assets are typically not for resale, and they are recorded on the balance sheet at their cost to the business less accumulated depreciation. Examples include land (which is not depreciable for most businesses), buildings, leasehold improvements, fixtures, furniture, machinery, tools, and equipment. A fixed asset is treated as a long-term cost, with the cost allocated as depreciation over the working life of the asset. Thus, the value of a fixed asset shown on the balance sheet is not necessarily the same as the resale value of the asset.

Fixed assets are relatively easy to estimate for a pro forma statement, since they usually don't change greatly from period to period. If you anticipate the need for more fixed assets, this should be taken into account in the cash budget and on row 65, buildings and equipment.

To enter

a label to identify this section of assets on the pro forma balance sheet as fixed assets

Type >**A64** and type **"<Fixed as** →
  >**B(A)64** and type **sets>** ↵

....

ROW 65 **Buildings and equipment** are fixed assets used in the normal course of business. They are carried on the balance sheet at their original cost plus the cost of permanent improvements. For equipment or machinery, delivery and installation costs are also included.

To enter

a label to identify this as the buildings and equipment line of the pro forma balance sheet
a value of $50,000 in cell D(B)65 as the opening balance on this line, which is the same as the closing buildings and equipment balance from the last period of the previous balance sheet
formulas in cells E(C)65 through P(N)65 that will carry the opening balance across the periods covered by the statement

Type >**A65** and type **Buildings** →
  >**B(A)65** and type **"(S)& equipm** →
  >**C(A)65** and type **ent** →
  >**D(B)65** and type **50000** →
  >**E(C)65** and type **+D(B)65** ↵

To replicate

from one cell to a range

Type >**E(C)65** and type **/R** ↵ **F(D)65.P(N)65** ↵
  Prompt line will read N=No change
  R=Relative
  Type **R**

Result The monthly figures should all be $50,000.

Accumulated depreciation is a deducted item (see row 64, fixed assets). *Depreciate* means to decrease in price or value. Each year, buildings and equipment depreciate as their usefulness declines, and over the years the depreciation adds up. Since the assets are worth less, their accumulated depreciation must be subtracted from their original cost. This "book value" is listed on the pro forma balance sheet. To get an accumulated depreciation amount, you figure the depreciation for each item during the projected accounting period, find the total for all items, and then add that sum to the total depreciation figure from the last accounting period. The depreciation for this forecast period would be equal to the depreciation expense on the income statement.

The amount of depreciation allowed each period and the useful life of assets is governed by Internal Revenue Service regulations and federal tax laws. Amortization, which is basically the same thing as depreciation, is taken for intangible assets such as leasehold improvements.

To enter

> *a label* to identify this as the depreciation line of the pro forma balance sheet
> *a value* of $30,000 in cell D(B)66 to represent the actual closing accumulated depreciation balance from the last period of the previous balance sheet
> *formulas* in cells E(C)66 through P(N)66 that will add monthly depreciation on row 41 of the pro forma income statement to the previous month's depreciation on this statement

Type >**A66** and type **Less accu** →
>**B(A)66** and type **m.depreci** →
>**C(A)66** and type **ation** →
>**D(B)66** and type **30000** →
>**E(C)66** and type **+D(B)66+E(C)41** ↵

To replicate

from one cell to a range

Type >**E(C)66** and type **/R** ↵ **F(D)66.P(N)66** ↵
Prompt line will read N=No change
R=Relative
Type **RR**

Result The monthly figures should be as follows. (If you don't get these results, press the **SHIFT** and **!** keys together four times.)

Cell	Month	Value	Cell	Month	Value
D(B)66	Beginning	$30,000	K(I)66	7	$38,750
E(C)66	1	$31,250	L(J)66	8	$40,000
F(D)66	2	$32,500	M(K)66	9	$41,250
G(E)66	3	$33,750	N(L)66	10	$42,500
H(F)66	4	$35,000	O(M)66	11	$43,750
I(G)66	5	$36,250	P(N)66	12	$45,000
J(H)66	6	$37,500			

Land is the property, other than buildings and equipment, owned by the business. It is a fixed asset which is carried at original cost and, for most firms, is not depreciable.

To enter

> *a label* to identify this as the land line of the pro forma balance sheet
> *a value* of $10,000 in cell D(B)67 to represent the actual closing land balance from the last period of the previous balance sheet
> *formulas* in cells E(C)67 through P(N)67 that will carry the beginning entry across the monthly columns of the statement

Type >**A67** and type **Land** → → →
>**D(B)67** and type **10000** →
>**E(C)67** and type **+D(B)67** ↵

To replicate

from one cell to a range

Type >**E(C)67** and type **/R** ↵ **F(D)67.P(N)67** ↵
Prompt line will read N=No change
R=Relative
Type **R**

Result The monthly figures should all be $10,000.

Net fixed assets is the total of buildings and equipment and land (property), less accumulated depreciation. The computer, using a formula you'll enter, will calculate net fixed assets for you.

To enter

> *a label* to identify this as the net fixed assets line of the pro forma balance sheet
> *formulas* in cells D(B)69 through P(N)69 that will add the fixed asset line items and subtract depreciation

Type >**A69** and type **Net fixed** →
>**B**(A)**69** and type **"(S)assets** → →
>**D**(B)**69** and type **+ D**(B)**65 + D**(B)**67-D**(B)**66** ↵

To replicate

from one cell to a range

Type >**D**(B)**69** and type **/R** ↵ **E**(C)**69.P**(N)**69** ↵
Prompt line will read N=No change
R=Relative
Type **RRR**

Result The monthly figures should be as follows. (If your results don't match these figures, press the **SHIFT** and ! keys together four times.)

Cell	Month	Value	Cell	Month	Value
D(B)69	Beginning	$30,000	K(I)69	7	$21,250
E(C)69	1	$28,750	L(J)69	8	$20,000
F(D)69	2	$27,500	M(K)69	9	$18,750
G(E)69	3	$26,250	N(L)69	10	$17,500
H(F)69	4	$25,000	O(M)69	11	$16,250
I(G)69	5	$23,750	P(N)69	12	$15,000
J(H)69	6	$22,500			

Step Four

Enter total assets.

	A	B(A)	C(A)	D(B)	E(C)	F(D)	G(E)	H(F)	I(G)	J(H)	K(I)	L(J)	M(K)	N(L)	O(M)	P(N)
52	Part 3: Pro forma balance sheet															
53	================															
54	Assets:															
55																
56	<Current assets>															
57	Cash			20000	21350	25100	28850	29600	33350	37100	37850	41600	45350	46100	49850	53600
58	Accounts receivable			60000	60000	60000	60000	60000	60000	60000	60000	60000	60000	60000	60000	60000
59	Inventory			30000	30000	30000	30000	30000	30000	30000	30000	30000	30000	30000	30000	30000
60	Prepaid expenses			2000	2000	2000	2000	2000	2000	2000	2000	2000	2000	2000	2000	2000
61																
62	Total current assets			112000	113350	117100	120850	121600	125350	129100	129850	133600	137350	138100	141850	145600
63																
64	<Fixed assets>															
65	Buildings & equipment			50000	50000	50000	50000	50000	50000	50000	50000	50000	50000	50000	50000	50000
66	Less accum.depreciation			30000	31250	32500	33750	35000	36250	37500	38750	40000	41250	42500	43750	45000
67	Land			10000	10000	10000	10000	10000	10000	10000	10000	10000	10000	10000	10000	10000
68																
69	Net fixed assets			30000	28750	27500	26250	25000	23750	22500	21250	20000	18750	17500	16250	15000
70																
71	Total assets			142000	142100	144600	147100	146600	149100	151600	151100	153600	156100	155600	158100	160600
72																

R O W 71 **Total assets** is the total of assets in all categories: current, fixed, and other. Notice that the assets are arranged from most liquid (covertible to cash) to least liquid on the balance sheet. Accounts receivable, for example, can be converted to cash faster than inventory, which can be converted to cash faster than equipment, and so forth.

To enter

a label to identify this as the total assets line of the pro forma balance sheet
formulas in cells D(B)71 through P(N)71 that will add current assets to net fixed assets

Type >**A71** and type **Total ass** →
>**B**(A)**71** and type **ets** → →
>**D**(B)**71** and type **+ D**(B)**62 + D**(B)**69** ↵

To replicate

from one cell to a range

Type >**D**(B)**71** and type **/R** ↵ **E**(C)**71.P**(N)**71** ↵
Prompt line will read N=No change
R=Relative
Type **RR**

Result The monthly figures should be as follows. (If your results don't match these figures, recalculate the worksheet by pressing the **SHIFT** and ! keys together four times.)

Cell	Month	Value	Cell	Month	Value
D(B)71	Beginning	$142,000	K(I)71	7	$151,100
E(C)71	1	$142,100	L(J)71	8	$153,600
F(D)71	2	$144,600	M(K)71	9	$156,100
G(E)71	3	$147,100	N(L)71	10	$155,600
H(F)71	4	$146,600	O(M)71	11	$158,100
I(G)71	5	$149,100	P(N)71	12	$160,600
J(H)71	6	$151,600			

Step Five

Enter a heading and ruled lines for liabilities.

	A	B(A)	C(A)	D(B)	E(C)	F(D)	G(E)	H(F)	I(G)	J(H)	K(I)	L(J)	M(K)	N(L)	O(M)	P(N)
73	Liabilities:															
74																
75																
76																
77																
78																
79																
80																
81																
82																
83																
84																
85																
86																
87																
88																
89																
90																
91																
92																
93																

R O W 73 **A heading and a double ruled line** for the liabilities section of the pro forma balance sheet will be entered.

To enter

a label to identify this as the liabilities section of sample pro forma balance sheet

double ruled lines to separate major sections of the liabilities section of the pro forma balance sheet

Type >**A73** and type **Liabiliti** →
>**B**(A)**73** and type **es:** ⏎

To replicate

from one cell to a range

Type >**A72** and type **/R.P**(N)**72** ⏎ **A93** ⏎

Result A label for the section is now entered and the double ruled line ending the income statement section of the example has been replicated to row 93 to mark the end of the balance sheet.

R O W 74 **Single ruled lines** will be entered using the same approach as for the double ruled lines.

To enter

a single ruled line from column A to column P(N)

Type >**A74** and type **/--** ⏎

To replicate

from one cell to a range

Type >**A74** and type **/R** ⏎ **B74.P**(N)**74** ⏎

from one range to another range

Type >**A74** and type **/R.P**(N)**74** ⏎ **A79** ⏎
>**A74** and type **/R.P**(N)**74** ⏎ **A81** ⏎
>**A74** and type **/R.P**(N)**74** ⏎ **A83** ⏎
>**A74** and type **/R.P**(N)**74** ⏎ **A85** ⏎
>**A74** and type **/R.P**(N)**74** ⏎ **A89** ⏎
>**A74** and type **/R.P**(N)**74** ⏎ **A91** ⏎

Result The first step should have put a single ruled line into cell A74. The first replication should have replicated it across to column P(N). The next series of replications should have copied the ruled line to rows 79, 81, 83, 85, 89, and 91.

Step Six

Enter current liabilities.

	A	B(A)	C(A)	D(B)	E(C)	F(D)	G(E)	H(F)	I(G)	J(H)	K(I)	L(J)	M(K)	N(L)	O(M)	P(N)
73	Liabilities:															
74																
75	<Current liabilities>															
76	Accounts payable			22500	22500	22500	22500	22500	22500	22500	22500	22500	22500	22500	22500	22500
77	Accrued wages & taxes			5500	4100	5100	6100	4100	5100	6100	4100	5100	6100	4100	5100	6100
78	Other current liabilities			4000	4000	4000	4000	4000	4000	4000	4000	4000	4000	4000	4000	4000
79																
80	Total current liabilities			32000	30600	31600	32600	30600	31600	32600	30600	31600	32600	30600	31600	32600
81																
82																
83																
84																
85																
86																
87																
88																
89																
90																
91																
92																
93																

ROW 75 **Current liabilities** are short-term obligations for the payment of cash, due on demand or within a specified period of less than a year. Such liabilities ordinarily include notes and accounts payable for merchandise, open loans payable, short-term bank loans, taxes, and accruals. Other short-term obligations, such as maturing debt obligations, also fall within the category of current liabilities.

To enter
> *a label* to identify the current liabilities section of the pro forma balance sheet

> **Type** >**A75** and type "**<Current** →
> >**B(A)75** and type **liabiliti** →
> >**C(A)75** and type **es**> ↵

....

ROW 76 **Accounts payable** include what a company owes others for goods or services that have been provided to that company. They are the result of others providing the firm with credit, and are sometimes known as *trade payables*, or *trade credit due*. Notes owed supplier companies or individuals can also be included under accounts payable.

This line item is difficult to project with precision. Few companies know, in advance, all the goods or services they will purchase from others during a projected period. You can start by identifying the known, upcoming items under accounts payable and then adjusting that figure up or down. Some managers estimate this item in relationship to sales in the last year: accounts payable as

a percentage of sales, such as 10 percent. Then they multiply the new projected sales by the percentage to determine the projected accounts payable.

In our example, the computer will use a formula to calculate accounts payable for you.

To enter
> *a label* to identify this as the accounts payable line of the pro forma balance sheet
> *a value* of $22,500 in cell D(B)76 to represent the actual closing accounts payable balance from the last period of the previous balance sheet
> *formulas* in cells E(C)76 through N(L)76 that will carry forward the previous month's closing accounts payable balance. This amount will then be increased by inventory purchases (from row 17) one month before they are paid for. Inventory purchases are deducted the month they are paid for on row 17. The formulas on this row that add inventory purchases to accounts payable refer to one month out on the inventory purchases row (17), which is referring one month into the future, hence a two month "lead" in respect to sales.
> *formulas* that will calculate accounts payable for the last month in the forecast. Because there is no "one month in the future" on the inventory purchases row for the last column on the forecast, the formula refers to the January period on the inventory purchases row. The example assumes the first month of the next year will have the same inventory purchases as the first month of the period covered by the example. For more detail on how this row relates to inventory

purchases and cost of goods, see TIPS, "Assumptions about inventory purchases," page 123.

Type >**A76** and type **Accounts** ⟶
>**B(A)76** and type **payable** ⟶⟶
>**D(B)76** and type **22500** ⟶
>**E(C)76** and type **+D(B)76+F(D)17-E(C)17** ⏎
>**P(N)76** and type **+O(M)76+E(C)17-P(N)17** ⏎

To replicate
from one cell to a range

Type >**E(C)76** and type **/R** ⏎ **F(D)76.O(M)76** ⏎
Prompt line will read N=No change
R=Relative
Type **RRR**

Result The total and monthly figures should all be $22,500. If they aren't, recalculate the worksheet by pressing the **SHIFT** and **!** keys together four times.

⋯⋯⋯⋯⋯⋯⋯⋯⋯⋯⋯⋯⋯⋯⋯⋯⋯⋯⋯⋯⋯⋯⋯⋯

ROW 77 **Accrued wages and taxes** is the line where the accumulated wages and taxes for the year are entered on the balance sheet. These expenses are charged against profits of the current year, although they will not be paid until later. Bonuses owed, but not paid, are included. Unpaid wages must be accounted for whenever the last day of the accounting period does not coincide with the last day of the pay period.

This line item is quite easy to project for a pro forma statement since it generally involves known figures or is based on other estimated items.

To enter
a label to identify this as the accrued wages and taxes line of the pro forma balance sheet
a value of $5,500 in cell D(B)77 to represent the actual closing accrued wages and taxes balance from the last period of the previous balance sheet
formulas in cells E(C)77 through P(N)77 that will put accrued taxes into the monthly columns. This formula carries forward the closing accrued taxes from the previous period, adds accrued taxes from row 48 of the income statement, and then deducts the quarterly tax payments from row 22 of the cash budget.

Type >**A77** and type **Accrued w** ⟶
>**B(A)77** and type **ages & ta** ⟶
>**C(A)77** and type **xes** ⟶
>**D(B)77** and type **5500** ⟶
>**E(C)77** and type **+D(B)77+E(C)48-E(C)22** ⏎

To replicate
from one cell to a range

Type >**E(C)77** and type **/R** ⏎ **F(D)77.P(N)77** ⏎
Prompt line will read N=No change
R=Relative
Type **RRR**

Result The monthly figures should all be $5,500 in column D(B) and then $4,100, $5,100, and $6,100 in the next three columns. The cycle of $4,100, $5,100, and $6,100 then repeats for the next three columns.

⋯⋯⋯⋯⋯⋯⋯⋯⋯⋯⋯⋯⋯⋯⋯⋯⋯⋯⋯⋯⋯⋯⋯⋯

ROW 78 **Other current liabilities** include any obligations that require payment within the next twelve months but are not listed separately under current liabilities. They can include seasonal and demand loans, notes payable, current portion of long-term debt, dividends payable, or unearned income. Unearned income arises when you receive payment in advance of providing goods or services. Some future service or product is due instead of cash. Therefore, unearned income is listed as a liability; you owe a service or product.

To enter
a label to identify this as the other current liabilities line of the pro forma balance sheet
a value of $4,000 in cell D(B)78 to represent the actual closing other current liabilities balance from the last period of the previous balance sheet
formulas in cells E(C)78 through P(N)78 that will add the previous month's other current liabilities to any loans entered on row 29 of the cash budget

Type >**A78** and type **Other cur** ⟶
>**B(A)78** and type **rent liab** ⟶
>**C(A)78** and type **ilities** ⟶
>**D(B)78** and type **4000** ⟶
>**E(C)78** and type **+D(B)78+E(C)29** ⏎

To replicate
from one cell to a range

Type >**E**(C)**78** and type **/R** ⏎ **F**(D)**78.P**(N)**78** ⏎
Prompt line will read N=No change
R=Relative
Type **RNR**

Result Begin by recalculating the worksheet four times. The beginning and monthly figures should all be $4,000 since no loans have been calculated on the loan line.

· ·

R O W
80 **Total current liabilities** is the total accounts payable, accrued wages and taxes, and other current liabilities.

To enter
a label to identify this as the total current liabilities line of the pro forma balance sheet
formulas in cells D(B)80 through P(N)80 that will add all current liabilities, which are between the ruled lines on rows 74 and 79

Type >**A80** and type **Total cur** →
>**B**(A)**80** and type **rent liab** →
>**C**(A)**80** and type **ilities** →
>**D**(B)**80** and type **@SUM(D**(B)**74.D**(B)**79)**⏎

To replicate
from one cell to a range

Type >**D**(B)**80** and type **/R** ⏎ **E**(C)**80.P**(N)**80** ⏎
Prompt line will read N=No change
R=Relative
Type **RR**

Result The monthly figures should be as follows. (If you don't get these results, try recalculating the worksheet by pressing the **SHIFT** and **!** keys together four times.)

Cell	Month	Value	Cell	Month	Value
D(B)80	Beginning	$32,000	K(I)80	7	$30,600
E(C)80	1	$30,600	L(J)80	8	$31,600
F(D)80	2	$31,600	M(K)80	9	$32,600
G(E)80	3	$32,600	N(L)80	10	$30,600
H(F)80	4	$30,600	O(M)80	11	$31,600
I(G)80	5	$31,600	P(N)80	12	$32,600
J(H)80	6	$32,600			

Step Seven

Enter long-term debt and total liabilities.

	A	B(A)	C(A)	D(B)	E(C)	F(D)	G(E)	H(F)	I(G)	J(H)	K(I)	L(J)	M(K)	N(L)	O(M)	P(N)
73	Liabilities:															
74																
75	<Current liabilities>															
76	Accounts payable			22500	22500	22500	22500	22500	22500	22500	22500	22500	22500	22500	22500	22500
77	Accrued wages & taxes			5500	3900	4700	5500	3900	4700	5500	3900	4700	5500	3900	4700	5500
78	Other current liabilities			4000	4000	4000	4000	4000	4000	4000	4000	4000	4000	4000	4000	4000
79																
80	Total current liabilities			32000	30400	31200	32000	30400	31200	32000	30400	31200	32000	30400	31200	32000
81																
82	Long term debt			40000	40000	40000	40000	40000	40000	40000	40000	40000	40000	40000	40000	40000
83																
84	Total liabilities			72000	70400	71200	72000	70400	71200	72000	70400	71200	72000	70400	71200	72000
85																
86																
87																
88																
89																
90																
91																
92																
93																

Long-term debt (also called fixed liabilities or bonds) includes all debts or loans not due for payment within the year.

To enter

a label to identify this as the long-term debt line of the pro forma balance sheet
a value of $40,000 in cell D(B)82 to represent the actual closing long-term debt balance from the last period of the previous balance sheet
formulas in cells E(C)82 through P(N)82 that will carry the closing long-term debt from the previous period across the monthly columns

Type >**A82** and type **Long term** →
>**B(A)82** and type **"(S)debt** → →
>**D(B)82** and type **40000** →
>**E(C)82** and type **+ D(B)82** ⏎

To replicate

from one cell to a range

Type >**E(C)82** and type **/R** ⏎ **F(D)82.P(N)82** ⏎
Prompt line will read N=No change
R=Relative
Type **R**

Result Long-term debt in each of the monthly columns on row 82 should be $40,000.

Total liabilities is the total debt, or current liabilities plus long-term debt, of the firm. It is also known as total debt.

To enter

a label to identify this as the total liabilities line of the pro forma balance sheet
formulas in cells D(B)84 through P(N)84 that will total current liabilities and long-term debt

Type >**A84** and type **Total lia** →
>**B(A)84** and type **bilities** → →
>**D(B)84** and type **+ D(B)80 + D(B)82** ⏎

To replicate

from one cell to a range

Type >**D(B)84** and type **/R** ⏎ **E(C)84.P(N)84** ⏎
Prompt line will read N=No change
R=Relative
Type **RR**

Result The monthly figures should be as follows. (If your figures don't match these, recalculate the worksheet by pressing the **SHIFT** and **!** keys together four times.)

Cell	Month	Value	Cell	Month	Value
D(B)84	Beginning	$72,000	K(I)84	7	$70,400
E(C)84	1	$70,400	L(J)84	8	$71,200
F(D)84	2	$71,200	M(K)84	9	$72,000
G(E)84	3	$72,000	N(L)84	10	$70,400
H(F)84	4	$70,400	O(M)84	11	$71,200
I(G)84	5	$71,200	P(N)84	12	$72,000
J(H)84	6	$72,000			

Step Eight

Enter owner equity.

	A	B(A)	C(A)	D(B)	E(C)	F(D)	G(E)	H(F)	I(G)	J(H)	K(I)	L(J)	M(K)	N(L)	O(M)	P(N)
73	Liabilities:															
74																
75	<Current liabilities>															
76	Accounts payable			22500	22500	22500	22500	22500	22500	22500	22500	22500	22500	22500	22500	22500
77	Accrued wages & taxes			5500	3900	4700	5500	3900	4700	5500	3900	4700	5500	3900	4700	5500
78	Other current liabilities			4000	4000	4000	4000	4000	4000	4000	4000	4000	4000	4000	4000	4000
79																
80	Total current liabilities			32000	30400	31200	32000	30400	31200	32000	30400	31200	32000	30400	31200	32000
81																
82	Long term debt			40000	40000	40000	40000	40000	40000	40000	40000	40000	40000	40000	40000	40000
83																
84	Total liabilities			72000	70400	71200	72000	70400	71200	72000	70400	71200	72000	70400	71200	72000
85																
86	<Owner equity>															
87	Common stock			50000	50000	50000	50000	50000	50000	50000	50000	50000	50000	50000	50000	50000
88	Retained earnings			20000	21200	22400	23600	24800	26000	27200	28400	29600	30800	32000	33200	34400
89																
90	Total owner equity			70000	71200	72400	73600	74800	76000	77200	78400	79600	80800	82000	83200	84400
91																
92																
93																

ROW 86   **Owner equity** (or *net worth, shareholder equity*) has two parts: the actual investment of the owner(s) in the firm, and retained earnings (any profits that are left to accumulate in the business or, in some cases, the firm's losses). Thus it is equal to the assets of a business minus its liabilities.

Owner equity will be recorded differently on a balance sheet according to the legal structure of a business. If the business is incorporated, its books will show capital stock accounts under owner equity. These accounts represent the total paid-in value of the shares issued to the owners of the business. Undistributed profits are recorded in a retained earnings account. If the business is a proprietorship (single owner) or a partnership, the heading under owner equity would read *capital* or *net worth*, and the capital accounts would appear under the name or names of the owner(s). Increases in equity as a result of undistributed earnings are also recorded there (as retained earnings), as are decreases in equity if the business shows a loss instead of a profit.

To enter
a label to identify this section of the pro forma balance sheet as owner equity

Type >**A86** and type **"<Owner eq** →
     >**B(A)86** and type **uity>** ↵

. . . .

ROW 87   **Common stock** (also called *common equity*) is equal to the total amount in money or value of services that stockholders have provided directly to the firm. If the stock was issued with a par value (that is, a dollar value that appears on the stock certificate), the common stock account may have two subaccounts. *Common stock* is the number of shares issued times the par value. *Paid-in capital* is the monetary difference between what the firm received for the stock and the common stock at par value. By law, paid-in capital must always be positive on the balance sheet. Common stock entries will not change often on the balance sheet.

To enter
a label to identify this as the common stock line of the pro forma balance sheet
a value of $50,000 in cell D(B)87 to represent the actual closing common stock balance from the last period of the previous balance sheet
formulas in cells E(C)87 through P(N)87 that will carry the value in D(B)87 across the balance sheet

Type >**A87** and type **Common st** →
     >**B(A)87** and type **ock** → →
     >**D(B)87** and type **50000** →
     >**E(C)87** and type **+D(B)87** ↵

To replicate
from one cell to a range

Type >**E(C)87** and type **/R** ↵ **F(D)87.P(N)87** ↵
     Prompt line will read N=No change
     R=Relative
     Type **R**

Result   The monthly figures should all be $50,000.

. . . .

ROW 88   **Retained earnings** is the accumulated amount of undistributed earnings of the company. Each year or accounting period, net profit, less any dividends paid, is added to the retained earnings account. If a company has a loss for the period, the amount of the loss is subtracted from the retained earnings account. If a company has a profit, that amount is added. Thus, the retained earnings account is the link between the balance sheet of the previous period and the balance sheet of the current one. It is also the link between the income statement and the balance sheet.

To enter
a label to identify this as the retained earnings line of the pro forma balance sheet
a value of $20,000 in cell D(B)88 to represent the actual closing retained earnings balance from the last period of the previous balance sheet
formulas in cells E(C)88 through P(N)88 that will add this month's net income on row 50 of the pro forma income statement to last month's retained earnings

Type >**A88** and type **Retained** →
     >**B(A)88** and type **earnings** → →
     >**D(B)88** and type **20000** →
     >**E(C)88** and type **+D(B)88+E(C)50** ↵

To replicate
from one cell to a range

Type >**E(C)88** and type **/R** ↵ **F(D)88.P(N)88** ↵
     Prompt line will read N=No change
     R=Relative
     Type **RR**

Result Press the **SHIFT** and **!** keys together once to recalculate the worksheet. The monthly figures should be as follows.

Cell	Month	Value	Cell	Month	Value
D(B)88	Beginning	$20,000	K(I)88	7	$28,400
E(C)88	1	$21,200	L(J)88	8	$29,600
F(D)88	2	$22,400	M(K)88	9	$30,800
G(E)88	3	$23,600	N(L)88	10	$32,000
H(F)88	4	$24,800	O(M)88	11	$33,200
I(G)88	5	$26,000	P(N)88	12	$34,400
J(H)88	6	$27,200			

....

ROW 90 **Total owner equity** is the total amount of money invested in the firm by various owners plus the amount earned and retained by the firm. It is also called *total net worth* or *net worth*. In our example, total owner equity is composed of common stock plus retained earnings.

To enter
a label to identify this as the total owner equity line of the pro forma balance sheet

formulas in cells D(B)90 through P(N)90 that will add all owner equity entries (which are between the ruled lines on rows 85 and 89)

Type >**A90** and type **Total own** (→)
>**B(A)90** and type **er equity** (→)(→)
>**D(B)90** and type **@SUM(D(B)85.D(B)89)**(⏎)

To replicate
from one cell to a range

Type >**D(B)90** and type **/R** (⏎) **E(C)90.P(N)90** (⏎)
Prompt line will read N=No change
R=Relative
Type **RR**

Result The monthly figures should be as follows.

Cell	Month	Value	Cell	Month	Value
D(B)90	Beginning	$70,000	K(I)90	7	$78,400
E(C)90	1	$71,200	L(J)90	8	$79,600
F(D)90	2	$72,400	M(K)90	9	$80,800
G(E)90	3	$73,600	N(L)90	10	$82,000
H(F)90	4	$74,800	O(M)90	11	$83,200
I(G)90	5	$76,000	P(N)90	12	$84,400
J(H)90	6	$77,200			

Step Nine

Enter total liabilities plus total owner equity.

	A B(A) C(A)	D(B)	E(C)	F(D)	G(E)	H(F)	I(G)	J(H)	K(I)	L(J)	M(K)	N(L)	O(M)	P(N)
73	Liabilities:													
74														
75	<Current liabilities>													
76	Accounts payable	22500	22500	22500	22500	22500	22500	22500	22500	22500	22500	22500	22500	22500
77	Accrued wages & taxes	5500	3900	4700	5500	3900	4700	5500	3900	4700	5500	3900	4700	5500
78	Other current liabilities	4000	4000	4000	4000	4000	4000	4000	4000	4000	4000	4000	4000	4000
79														
80	Total current liabilities	32000	30400	31200	32000	30400	31200	32000	30400	31200	32000	30400	31200	32000
81														
82	Long term debt	40000	40000	40000	40000	40000	40000	40000	40000	40000	40000	40000	40000	40000
83														
84	Total liabilities	72000	70400	71200	72000	70400	71200	72000	70400	71200	72000	70400	71200	72000
85														
86	<Owner equity>													
87	Common stock	50000	50000	50000	50000	50000	50000	50000	50000	50000	50000	50000	50000	50000
88	Retained earnings	20000	21200	22400	23600	24800	26000	27200	28400	29600	30800	32000	33200	34400
89														
90	Total owner equity	70000	71200	72400	73600	74800	76000	77200	78400	79600	80800	82000	83200	84400
91														
92	Total liab. & owner equity	142000	141600	143600	145600	145200	147200	149200	148800	150800	152800	152400	154400	156400
93														

Total liabilities and equity is the sum of all liabilities plus owner equity. It always equals total assets, and therefore the balance sheet "balances."

To enter

a label to identify this as the total liabilities and equity line of the pro forma balance sheet

formulas in cells D(B)93 through P(N)92 that will add total liabilities to total owner equity

Type >**A92** and type **Total lia** →
>**B(A)92** and type **b. & owne** →
>**C(A)92** and type **r equity** →
>**D(B)92** and type **+D(B)84+D(B)90** ↵

To replicate

from one cell to a range

Type >**D(B)92** and type **/R** ↵ **E(C)92.P(N)92** ↵
Prompt line will read N=No change
R=Relative
Type **RR**

Result The monthly figures should be as follows.

Cell	Month	Value	Cell	Month	Value
D(B)92	Beginning	$142,000	**K(I)92**	7	$148,800
E(C)92	1	$141,600	**L(J)92**	8	$150,800
F(D)92	2	$143,600	**M(K)92**	9	$152,800
G(E)92	3	$145,600	**N(L)92**	10	$152,400
H(F)92	4	$145,200	**O(M)92**	11	$154,400
I(G)92	5	$147,200	**P(N)92**	12	$156,400
J(H)92	6	$149,200			

Step Ten

Formatting, protecting, and saving.

Formatting the balance sheet. If you are using the Advanced Version, you can format a worksheet after it has been finished. This allows you to experiment with a number of different formats without having to replicate formulas and data as you would with the regular Visi-Calc version. In this example, we are going to format all numbers so that they have commas separating thousands, and negative numbers appear in parentheses.

AV To format

the balance sheet

Type >**D(B)52** and type **/AV,(** ↵ ↵

To replicate

from one cell to a range

Type >**B52** and type **/R**
The prompt line will read Replicate: (, Source range or ENTER
Type **(**
The prompt line will read Replicate:Limit: ACNR)
Type **A)**
Type ↵ **B32.B51** ↵

from one range to other ranges

Type **B52** and type **/R**
The prompt line will read Replicate: (, Source range or ENTER

Type **(**
The prompt line will read Replicate:Limit: ACNR)
Type **A)**
Type ↵ **.B93** ↵ **C52.N52** ↵

Result The entire balance sheet will now be formatted. All dollar values should appear with commas separating thousands and negative numbers should be in parentheses.

Protecting the balance sheet. If you are using the Advanced Version, you can protect all of the cells on the balance sheet so they aren't inadvertently overwritten or erased. Since no data has to be entered into this section of the example, protecting the entire sheet is suggested.

AV To protect

the balance sheet

Type >**A52** and type **/AMP** ↵ ↵

To replicate

from one cell to a range

Type >**A52** and type **/R**
The prompt line will read Replicate: (, Source range or ENTER
Type **(**
The prompt line will read Replicate:Limit:

ACNR)
Type **A)**
Type ⏎ **A53.A93** ⏎

from one range to other ranges

Type >**A52** and type **/R**
The prompt line will read Replicate: (, Source range or ENTER
Type **(**
The prompt line will read Replicate:Limit: ACNR)
Type **A)**
Type ⏎ **.A93** ⏎ **B52.N52** ⏎

Result The entire balance sheet will now be protected. To check that it is, go to any cell and try entering a value, label, or formula. The new entry shouldn't be accepted; you should get a message telling you the cell is protected.

Save your work. Again, it's advisable to save your work before you proceed to the "What Ifs" in the next chapter.

IBM PC TIPS What's on your diskettes

Once you have completed many files, it's hard to remember which files are stored on which diskettes. You can make a list of a diskette's files appear on the screen or a printout by using the DOS System Master Diskette for the IBM PC. A printed list of the contents of each numbered diskette can serve as an index to your diskette files. The printed list gives you important information.

To print a directory of the files on a diskette on the IBM PC:

Step 1. Boot your DOS System Master Diskette by inserting it into drive A and turning on the computer. Insert the diskette for which you want a directory in drive B.

Step 2. When the cursor appears and the drive stops, you must decide whether you want the directory displayed on the screen or on the printout. If you want it on the screen, go to the next step. If you want it printed out, however, see your owner's manual on how to address your printer.

Step 3. When the cursor reappears, i.e., >A, type **Dir B:** ⏎ and the directory will begin to print out. It will give you the name of the files on the diskette, including a suffix indicating if they are VisiCalc files (.VC), Disk interchange format files (.DIF), or print files (.PF). The directory also indicates the size of the files in kilobytes (thousands of bytes) and the date and time they were saved.

6 Exploring the cash budget and pro forma statements

Now that the example has been entered, your fun begins. Building a cash budget directly linked to a pro forma income statement and balance sheet on the computer is time-consuming the first time it's done. But you now have a working model, ready to be used to explore the future of your business.

Financial forecasting is a continual and repetitive process. Forecasts and assumptions about basic elements are made and put into your model. Then, based on the initial results, you can consider various scenarios that might improve your firm's cash flow, performance, and condition. These scenarios can be evaluated in terms of their benefits to your firm and of their likelihood of actually occurring. A business manager should at least prepare a worst case scenario to determine ahead of time what action would be necessary to address or resolve the worst problems that might arise. Working through these various "What Ifs" will not solve all your potential problems. But it will focus your attention on the critical areas of your business, so that you can track performance with a closer eye.

In this chapter, we'll illustrate how easy it is to examine assumptions, explore alternatives, and assess results. A special "What If" column has been built into the example to make it all easier.

Column D(B) and row 6 contain the cells that can be changed. When any changes are made, the results will be reflected throughout the entire example. Since only part of the example can be seen on the screen at one time, printouts of the "What Ifs" are illustrated beginning on page 127. To compare the results of changes you make in each "What If," you can refer to the illustration opposite, which is a printout of the original example.

What if sales follow a seasonal pattern?

WHAT IF 1 **Sales follow a seasonal pattern.** In the sample cash budget entered in Chapter 3, a major assumption was that sales would be evenly distributed throughout the year. The result of such an even sales pattern was a consistently positive monthly net cash flow (row 26) and an ending cash balance (row 30) that grew steadily from $20,000 at the beginning of the year to $49,400 at the end. Any manager or business owner would like to have such a predictable sales pattern and positive cash flow.

But what if your firm doesn't follow an even sales pattern; what if it has a strong seasonal variation in sales? That's a more realistic description of most companies. How will a seasonal pattern affect net cash flow and cash position, as shown on the cash budget? What will happen on the pro forma income statement and balance sheet?

Let's use the computer and the example you entered to explore the possibilities. Assume that sales are seasonal and you expect them to follow this pattern: 30 percent of total annual sales will be evenly distributed throughout the first six months (5 percent each month), 50 percent of sales will be evenly distributed across the next five months (10 percent each month), and 20 percent of sales will occur in a strong last month.

(Note: Since you don't want to save the "What If" examples, check that you have put a piece of tape that came with your diskette over the square write-protect cutout on the diskette.)

To enter

a change in the percentages describing the seasonal pattern of sales on row 6

Note: If you are using the Advanced Version and you formatted the cells on row 6 of the cash budget to display the percentages as whole numbers followed by percent signs, you will have to enter the changes below as decimals rather than as whole numbers. To do so, follow the instructions under "AV Type" below and in all subsequent "What Ifs."

Part 1: Cash budget

Item:	What if column	1 1984	2 1984	3 1984	4 1984	5 1984	6 1984	7 1984	8 1984	9 1984	10 1984	11 1984	12 1984
Seasonal pattern*	100	8	8	8	8	8	8	8	8	8	8	8	8
Net sales; monthly*	450000	37500	37500	37500	37500	37500	37500	37500	37500	37500	37500	37500	37500
Cash receipts:													
% collected within 30 days*	60	22500	22500	22500	22500	22500	22500	22500	22500	22500	22500	22500	22500
% collected within 60 days*	20	7500	7500	7500	7500	7500	7500	7500	7500	7500	7500	7500	7500
% collected within 90 days*	20	7500	7500	7500	7500	7500	7500	7500	7500	7500	7500	7500	7500
Other cash receipts*	0	($)	($)	($)	($)	($)	($)	($)	($)	($)	($)	($)	($)
Total cash receipts		37500	37500	37500	37500	37500	37500	37500	37500	37500	37500	37500	37500
Inventory purchases*	60	22500	22500	22500	22500	22500	22500	22500	22500	22500	22500	22500	22500
Gen.& admin.*	20	7500	7500	7500	7500	7500	7500	7500	7500	7500	7500	7500	7500
Selling expenses*	10	3750	3750	3750	3750	3750	3750	3750	3750	3750	3750	3750	3750
Interest expense*	15	500	500	500	500	500	500	500	500	500	500	500	500
Other expense*	0	($)	($)	($)	($)	($)	($)	($)	($)	($)	($)	($)	($)
Taxes*	40	2400			2400			2400			2400		
Total cash disbursements		36650	34250	34250	36650	34250	34250	36650	34250	34250	36650	34250	34250
Net cash flow		850	3250	3250	850	3250	3250	850	3250	3250	850	3250	3250
Opening cash balance		20000	20850	24100	27350	28200	31450	34700	35550	38800	42050	42900	46150
Loans required	0	0	0	0	0	0	0	0	0	0	0	0	0
Ending cash balance*	20000	20850	24100	27350	28200	31450	34700	35550	38800	42050	42900	46150	49400

Part 2: Pro forma income statement

Item:	What if column	1 1984	2 1984	3 1984	4 1984	5 1984	6 1984	7 1984	8 1984	9 1984	10 1984	11 1984	12 1984
Net sales	450000	37500	37500	37500	37500	37500	37500	37500	37500	37500	37500	37500	37500
Cost of goods sold	270000	22500	22500	22500	22500	22500	22500	22500	22500	22500	22500	22500	22500
Gross profit	180000	15000	15000	15000	15000	15000	15000	15000	15000	15000	15000	15000	15000
General & administrative	90000	7500	7500	7500	7500	7500	7500	7500	7500	7500	7500	7500	7500
Selling expenses	45000	3750	3750	3750	3750	3750	3750	3750	3750	3750	3750	3750	3750
Depreciation	15000	1250	1250	1250	1250	1250	1250	1250	1250	1250	1250	1250	1250
Operating income	30000	2500	2500	2500	2500	2500	2500	2500	2500	2500	2500	2500	2500
Interest expense	6000	500	500	500	500	500	500	500	500	500	500	500	500
Other income/expense*	0	($)	($)	($)	($)	($)	($)	($)	($)	($)	($)	($)	($)
Income before taxes	24000	2000	2000	2000	2000	2000	2000	2000	2000	2000	2000	2000	2000
Taxes	9600	800	800	800	800	800	800	800	800	800	800	800	800
Net income	14400	1200	1200	1200	1200	1200	1200	1200	1200	1200	1200	1200	1200

Part 3: Pro forma balance sheet

Assets:

Item:	What if column	1 1984	2 1984	3 1984	4 1984	5 1984	6 1984	7 1984	8 1984	9 1984	10 1984	11 1984	12 1984
<Current assets>													
Cash	20000	20850	24100	27350	28200	31450	34700	35550	38800	42050	42900	46150	49400
Accounts receivable	60000	60000	60000	60000	60000	60000	60000	60000	60000	60000	60000	60000	60000
Inventory	30000	30000	30000	30000	30000	30000	30000	30000	30000	30000	30000	30000	30000
Prepaid expenses	2000	2000	2000	2000	2000	2000	2000	2000	2000	2000	2000	2000	2000
Total current assets	112000	112850	116100	119350	120200	123450	126700	127550	130800	134050	134900	138150	141400
<Fixed assets>													
Buildings & equipment	50000	50000	50000	50000	50000	50000	50000	50000	50000	50000	50000	50000	50000
Less accum.depreciation	30000	31250	32500	33750	35000	36250	37500	38750	40000	41250	42500	43750	45000
Land	10000	10000	10000	10000	10000	10000	10000	10000	10000	10000	10000	10000	10000
Net fixed assets	30000	28750	27500	26250	25000	23750	22500	21250	20000	18750	17500	16250	15000
Total assets	142000	141600	143600	145600	145200	147200	149200	148800	150800	152800	152400	154400	156400

Liabilities:

Item:	What if column	1 1984	2 1984	3 1984	4 1984	5 1984	6 1984	7 1984	8 1984	9 1984	10 1984	11 1984	12 1984
<Current liabilities>													
Accounts payable	22500	22500	22500	22500	22500	22500	22500	22500	22500	22500	22500	22500	22500
Accrued wages & taxes	5500	3900	4700	5500	3900	4700	5500	3900	4700	5500	3900	4700	5500
Other current liabilities	4000	4000	4000	4000	4000	4000	4000	4000	4000	4000	4000	4000	4000
Total current liabilities	32000	30400	31200	32000	30400	31200	32000	30400	31200	32000	30400	31200	32000
Long term debt	40000	40000	40000	40000	40000	40000	40000	40000	40000	40000	40000	40000	40000
Total liabilities	72000	70400	71200	72000	70400	71200	72000	70400	71200	72000	70400	71200	72000
<Owner equity>													
Common stock	50000	50000	50000	50000	50000	50000	50000	50000	50000	50000	50000	50000	50000
Retained earnings	20000	21200	22400	23600	24800	26000	27200	28400	29600	30800	32000	33200	34400
Total owner equity	70000	71200	72400	73600	74800	76000	77200	78400	79600	80800	82000	83200	84400
Total liab. & owner equity	142000	141600	143600	145600	145200	147200	149200	148800	150800	152800	152400	154400	156400

Exploring "What Ifs"

Type	>**E**(C)**6** and type **5** →
	>**F**(D)**6** and type **5** →
	>**G**(E)**6** and type **5** →
	>**H**(F)**6** and type **5** →
	>**I**(G)**6** and type **5** →
	>**J**(H)**6** and type **5** →
	>**K**(I)**6** and type **10** →
	>**L**(J)**6** and type **10** →
	>**M**(K)**6** and type **10** →
	>**N**(L)**6** and type **10** →
	>**O**(M)**6** and type **10** →
	>**P**(N)**6** and type **20** ↵

⬛AV **Type**	>**C6** and type **.5** →
	>**D6** and type **.5** →
	>**E6** and type **.5** →
	>**F6** and type **.5** →
	>**G6** and type **.5** →
	>**H6** and type **.5** →
	>**I6** and type **.10** →
	>**J6** and type **.10** →
	>**K6** and type **.10** →
	>**L6** and type **.10** →
	>**M6** and type **.10** →
	>**N6** and type **.20** ↵

Result Begin by using the **SHIFT** and **!** keys to recalculate the worksheet three times to insure that all of the formulas have calculated the correct values. As you can see by looking at the screen or the printout on page 127, the introduction of seasonality in sales significantly changes the firm's cash flow pattern and cash position. Monthly net cash flow on row 26 becomes negative (-$2,750) in the fifth month (May) and remains negative for the next three months, until increasing sales make it positive in September ($1,750). It becomes negative again in November when inventory purchases (the $54,000 in cell O(M)17) are made for December, your strongest sales month.

The negative monthly net cash flows deplete the cash balance of the firm, so a loan is required. The amount needed (shown on row 29) is calculated by the computer. The formula is designed to indicate how much cash is needed to keep the closing balance from becoming negative. When the monthly net cash flow plus the opening balance is less than zero, the formula on the loan line enters the difference in the month(s) where money is needed. In our example, the computer shows that a loan or some other form of financing in the amount of $16,759 is needed in November (cell O(M)29).

This is calculated as follows:

VISICALC TIPS Windows and fixed titles

With a small screen and a large VisiCalc worksheet, only a small section of your work can be seen at one time. There are, however, two commands that can greatly expand what you can see, the *window* and *fixed titles* commands.

The *window* command splits the screen into two parts, either horizontally (/**WH**) or vertically (/**WV**). The two screens can be scrolled together (/**WS**) or independently (/**WSU**). You can use this command to hold columns A-C (column A on the Advanced Version) on the screen in the left-hand window while scrolling across columns on the right-hand side of the template in the other window. When you explore "What Ifs" you can also use this command to keep one row, the current ratio for example, in the lower window while using the upper window to scroll up and down the example to enter data. The command /**W1** clears the screen of windows.

The *fixed titles* command can be used independently or in conjunction with the window command to hold specific rows or columns on the screen when scrolling. You can fix titles on the screen horizontally (/**TH**), vertically (/**TV**), or both horizontally and vertically (/**TB**). The rows or columns that are fixed with this command depend on the position of the cursor at the time the command is entered. Rows on or to the left of the cursor position and columns on or above the cursor position are the ones that will be fixed. The command /**TN** clears the screen of this command.

When you use the window and fixed titles commands simultaneously, different fixed title settings can be made in each window.

Net cash flow (cell O(M)26)	−$20,959
Plus opening cash balance (cell O(M)28)	4,200
Loans required (cell O(M)29)	16,759

ANALYSIS This "What If" demonstrates the usefulness of the cash budget for anticipating periods of cash shortage. It also shows the effects of a seasonal sales pattern on the budget, pro forma income statement, and balance sheet. Let's examine some of these effects:

The cash budget: Total cash receipts begin to decline in the early months due to lower sales in that period. Cash disbursements in the same period are relatively stable, with the exception of negative tax payments in two months (cells H(F)22 and K(I)22). These occur because tax payments are calculated as a percentage of the income before taxes for the previous three months.

Normally you will never have negative tax payments. You would use tax losses to offset taxes due during profitable periods. In actuality you would be making no tax payments during these months. The effect of keeping the tax payment formula simple is to understate your total cash disbursements during those months in which negative tax payments are indicated, which in turn overstates the net cash flow. A more complicated formula would eliminate this problem. If you decide to use such a complex formula, we suggest that your accountant review the logic before you actually enter and use it for forecasting purposes.

The overall result of changing an even sales pattern to a seasonal one is a gradual deterioration in monthly net cash flow from $9,850 in the first month to −$16,250 in the sixth. In the second half of the year net cash flow falls even further, as inventory purchases begin to increase faster than either sales or cash receipts. There is a built-in lag between the time of an inventory purchase and the time the inventory is sold. There is an additional lag between the time it is sold and the time you are paid. The effect of these lags is to decrease cash flow and, in some cases, increase borrowing requirements. This situation is common as firms move into their peak selling periods or experience fast growth. (In the next "What If," we'll explore what can be done to reduce the effects of this lag.)

By the end of the year the cash flow and position improves, since sales and cash receipts are up while inventory purchases are down substantially due to lower inventory requirements for the first half of the next year (not shown on the forecast). In the last month enough cash is left to repay the loan required in the previous month.

The pro forma income statement: Net income on the pro forma income statement is negative at the beginning of the year, but as sales pick up it turns positive and the year ends on a strong note (net income of $13,674 in December). The income statement doesn't reflect the swings in inventory purchases (calculated at 60 percent of net sales) as closely as the cash budget does, since they are only recorded on this statement when inventory is sold (or written off) and not when it is purchased. You can see, though, that interest expense on row 44 (and also on row 20 of the cash budget) has increased in the last two months to reflect the loan required to finance operations.

The balance sheet: In the original example total assets (row 71) and retained earnings (row 88) grew gradually throughout the year. Total assets increased from $142,000 to $183,541. Retained earnings, which are derived from net income, increased from $20,000 to $34,149.

Introducing seasonality in sales changed both of these items. Total assets began by falling from $142,000 in January to a low point of $127,600 in March before they started climbing again, to reach a high of $183,541 in the last month. The fall was caused by a decline in accounts receivable due to lower sales in the first half of the year. Assets began to increase primarily as a result of the build-up in inventory needed to support sales in the second half of the year. This increase in inventory is matched by an increase on the accounts payable line (row 76).

Retained earnings started the year at $20,000 and declined steadily through the first six months, when net income was negative. They began increasing in July as sales and net income improved, and ended the year on a high of $34,149 in December.

As you can see, the beginning and end of the year are the company's strongest periods in terms of performance (the pro forma income statement) and condition (the pro forma balance sheet). Both profitability and financial strength deteriorated through the first part of the year due to the dropping off of collection on the prior year's strong sales and the high fixed expenses, relative to sales. Profits declined and the asset base and retained earnings decreased. As sales began to pick up, the immediate result was further weakening in cash flow and the balance sheet because inventory to support the higher sales was purchased in advance of its actual sale. As the collections on the higher sales began to come in, cash flow, profits, and the asset base strengthened. Swings like these in cash flow, performance, and condition make it clear that there are certain times of the year in which a firm looks stronger from a financial standpoint than in others. This is why many businesses select their strongest period as their year-end.

Here are some lines on the pro forma balance sheet to look at and think about:

Cash (row 57): This line is taken directly from the ending balance line (row 30) of the cash budget.

Accounts receivable (row 58): This line is calculated by taking accounts receivable from the previous month on this row, adding this month's sales (row 7), and then subtracting this month's cash receipts (row 15).

This row starts high ($45,000 in January) due to receivables not yet collected from the previous period. Receivables then decline along with the low sales of the first half and begin to pick up as sales pick up. They close very high ($117,000 in December) because of the high sales that month and the uncollected receivables from the relatively high sales periods in the previous months of the second half of the year.

Inventory (row 59): This line is calculated by taking inventory from the previous month on this row, adding the current month's inventory purchases (row 17) and subtracting this month's cost of goods sold (row 35) on the income statement.

This row starts low ($30,000 in January) and then climbs as inventory purchases increase in anticipation of higher sales in the second half of the year. They decline in the last month (December) because the inventory is sold during this month, the month with the highest sales level of the year. Since next month's sales (January) are expected to be much lower than December's, the inventory requirement is proportionately lower. We have assumed that next year will have no growth and the same seasonality as this forecast by having the formula that calculates the last month refer to the first month of this forecast.

Accounts payable (row 76): This line is calculated by a formula that takes the previous month's accounts payable, adds the inventory purchase for two months out (row 17) and then subtracts this month's inventory purchases. The built-in assumption is that inventory purchases are made two months in advance and paid for one month in advance of their sale. They are entered in accounts payable when they are ordered and are deducted when they are paid for.

Like the inventory line the formulas in the last month of this row refers back to the first month on the forecast (column E(C)) instead of the next month since this doesn't appear on the forecast. As a result the row peaks in November (column O(M)) reflecting inventory purchases in November ($54,000 in cell O(M)17) ordered in anticipation of the large sale in December.

Accrued wages and taxes (row 77): This row is calculated by a formula that carries forward the accrued wages and taxes from the previous month, adds taxes due from the income statement (row 48) based on this month's net income, and subtracts quarterly payments shown on the cash budget (row 22).

This row fluctuates as net income and taxes due fluctuate. It doesn't drop each quarter (January, April, July, and October) as expected when quarterly tax payments are made. This is because taxes are calculated as negative figures. The result is that cash actually improves in the example. In the real world, of course, quarterly rebates of tax payments aren't actually received.

VISICALC TIPS Displaying numbers with more precision

The global format for many financial statements should be set to integer (/GFI), since the display of cents adds no information of value. Although this setting simplifies the screen display and printed reports, it doesn't change the actual values in memory. However, in some cases you may want to see a value unrounded and displayed out to several decimal places. Here are three ways to do this:

■ **The # command:** Place the cursor into the cell of interest and type # (using the **SHIFT** key). The precise value of the cell will be displayed on the edit line. Be careful if you use this command in a cell containing a formula. Hitting the ⏎ key will convert the formula in the cell into the value displayed at the time the key was pressed. Use the backspace key to terminate the display without changing the formula.

■ **The /F command:** You can use the /F command to put a local format into any cell you choose. Begin by positioning the cursor in the cell and then type /F followed by one of the following: $ to display the value out to two decimal places; or G to display the value out to the maximum number of decimals that can be contained in the column width you are using.

■ The Advanced Version allows you to spell out precisely the number of decimal places to be displayed or printed. Type **/AV2F** for two decimal places, **/AV3F** for three decimal places, **/AV4F** for four, and so forth.

WHAT IF 2 **Collections are improved.** In the previous "What If," seasonal sales patterns were introduced into the example and their effects on the cash budget and pro forma income statement and balance sheet were explored. Let's leave the seasonality pattern unchanged and explore what can be done to reduce its effect on cash flow. Any improvements that can be made will reduce the loans required to finance operations.

Assume that collections are improved by either better collection procedures or tighter credit policies. In the original example, the collection pattern was 60 percent collected within 30 days of a sale, 20 percent within 60 days, and 20 percent within 90 days. Let's improve that to 80 percent collected within 30 days, 10 percent within 60 days, and 10 percent within 90 days. The computer will recalculate the entire example so that you can immediately see the effects of this change.

To enter

changes in collections in cells D(B)10, 11, and 12 from 60 percent, 20 percent, and 20 percent to 80 percent, 10 percent, and 10 percent (See page 84 for Advanced Version explanation.)

Type >**D**(B)**10** and type **80** ⏎
>**D**(B)**11** and type **10** ⏎
>**D**(B)**12** and type **10** ⏎

AV **Type** >**B10** and type **.80** ⏎
>**B11** and type **.10** ⏎
>**B12** and type **.10** ⏎

Result Begin by using the **SHIFT** and **!** keys to the worksheet five times. Since there are several forward references in the example, a series of recalculations is always required to make all the changes.

Total cash receipts on row 15 closely parallel those of the first "What If," due to the effects of collections carried forward from the previous period (not covered by this budget). The collection change begins to have a dramatic effect in August (column L(J)), when collections for the sales increase in July come in. This improvement is retained for a month and then levels out in October.

The real effect can be seen on the loans required line. In the previous "What If," $16,759 was required in November to keep the closing balance from becoming negative. With collections speeded up, this loan requirement is reduced to $3,089.

ANALYSIS When payments are delayed, you must finance inventory purchases with your own resources, either cash on hand or loans. When collections are improved, the cash you had invested in accounts receivable becomes available, and the amount of money you need to borrow is reduced.

Notice that the closer in time your collections and payments are to the month of sale, the more closely the cash budget resembles the pro forma income statement. Faster collections also reduce accounts receivable because customers are paying you more promptly.

Also note that in the example net income (row 50) increased slightly in the last two months since less interest is paid out because you have a smaller loan. In the next "What Ifs" we'll take a look at loans and interest rates, and their possible effect on an expected financial position.

What if debt increases?

<u>**W H A T   I F**</u>
3 **Debt increases.** Suppose you plan to expand your business and incur higher debt to do so. What would happen to your interest payments?

Let's see what happens when long-term debt is increased from $40,000 to $80,000 and interest rates are at 10 percent. The opening cash balance will be increased $40,000 (from $20,000 to $60,000) to keep the balance sheet balanced when long-term debt is increased.

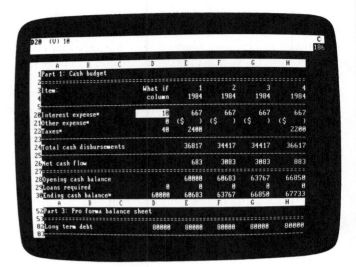

To restore

the example to its original state

Note: If you are using the Advanced Version, and you formatted the cells on row 6 of the cash budget to display the percentages as whole numbers followed by percent signs, you will have to enter different formulas to restore the example. To do so, follow the "[AV] Type" instructions here and in subsequent "What Ifs."

Type >**E**(C)**6** and type **100/12**
>**D**(B)**10** and type **60** ⏎
>**D**(B)**11** and type **20** ⏎
>**D**(B)**12** and type **20** ⏎

[AV] **Type** >**C6** and type **1/12** ⏎
>**B10** and type **.60** ⏎
>**B11** and type **.20** ⏎
>**B12** and type **.20** ⏎

To replicate

from one cell to a range

Type >**E**(C)**6** and type **/R** ⏎ **F**(D)**6.P**(N)**6** ⏎
Use the **SHIFT** and **!** keys to recalculate the worksheet three times.

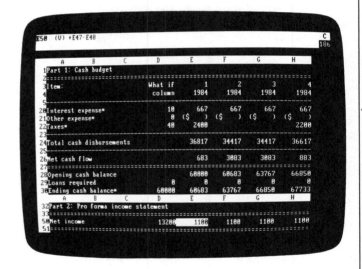

Type >**D**(B)**20** and type **10** ⏎
>**D**(B)**30** and type **60000** ⏎
>**D**(B)**82** and type **80000** ⏎

[AV] **Type** >**B20** and type **.10** ⏎
>**B30** and type **60000** ⏎
>**B82** and type **80000** ⏎

To enter

a change in interest rates from 15 percent to 10 percent (cell D(B)20)

a change in the previous period's ending cash balance (the same as the first month's opening cash balance) from $20,000 to $60,000 (cell D(B)30)

a change in long-term debt from $40,000 to $80,000 (cell D(B)82)

Result Begin by using the **SHIFT** and **!** keys to recalculate the worksheet at least twice. Monthly interest payments (rows 20 and 44) are now $667 and net income (row 50) moves from a monthly $1200 in the original example to $1100.

ANALYSIS The high opening cash balance made the short-term loans required (row 29) unnecessary, but the increase in long-term debt increases interest payments to $667. Now let's see what would happen if the loan had a variable rate and the interest rate increased to 18 percent.

. . . .

WHAT IF 4 **The interest rates increase.** This is a situation that many business people have encountered in the last several years. Intuitively, you know that an increase in interest rates means an increase in cost; but your question is, "How much of an impact does it have?" Suppose, for example, the interest rate goes from 10 percent to 18 percent.

To enter

a change in interest rates in cell D(B)20 from 10 percent to 18 percent

Type >**D**(B)**20** and type **18** ⏎

[AV] **Type** >**B20** and type **.18** ⏎

Result Begin by using the **SHIFT** and **!** keys to recalculate the worksheet at least twice. Interest expenses (rows 20 and 44) increase from the previous $667 to $1,200 a month. This both reduces monthly net cash flow (row 26) and reduces net income (row 50) from $1100 in the previous "What If" to $780 per month due to increased interest payments.

ANALYSIS Wide swings in interest rates have recently been a serious problem for firms of all sizes. While high debt works to one's advantage when interest rates are stable and inflation is high (loans are paid back with cheaper dollars), it has the opposite effect when rates swing wildly and inflation slows down. In today's environment, good planning looks at the possible effects of increased interest rates to insure that the firm isn't vulnerable to changes outside of its control. If a change in interest rates makes the difference between positive and negative cash flow or between profit and loss, the planned debt should be avoided or other forms of financing sought.

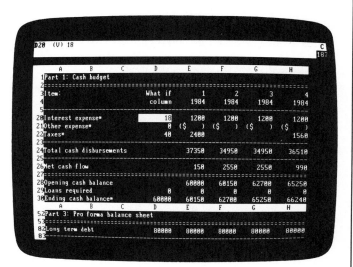

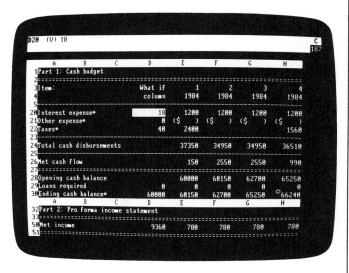

What if cost of goods goes up?

WHAT IF 5 **Cost of goods goes up.** Let's see how a change in one line item, such as cost of goods, can affect both the cash budget and pro forma income statement. Remember that the example is modeled on a retail operation, so cost of goods is made up entirely of inventory purchases. (Cost of goods for manufacturing and service businesses is described on page 116.) Let's look at what happens to net cash flow (row 26 on the cash budget) and net income (row 50 on the income statement) if cost of goods increases. Assume that net sales receipts remain unchanged because these cost increases are not passed on to customers through price increases. In effect, prices remain the same while costs rise.

To explore this situation, you'll enter a change in the inventory purchases percentage figure in cell D(B)17. The example calculates the cost of inventory purchases by multiplying this figure (now .60 or 60 percent) by the next month's net sales. (It assumes you order inventory two months prior to its sale and pay for it one month before it is sold.) Suppose this percentage is raised to 65 percent. How will this change affect net cash flow and net income on a month-by-month and annual basis?

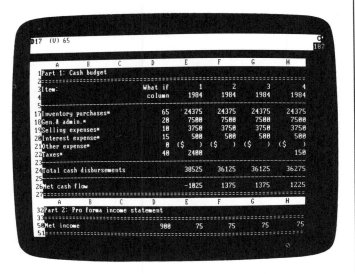

To restore
the example to its original state

Type >D(B)**20** and type **15** ⏎
    >D(B)**30** and type **20000** ⏎
    >D(B)**82** and type **40000** ⏎
    Use the **SHIFT** and **!** keys to recalculate the worksheet at least twice.

AV **Type** >B**20** and type **.15** ⏎
    >B**30** and type **20000** ⏎
    >B**82** and type **40000** ⏎

To enter
a change in the cost of inventory purchased (cell D(B)17 from 60 percent of net sales to 65 percent

Type >D(B)**17** and type **65** ⏎

AV **Type** >B**17** and type **.65** ⏎

Result Begin by using the **SHIFT** and **!** keys to recalculate the sheet three times. You can see that the higher cost of inventory reduces both net cash flow on row 26

and net income on row 50. (You can use the WINDOW command to see both of these rows at the same time.) Net cash flow falls from a monthly $3,250 in the original example ($850 in those months when quarterly tax payments on row 22 are made) to a smaller but still positive $1,375 ($1,225 in those months when quarterly tax payments are made). The ending cash balance (row 30) also declines each month but the year-end cash balance of $33,650 is still higher than the opening cash balance of $20,000. Before the change in inventory cost, though, the ending cash balance improved from $20,000 to $49,400. The 8 percent increase in inventory cost reduces the ending balance by almost 30 percent.

Net income is even more seriously affected. It falls from $1,200 a month to a very slim $75 a month. Obviously, this is a turn for the worse and action is necessary to improve profits.

This "What If" clearly demonstrates the importance of watching the cost of goods sold and the resulting gross profit you obtain (gross profit equals sales minus cost of goods). The relationship between these two line items is extremely important for both good cash flow and profitability.

ANALYSIS The cause of the decrease in net cash flow and net income is obvious. The 8 percent increase in cost of goods sold (from 60 percent to 65 percent of sales) produced both the drop in net cash flow and the deterioration in net income.

You still do not need to borrow any money because there is a stable and positive net cash flow throughout the year. But the decline in profits is a concern. If you did need to borrow, bankers might be reluctant to lend to you unless you could take some action to improve the profit picture.

But why the difference in the drop of net cash flow and net income? Should net income be positive if net cash flow is? Not necessarily. The cash budget, which gives you net cash flow and your cash position, reflects cash as it is received and paid out. It is basically what you expect to happen in your checkbook for the next year. Net income is derived from the pro forma income statement and does not usually reflect the flow of cash into and out of your business as you expect it to occur. In addition, the income statement includes depreciation, which is not an actual cash expense, so it's not reflected in the cash budget. In our example, depreciation amounts to $1,250 per month. That accounts for the difference between the $75 monthly net cash flow and the $1,325 monthly net income.

What can you do to improve your profit picture? In this "What If," we assumed that the higher inventory costs could not be passed on to your customers in the form of higher prices. But increasing prices is an obvious action you could take to improve profits. Another alternative is to reduce other expenses enough to offset the higher inventory cost. You would have to save $3,750 to restore net income to its original level of $1,200 per month. Just to break even in terms of net income (no net income, but no loss), you would have to generate $2,625 in cost reductions.

Another possible action would be to increase sales to the point where the additional gross profit offsets the higher inventory cost and covers operating and interest expenses. Any of these alternatives or a combination of them should improve both net income and net cash flow.

This "What If" shows how one change, entered into the computer, affects both the cash budget and pro forma income statement. It also demonstrates how you can use these statements to gain better financial awareness and thus better control of your company. You can explore what will happen instead of simply reacting to what has happened. The income statement and cash budget, while not crystal balls that can forecast the future, do allow you to anticipate situations and plan for better cash flow and higher profits: a vital aspect of improving control.

....

WHAT IF 6 **Cost of goods increases can't be passed on to customers to restore profitability.** Suppose you can't raise prices to cover the increased cost of goods. This situation can arise in periods when high inflation begins to slow down. Costs can no longer be easily passed along. During such periods, careful planning of controllable expenses is needed to offset the increases in costs that can't be avoided.

In this "What If" we will explore how the increase in inventory purchase costs in the previous "What If" (from 60 to 65 percent) might be offset by a reduction in general and administrative expenses. Suppose these costs can be reduced from 20 percent of net sales to 15 percent. How will this reduction affect cash flow and profits?

To enter

a change in general and administrative expenses as a percentage of net sales from 20 percent to 15 percent (cell D(B)18)

Type >D(B)**18** and type **15** ⏎

AV **Type** >B18 and type .15 ⏎

Result Begin by using the **SHIFT** and **!** keys to recalculate the sheet at least once. The reduction in G&A expenses exactly offsets the increase in inventory purchase costs. Monthly net cash flow (row 26) and net income (row 50) return to the same values they had in the original example. Net cash flow has increased, back to a monthly $3,250 ($850 in those months when quarterly tax payments on row 22 are made) and net income is back to $1,200 a month.

Exploring "What Ifs," Continued

ANALYSIS This "What If" demonstrates the relationship between inventory costs, operating expenses (of which G&A is one), and cash flow and net income. Changes in costs as a percentage of net sales must be offset by changes in expenses to maintain the same financial results. When inventory costs go down and operating expenses remain the same, an increase in both cash flow and net income can be expected.

If this situation had included a seasonal sales pattern, the higher inventory cost would magnify the swings in net cash flow and profits, while the reduction in G&A would dampen this effect.

What if sales exceed expectations?

WHAT IF 7 **Sales exceed expectations.** Many expenses are directly related to sales. If sales fall below projections, you worry about covering fixed expenses that do not vary with sales. But when sales exceed what you expected, you must be concerned with the expenses that do vary with sales. This is particularly true when sales follow a seasonal pattern and the collection on sales lags behind the cash expenditures necessary to generate the sales.

Let's explore what the effect on net cash flow and net income would be if sales are $600,000 instead of the expected $450,000.

To restore
the example to its original state

Type >D(B)**17** and type **60** ⏎
>D(B)**18** and type **20** ⏎
Use the **SHIFT** and **!** keys to recalculate the worksheet twice.

AV **Type** >B**17** and type **.60** ⏎
>B**18** and type **.20** ⏎

To enter
a change in net sales (cell D(B)7) from $450,000 to $600,000

Type >D(B)**7** and type **600000** ⏎

Result Begin by recalculating the sheet at least three times. If your results don't match those given, try recalculating again. Monthly sales increase $12,500, from $37,500 to $50,000. Since the only expenses that are directly related to sales in the template you built are inventory purchases, cost of goods sold, and taxes, the increase in sales should produce better cash flow and profits and strengthen the balance sheet.

Net income (row 50) does improve, from $1,200 to $1,950 a month. Net cash flow (row 26) is higher during the months that taxes are not paid ($4,500 versus $3,250) except for the first three months of the year. The ending cash balance (row 30) increases from $20,000 at the beginning of the year to $39,900 at the end of the year. This is lower than the original ending cash balance of $49,400, based on sales of $450,000.

The balance sheet is strengthened by higher accounts receivable, inventory, and retained earnings. Current assets increase steadily throughout the year, while current liabilities remain constant except for the months during which accrued taxes are reduced by the amount of your tax payments.

ANALYSIS The higher sales produced higher profits and a stronger balance sheet. But why did the cash flow and cash position deteriorate in comparison to the original example? The answer lies in one of the paradoxes of doing business. Sales growth will almost always generate higher dollar profits. At the same time, rapid growth will almost always produce a cash drain.

Let's look at what happened. The negative net cash flows during January and February were the result of higher inventory purchase payments, necessary to support the higher sales. During those same months your receipts were based on a lower level of sales for the previous year. The net effect is a cash drain that you do not recover from fully by the end of the year. The result is a lower ending cash balance.

A second factor that affects your cash flow and cash position is the higher level of operating costs (general and administrative and selling expenses). These are tied directly to sales (they are a percentage of sales). So when sales increase, these expenses will also increase. For small sales increases, these expenses are likely to remain relatively constant. But under this scenario, sales increased by more than 30 percent. Under these circumstances, you would expect general and administrative and selling expenses to increase as well.

7 Adapting the example to your company

Our approach

The example cash budget, pro forma income statement, and pro forma balance sheet you entered in Chapters 3, 4, and 5 (Example) can be adapted to your business with little extra effort. To do so, you first have to generate your own data for a number of the line items on the cash budget.

Look at the information in this chapter as a starting point. Every business is unique and no single approach or model can anticipate or cover every aspect of your business. For this reason, numerous examples and techniques are provided. Choose those that best serve your needs. Also included are some "shopping lists," detailed breakdowns of certain line items. Few businesses have all of the revenue sources or expense items listed, so select those you want to use and ignore the rest.

As you gain experience with both the VisiCalc program and your own business requirements, you will find it easy to expand on the model we've provided. The example and templates described are not fixed. One of the advantages of using a computer is that you can continue to improve and expand upon your model as you learn. All new knowledge can be incorporated into your model and lead to better control and more accurate planning and budgeting.

In this chapter, we'll show you how to develop and adapt a general forecasting template (Template) for use with the cash budget and the pro formas. This template can be used to forecast line items and will improve and speed up the assembly of information. Here is an overview of this chapter and what aids you can develop as you proceed through it.

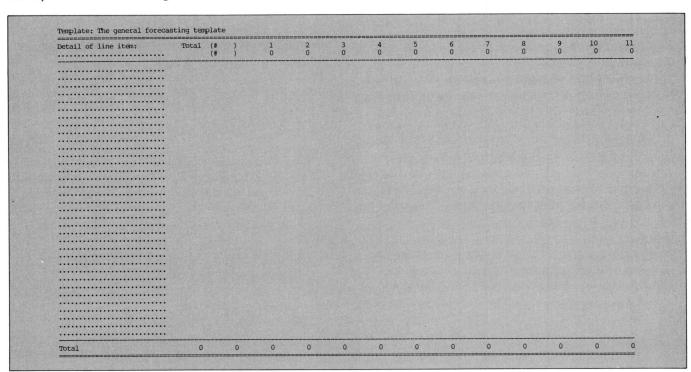

The general forecasting template *will be entered into the computer. This basic template can be saved and then reloaded and adapted to a number of specific applications including forecasting sales and expenses such as cost of goods.*

Detail of line item:	Total	1 1984	2 1984	3 1984	4 1984	5 1984	6 1984	7 1984	8 1984	9 1984	10 1984	11 1984	12 1984
Office rent	9000	750	750	750	750	750	750	750	750	750	750	750	750
Insurance payments	1600	($)	($)	400	($)	($)	400	($)	($)	400	($)	($)	400
Heat	6000	1200	900	600	300	0	0	0	0	300	600	900	1200
Total	16600	1950	1650	1750	1050	750	1150	750	750	1450	1350	1650	2350

▲ **Adapting the template**. *You'll see how to adapt the general forecasting template by adding formulas that speed the entry of expenses or sales revenues that occur on a regular monthly basis, those that occur irregularly, or on a periodic but non-monthly basis, and those that occur seasonally.*

▼ **Forecasting your own sales**. *After describing some general methods of forecasting sales, we'll show you how to how to forecast sales by dollars, units, or a combination of both and adapt the template.*

Template: The general forecasting template

Detail of line item: Sales revenue	Total	1 1984	2 1984	3 1984	4 1984	5 1984	6 1984	7 1984	8 1984	9 1984	10 1984	11 1984	12 1984
Monthly service:													
Client # 1	1200	100	100	100	100	100	100	100	100	100	100	100	100
Client # 2	1200	100	100	100	100	100	100	100	100	100	100	100	100
Client # 3	1200	100	100	100	100	100	100	100	100	100	100	100	100
Client # 4	1200	100	100	100	100	100	100	100	100	100	100	100	100
Client # 5	1200	100	100	100	100	100	100	100	100	100	100	100	100
Client # 6	1200	100	100	100	100	100	100	100	100	100	100	100	100
Client # 7	1200	100	100	100	100	100	100	100	100	100	100	100	100
Client # 8	1200	100	100	100	100	100	100	100	100	100	100	100	100
Client # 9	1200	100	100	100	100	100	100	100	100	100	100	100	100
Quarterly service:													
Client # 11	1200	300	($)	($)	300	($)	($)	300	($)	($)	300	($)	($)
Client # 12	1200	300	($)	($)	300	($)	($)	300	($)	($)	300	($)	($)
Client # 13	1200	300	($)	($)	300	($)	($)	300	($)	($)	300	($)	($)
Client # 14	1200	300	($)	($)	300	($)	($)	300	($)	($)	300	($)	($)
Client # 15	1200	300	($)	($)	300	($)	($)	300	($)	($)	300	($)	($)
Client # 16	1200	300	($)	($)	300	($)	($)	300	($)	($)	300	($)	($)
Client # 17	1200	300	($)	($)	300	($)	($)	300	($)	($)	300	($)	($)
Client # 18	1200	300	($)	($)	300	($)	($)	300	($)	($)	300	($)	($)
Client # 19	1200	300	($)	($)	300	($)	($)	300	($)	($)	300	($)	($)
Client # 20	1200	300	($)	($)	300	($)	($)	300	($)	($)	300	($)	($)
Annual service:													
Client # 30	400	($)	($)	($)	($)	($)	($)	($)	($)	($)	($)	($)	400
Client # 31	400	($)	($)	($)	($)	($)	($)	($)	($)	($)	($)	($)	400
Client # 32	400	($)	($)	($)	($)	($)	($)	($)	($)	($)	($)	($)	400
Client # 33	400	($)	($)	($)	($)	($)	($)	($)	($)	($)	($)	($)	400
Client # 34	400	($)	($)	($)	($)	($)	($)	($)	($)	($)	($)	($)	400
Client # 35	400	($)	($)	($)	($)	($)	($)	($)	($)	($)	($)	($)	400
Client # 36	400	($)	($)	($)	($)	($)	($)	($)	($)	($)	($)	($)	400
Client # 37	400	($)	($)	($)	($)	($)	($)	($)	($)	($)	($)	($)	400
Total	26000	3900	900	900	3900	900	900	3900	900	900	3900	900	4100

```
Templa:Forecasting unit sales, sales revenue, and cost of goods
```

Detail of line item: Unit sales forecast	Total units	1 1984	2 1984	3 1984	4 1984	5 1984	6 1984	7 1984	8 1984	9 1984	10 1984	11 1984	12 1984
Product number 1	1200	96	96	96	120	120	120	120	120	120	72	48	72
Product number 2	1200	24	24	24	48	48	48	60	96	180	216	216	216
Product number 3	500	(#)	(#)	250	250	(#)	(#)	(#)	(#)	(#)	(#)	(#)	(#)
Product number 4	2000	(#)	(#)	(#)	(#)	(#)	(#)	(#)	(#)	(#)	(#)	(#)	2000
Product number 5	4000	333	333	333	333	333	333	333	333	333	333	333	333
Product number 6	100	8	8	8	8	8	8	8	8	8	8	8	8
Product number 7	0	(#)	(#)	(#)	(#)	(#)	(#)	(#)	(#)	(#)	(#)	(#)	(#)
Product number 8	0	(#)	(#)	(#)	(#)	(#)	(#)	(#)	(#)	(#)	(#)	(#)	(#)
Product number 9	0	(#)	(#)	(#)	(#)	(#)	(#)	(#)	(#)	(#)	(#)	(#)	(#)
Product number 10	0	(#)	(#)	(#)	(#)	(#)	(#)	(#)	(#)	(#)	(#)	(#)	(#)
Product number 11	0	(#)	(#)	(#)	(#)	(#)	(#)	(#)	(#)	(#)	(#)	(#)	(#)
Total unit sales	9000	462	462	712	760	510	510	522	558	642	630	606	2630

Detail of line item: Sales revenue forecast	Total sales	1 1984	2 1984	3 1984	4 1984	5 1984	6 1984	7 1984	8 1984	9 1984	10 1984	11 1984	12 1984	Net price	Dis-count	List price
Product number 1	4800	384	384	384	480	480	480	480	480	480	288	192	288	4.00 (%)		4.00
Product number 2	7200	144	144	144	288	288	288	360	576	1080	1296	1296	1296	6.00 (%)		6.00
Product number 3	1200	0	0	600	600	0	0	0	0	0	0	0	0	2.40	20	3.00
Product number 4	9000	0	0	0	0	0	0	0	0	0	0	0	9000	4.50 (%)		4.50
Product number 5	32700	2725	2725	2725	2725	2725	2725	2725	2725	2725	2725	2725	2725	8.18	50	16.35
Product number 6	735	61	61	61	61	61	61	61	61	61	61	61	61	7.35 (%)		7.35
Product number 7	0	0	0	0	0	0	0	0	0	0	0	0	0	9.25 (%)		9.25
Product number 8	0	0	0	0	0	0	0	0	0	0	0	0	0	0.00 (%)		($)
Product number 9	0	0	0	0	0	0	0	0	0	0	0	0	0	0.00 (%)		($)
Product number 10	0	0	0	0	0	0	0	0	0	0	0	0	0	0.00 (%)		($)
Product number 11	0	0	0	0	0	0	0	0	0	0	0	0	0	0.00 (%)		($)
Total sales revenue	55635	3314	3314	3914	4154	3554	3554	3626	3842	4346	4370	4274	13370	6.18		

Detail of line item: C.O.G forecast	Total sales	1 1984	2 1984	3 1984	4 1984	5 1984	6 1984	7 1984	8 1984	9 1984	10 1984	11 1984	12 1984	Unit cost	C.O.G. %	Gross margin
Product number 1	2400	192	192	192	240	240	240	240	240	240	144	96	144	2.00	50	50
Product number 2	3240	65	65	65	130	130	130	162	259	486	583	583	583	2.70	45	55
Product number 3	650	0	0	325	325	0	0	0	0	0	0	0	0	1.30	54	46
Product number 4	4320	0	0	0	0	0	0	0	0	0	0	0	4320	2.16	48	52
Product number 5	30760	2563	2563	2563	2563	2563	2563	2563	2563	2563	2563	2563	2563	7.69	94	6
Product number 6	400	33	33	33	33	33	33	33	33	33	33	33	33	4.00	54	46
Product number 7	0	0	0	0	0	0	0	0	0	0	0	0	0	0 ($)	0	0
Product number 8	0	0	0	0	0	0	0	0	0	0	0	0	0	0 ($)	0	0
Product number 9	0	0	0	0	0	0	0	0	0	0	0	0	0	0 ($)	0	0
Product number 10	0	0	0	0	0	0	0	0	0	0	0	0	0	0 ($)	0	0
Product number 11	0	0	0	0	0	0	0	0	0	0	0	0	0	0 ($)	0	0
Total cost of goods	41770	2853	2853	3178	3219	2966	2966	2999	3096	3323	3324	3276	7644	4.64	75	25

Forecasting expenses. Expenses such as cost of goods sold, salaries, general and administrative expenses, and selling expenses can be forecast to form the basis of a budget. We'll show you some typical ways to break down key expense categories. Then you'll see how to adapt the general forecasting template as you did for sales to speed the entry of expenses that occur on a constant monthly basis, those that occur on an irregular or non-monthly periodic basis, and those that occur seasonally. We'll illustrate how to estimate cost of goods directly from the sales forecast by linking it to a cost-of-goods worksheet.

Entering the general forecasting template

The general purpose template, with the file name Template, can be used to assemble the data needed for forecasting sales and expenses for your own budget and pro formas. Many of the key lines on the cash budget, pro forma income statement, and pro forma balance sheet in the previous chapters have been consolidated to reduce the number of lines on the example. This consolidation into major line items is a common business practice, since it makes the budget easier to interpret. For your own firm or department, though, the budget for some of the lines on the statements may need more detail. Line items such as sales, cost of goods sold, operating expenses, interest, and taxes need to be built from the bottom up. The general forecasting template is designed so that you

can customize it to meet this need. Any individual line item can be broken down on this template into its basic elements and the results then transferred to the sample statements using the DIF command.

Our approach

First you will enter the basic template, consisting of descriptive headings, column headings, label entry spaces, and formulas, to total the entries. Next you will see how to set up additional formulas to speed data entry into the template. Three kinds of formulas cover the basic patterns in which sales and expenses occur: monthly, irregular, and seasonal.

	A	B(A)	C(A)	D(B)	E(C)	F(D)	G(E)	H(F)	I(G)	J(H)	K(I)	L(J)	M(K)	N(L)	O(M)	P(N)
1	Template: The general forecasting template															
2	===															
3	Detail of line item:			Total	(# |)	1	2	3	4	5	6	7	8	9	10	11
4	....				(# |)	0	0	0	0	0	0	0	0	0	0	0
5																
6	....															
7	....															
8	....															
9	....															
10	....															
11	....															
12	....															
13	....															
14	....															
15	....															
16	....															
17	....															
18	....															
19	....															
20	....															
21	....															
22	....															
23	....															
24	....															
25	....															
26	....															
27	....															
28	....															
29	....															
30	....															
31	....															
32	....															
33	....															
34	....															
35	....															
36	....															
37	....															
38	....															
39	....															
40	....															
41	....															
42	Total				0	0	0	0	0	0	0	0	0	0	0	0
43	===															

ROW 1 **Template heading and ruled lines** are entered. Template is a master template that can be saved and then reloaded and adapted to a number of applications. Each of these adaptations can then be saved under a different file name. The master template will not have formulas in either the monthly or total columns since the kinds of formulas you enter depend on the pattern of your individual income or expense line items. How to enter formulas for monthly, irregular, and seasonal patterns are covered starting on page 102.

To enter

a label to identify this as Template, the master general forecasting template

single ruled lines from column A through column P(N) that will separate major sections of the template

double ruled lines from column A through column P(N) that will separate major sections of the template

phantom instructions identifying the lower right-hand corner of the template (These phantom instructions won't appear in printouts and can't be seen unless the cursor is positioned in the cell containing them.)

Type >**A1** and type **Template:Print to P(N)43** →
>**B(A)1** and type **"(S)The gene** →
>**C(A)1** and type **ral forec** →
>**D(B)1** and type **asting te** →
>**E(C)1** and type **mplate** ↵

>**A2** and type **/-=** ↵

>**A5** and type **/--** ↵

To replicate

from one cell to a range

Type >**A2** and type **/R** ↵ **B2.P(N)2** ↵
>**A5** and type **/R** ↵ **B5.P(N)5** ↵

from one range to another range

Type >**A2** and type **/R.P(N)2** ↵ **A43** ↵
>**A5** and type **/R.P(N)5** ↵ **A41** ↵

Result The template should have double ruled lines on rows 2 and 43 from column A to column P(N) and single ruled lines between the same columns on rows 5 and 41.

. . . .

⌐ROWS⌐
3-4 **Column headings and dates** are entered. These will adjust automatically whenever the first month and year are entered or changed.

To enter

labels to identify the line item and total columns of the template
formulas on rows 3 and 4 that will label the monthly columns and change them automatically if the beginning month and year are changed

Type >**A3** and type **Detail of** →
>**B(A)3** and type **"(S)line ite** →
>**C(A)3** and type **m:** →
>**D(B)3** and type **/FR Total** →
>**E(C)3** and type **/FR "(#)** →
>**F(D)3** and type **@IF(E(C)3=12,1,E(C)3+1** ↵

>**A4** and type **/-.** → → → →
>**E(C)4** and type **/FR "(#)** →
>**F(D)4** and type **@IF(E(C)3=12,E(C)4+1,E(C)4** ↵

To replicate

from one cell to a range

Type >**F(D)3** and type **/R** ↵ **G(E)3.P(N)3** ↵
Prompt line will read N=No change
R=Relative
Type **RR**

from one cell to a range (This step isn't required for Advanced Version users.)

Type >**A4** and type **/R** ↵ **B4.C(A)4** ↵

from one cell to a range

Type >**F(D)4** and type **/R** ↵ **G(E)4.P(N)4** ↵
Prompt line will read N=No change
R=Relative
Type **RRR**

Result The template should now have headings and a series of formulas that will automatically date the monthly columns when the beginning month and year are entered. To check that they work, go to cell D(B)3 and type **10** (for the month of October). Now go to D(B)4 and enter **1984**. Press the **SHIFT** and **!** keys together to recalculate the sheet. Row 3, containing the monthly labels, should change from 10 in column D(B) to 9 (for September) in column O(M). At cell G(E)3, where the column is now dated 1 for January, the year should have changed to 1985.

. . . .

⌐COLUMN⌐
A-C **Label entry spaces** can now be entered between row 6 and row 40. These spaces can guide you when you organize the specific line items to be included in the breakdown. They are helpful when entering data on the computer or when the blank template is printed out as a worksheet.

To enter

label entry spaces in columns A through C(A) that can be used to list line items to be included in the breakdown

Type >**A6** and type **/-.** ↵

To replicate

from one cell to a range (This step isn't necessary for Advanced Version users.)

Type >**A6** and type **/R** ↵ **B6.C(A)6** ↵

from one range to a number of ranges

Type >**A6** and type **/R.C**(A)**6** ⏎ **A7.A40** ⏎

Result Columns A through C (column A for Advanced Version users) should now contain a series of label entry spaces between row 6 and row 40.

....

ROW
42

The bottom line contains the total monthly column entries, and the grand total in column D(B).

To enter

a label to identify row 42 as the row containing the monthly totals and the grand total for the line item *formulas* on row 42 that will add all of the entries in the monthly columns between rows 5 and 41

Type >**A42** and type **Total** → → →
    >**D**(B)**42** and type **@SUM(D**(B)**5.D**(B)**41)** ⏎

To replicate
from one cell to a range

Type >**D**(B)**42** and type **/R** ⏎ **E**(C)**42.P**(N)**42** ⏎
    Prompt line will read N=No change
    R=Relative
    Type **RR**

Result The template should now have a series of zeros on row 42 between columns D(B) and P(N). If any data is entered in the monthly column it will be totaled on this row. The same entries will be totaled across the rows and the sum will appear in column D(B). The grand total will appear in cell D(B)42.

Save your work. It's advisable to save your work at this point before proceeding.

VISICALC TIPS Adding and deleting rows

Once your template is completed, you can add or delete rows used to enter line labels and data. All formulas will continue working correctly. Be sure never to delete rows containing formulas that calculate totals, such as net sales revenue, total assets, and so forth. When rows are added, new data entry spaces and formulas used to calculate percentages must be replicated from adjoining rows.

To delete line item rows from the completed template: Position your cursor on the row to be deleted. Type **/DR**, and you will delete the row.

To add line item rows to the completed template: Position the cursor in the row below the one in which you want to insert the new row. Type **/IR**. After a moment, a blank row will appear.

This new row contains no data entry spaces or formulas to calculate percentages. To enter these, position your cursor in column A of the nearest row containing these entries and type **/R**. Then type the coordinate of the cell on the end of the row from which you are replicating (in most cases column K(I) for the income statement and column G(E) for the balance sheet will suffice). Next, type ⏎ followed by the coordinate of the first cell in the row to which you want to replicate; type ⏎ again. You will now have to specify each formula reference, using **N** for no change, or **R** for relative.

Adapting the template

The general forecasting template has a simple but flexible structure that you can adapt by entering formulas or adding supplements. If you were working in the traditional way, with ledger sheets and a pencil, you would enter a label for each line item and then use a calculator to determine monthly entries and totals. With your computer and the VisiCalc program there are simpler, faster, and more accurate ways to enter the data you need. These techniques are faster than traditional methods the first time through the budget, but their real power is most obvious when you start making revisions to fine tune your plans.

In this section we'll show you how to adapt the general forecasting template to speed the entry of estimated sales and expenses that follow three common patterns:

■ Those that occur on a regular monthly basis, such as rent payments.

■ Those that occur on a regular but non-monthly basis, such as quarterly insurance or tax payments, or that follow no pattern at all, such as equipment purchases.

■ Those that follow a seasonal pattern, such as heat or air-conditioning expenses.

	A	B(A)	C(A)	D(B)	E(C)	F(D)	G(E)	H(F)	I(G)	J(H)	K(I)	L(J)	M(K)	N(L)	O(M)	P(N)
1	Template: The general forecasting template															
2																
3	Detail of line item:			Total	1	2	3	4	5	6	7	8	9	10	11	12
4					1984	1984	1984	1984	1984	1984	1984	1984	1984	1984	1984	1984
5																
6	Office rent			9000	750	750	750	750	750	750	750	750	750	750	750	750
7	Insurance payments			1600	($)	($)	400	($)	($)	400	($)	($)	400	($)	($)	400
8	Heat			6000	1200	900	600	300	0	0	0	0	300	600	900	1200
9																
42	Total			16600	1950	1650	1750	1050	750	1150	750	750	1450	1350	1650	2350

Revenues or expenses that occur on a regular monthly basis. *Rent, entered in row 6 of the illustration above, is typical of revenues or expenses that occur on a regular monthly basis. The best way to enter revenues or expenses that follow this pattern is to enter the anticipated total annual amount in the total column and then enter formulas in each of the monthly columns to divide the total by 12.*

Entering sales or expenses that occur on a regular monthly basis can be made faster by setting up the rows on which they are to be entered so that any annual total entered in the total column is automatically divided by 12 (the number of months covered by the forecast). You may need one or more rows set up this way. The rows you'll be entering the formulas on and those that you'll replicate from or to will vary according to your needs. For this reason all typing instructions below indicate the row number with a question mark (**?**). Enter the column letter given. When entering formulas, follow the instructions until you come to a question mark; then enter the row number on which you are entering the formulas. Do the same if you are replicating, but when the source range is requested on the prompt line enter the row you are replicating from; when prompted for the target range enter the row number(s) you are replicating to.

To enter

data entry spaces ($) in column D(B) where you can enter the annual amount that is to be spread evenly throughout the monthly columns
formulas on the rows where you will enter sales or expenses that occur on a regular monthly basis, so that any number entered in the total column will be divided by 12 in each of the monthly columns

Type >**D**(B)(**?**) and type **/FR** "**($)** ⟶
      >**E**(C)(**?**) and type **+D**(B)(**?**)**/12** ⟵

To replicate

from one cell to a range

Type >**E**(C)(**?**) and type **/R** ⟵ **F**(D)(**?**).**P**(N)(**?**) ⟵
      Prompt line will read N=No change
      R=Relative
      Type **N**

from one range to a number of ranges (if you want to set up more than one row this way)

Type >**D**(B)(**?**) and type **/R.P**(N)(**?**) ⟵ **D**(B)(**?**).**D**(B)(**?**) ⟵
      Prompt line will read N=No change
      R=Relative
      Type **RRRRRRRRRRRR** (12 **R**s)

Result The first replication should have copied the formula (total divided by 12) across the monthly columns on the row you selected. The second replication should have copied that row, including the data entry space in column D(B), to other rows where you

want to distribute sales or expenses. Until data is entered in the total column, D(B), all of the formula results on the screen should be 0. Try entering a number in the total column and pressing the **SHIFT** and ! keys together to recalculate. Each monthly column on the row in which you entered the total should show 1/12 of the total amount. If you do this, be sure to replace the number with a blank entry space before saving the template.

VISICALC TIPS Calculating and displaying percentages

In most financial statements, percentages are shown rounded off, without decimal places. To obtain this result with the VisiCalc program, you first enter the formula — for instance, cost of goods sold divided by net sales — and then multiply by 100: (cost of goods/net sales)*100. Multiplying by 100 eliminates the decimal, so percentages appear on the screen and in printouts as whole numbers (10, 20, 30, etc.) rather than as decimals (.10, .20, .30).

If you are using the Advanced Version, you can use the **/AV%** command instead of multiplying by 100. The **/AV%** command simultaneously multiplies the calculated result of the formula you enter by 100 and displays the answer followed by a % sign: 10%, 20%, 30%.

The display of calculated percentages in the cells can also be changed as needed to obtain the degree of precision desired. **/FI** will display the calculated percentage as a rounded-off whole number (for example, 20), **/F$** will display it out to two decimal places (20.34), and **/FG** will display it out to the maximum number of decimals allowed by the column width setting (20.3411234). To see even more decimals when using the **/FG** format, you can temporarily change the column width by using the **/GC** command. You can enter any of these formats before or after entering formulas.

	A	B(A)	C(A)	D(B) Total	E(C) 1 1984	F(D) 2 1984	G(E) 3 1984	H(F) 4 1984	I(G) 5 1984	J(H) 6 1984	K(I) 7 1984	L(J) 8 1984	M(K) 9 1984	N(L) 10 1984	O(M) 11 1984	P(N) 12 1984
1	Template: The general forecasting template															
2																
3	Detail of line item:			Total	1 1984	2 1984	3 1984	4 1984	5 1984	6 1984	7 1984	8 1984	9 1984	10 1984	11 1984	12 1984
4																
5																
6	Office rent			9000	750	750	750	750	750	750	750	750	750	750	750	750
7	Insurance payments			1600	($)	($)	400	($)	($)	400	($)	($)	400	($)	($)	400
8	Heat			6000	1200	900	600	300	0	0	0	0	300	600	900	1200
42	Total			16600	1950	1650	1750	1050	750	1150	750	750	1450	1350	1650	2350

Revenues or expenses that occur on an irregular basis.
Most sales and revenues are not distributed equally throughout each month of a year. Some occur regularly but not monthly, such as the quarterly insurance payments shown on row 7 above. Others follow no pattern of any kind. The best way to distribute these revenues and expenses is to enter the monthly amounts and then enter a formula in the total column to add all entries made on the row. Data entry spaces, ($) can be added in the monthly columns to guide you in entering the data either while working on the computer or when gathering and assembling information on a printout of the template used as a worksheet.

ROWS 6–40 **Entering income or expenses that occur on an irregular basis** can be made faster by setting up the rows on which they are to be entered so that any monthly entry is automatically totaled in the total column, D(B). You may need one or more rows set up this way. Since the rows you'll be entering the formulas on or those that you'll replicate from or to will vary according to your needs, all typing instructions below indicate the row number with a question mark (?). Enter the column letter given. When entering formulas, follow the instructions until you come to a question mark; then enter the row number on which you are entering the formulas. Do the same if you are replicating, but when the source range is requested on the prompt line enter the row you are replicating from; when prompted for the target range enter the row number(s) you are replicating to.

To enter

formulas in the total column on the rows where you will enter income or expenses that occur on an irregular basis, so that any number entered in the monthly columns will be automatically totaled in column D(B)

data entry spaces ($) on the rows you are using between column D(B) and column P(N)

Type >**D**(B)(**?**) and type @**SUM(E**(C)(**?**)**.P**(N)(**?**)**)** ⏎
    >**E**(C)(**?**) and type **/FR** "**($** **)** ⏎

To replicate

from one cell to a range

Type >**E**(C)(**?**) and type **/R** ⏎ **F**(D)(**?**)**.P**(N)(**?**) ⏎

from one range to a number of ranges (if you want to set up more than one row this way)

Type >**D**(B)(**?**) and type **/R.P**(N)(**?**) ⏎ **D**(B)(**?**)**.D**(B)(**?**) ⏎
    Prompt line will read N=No change
    R=Relative
    Type **RR**

Result The first replication should have copied the data entry spaces across the monthly columns covered by the forecast. The second replication should have copied these spaces and the formula used to calculate the total in column D(B) to other rows you want to apportion the same way. Until data is entered in one of the monthly columns, the total column, D(B), will read 0. Try entering a number in one of the data entry spaces and pressing the **SHIFT** and ! keys together to recalculate. The total column should automatically pick up the number you entered. If you do this, be sure to replace the number with a blank data entry space before saving the template.

VISICALC TIPS Quick and easy graphing

Columns of raw numbers are sometimes hard to evaluate because their relationships are hidden in a mass of digits. Percentages such as those used on the common-sized income statements and balance sheets help. They reduce a long series of numbers to their relationships to each other. Graphs are even more revealing because they give a visual image of trends. With the VisiCalc or VisiCalc Advanced Version programs, you can make a quick graph of any dollar or percent column.

The graph will show the size of numbers in relationship to each other, and express this relationship using multiplication signs. For instance, the number 400 could be represented by 4 multiplication signs and the number 100 could be represented by 1 sign.

To make the graph, type **/GF*** (multiplication sign). All the numbers on the worksheet will then be converted to multiplication signs. Since the signs may not fit into the space (width) of the worksheet, you'll probably have to adjust the column width or divide all the numbers by the same number to reduce them equally, and thereby have them fit on the worksheet. Then you can print out your graph.

VISICALC TIPS Confidentiality

Do you have any numbers on your worksheets that you don't want others to see, either on the screen or in printed-out reports? How about individual's salaries and bonuses, or maybe the line-item breakdown of your expense report? The Advanced Version lets you do this. Just place the cursor in the cell you want to conceal and type **/AHY.** When you want to see the cell contents, type **/AHN.**

	A	B(A)	C(A)	D(B)	E(C)	F(D)		Q(O)	R(P)	S(Q)	T(R)	U(S)	V(T)	W(U)	X(V)	Y(W)	Z(X)	AA(Y)	AB(Z)	AC(AA)
1	Template: The general forecasting template							Seasonal patterns:												
2	============							===========												
3	Detail of line item:			Total	1	1		Total	1	2	3	4	5	6	7	8	9	10	11	12
4					1984	1984		%	1984	1984	1984	1984	1984	1984	1984	1984	1984	1984	1984	1984
5																				
6	Office rent			9000	750	750		0	(%)	(%)	(%)	(%)	(%)	(%)	(%)	(%)	(%)	(%)	(%)	(%)
7	Insurance payments			1600	($)	($)		0	(%)	(%)	(%)	(%)	(%)	(%)	(%)	(%)	(%)	(%)	(%)	(%)
8	Heat			6000	1200	90		100	20	15	10	5	(%)	(%)	(%)	(%)	5	10	15	20
9								0	(%)	(%)	(%)	(%)	(%)	(%)	(%)	(%)	(%)	(%)	(%)	(%)
10								0	(%)	(%)	(%)	(%)	(%)	(%)	(%)	(%)	(%)	(%)	(%)	(%)
11								0	(%)	(%)	(%)	(%)	(%)	(%)	(%)	(%)	(%)	(%)	(%)	(%)
12								0	(%)	(%)	(%)	(%)	(%)	(%)	(%)	(%)	(%)	(%)	(%)	(%)
13								0	(%)	(%)	(%)	(%)	(%)	(%)	(%)	(%)	(%)	(%)	(%)	(%)
14								0	(%)	(%)	(%)	(%)	(%)	(%)	(%)	(%)	(%)	(%)	(%)	(%)
15								0	(%)	(%)	(%)	(%)	(%)	(%)	(%)	(%)	(%)	(%)	(%)	(%)
16								0	(%)	(%)	(%)	(%)	(%)	(%)	(%)	(%)	(%)	(%)	(%)	(%)
17								0	(%)	(%)	(%)	(%)	(%)	(%)	(%)	(%)	(%)	(%)	(%)	(%)
18								0	(%)	(%)	(%)	(%)	(%)	(%)	(%)	(%)	(%)	(%)	(%)	(%)
19								0	(%)	(%)	(%)	(%)	(%)	(%)	(%)	(%)	(%)	(%)	(%)	(%)
20								0	(%)	(%)	(%)	(%)	(%)	(%)	(%)	(%)	(%)	(%)	(%)	(%)
21								0	(%)	(%)	(%)	(%)	(%)	(%)	(%)	(%)	(%)	(%)	(%)	(%)
22								0	(%)	(%)	(%)	(%)	(%)	(%)	(%)	(%)	(%)	(%)	(%)	(%)
23								0	(%)	(%)	(%)	(%)	(%)	(%)	(%)	(%)	(%)	(%)	(%)	(%)
24								0	(%)	(%)	(%)	(%)	(%)	(%)	(%)	(%)	(%)	(%)	(%)	(%)
25								0	(%)	(%)	(%)	(%)	(%)	(%)	(%)	(%)	(%)	(%)	(%)	(%)
26								0	(%)	(%)	(%)	(%)	(%)	(%)	(%)	(%)	(%)	(%)	(%)	(%)
27								0	(%)	(%)	(%)	(%)	(%)	(%)	(%)	(%)	(%)	(%)	(%)	(%)
28								0	(%)	(%)	(%)	(%)	(%)	(%)	(%)	(%)	(%)	(%)	(%)	(%)
29								0	(%)	(%)	(%)	(%)	(%)	(%)	(%)	(%)	(%)	(%)	(%)	(%)
30								0	(%)	(%)	(%)	(%)	(%)	(%)	(%)	(%)	(%)	(%)	(%)	(%)
31								0	(%)	(%)	(%)	(%)	(%)	(%)	(%)	(%)	(%)	(%)	(%)	(%)
32								0	(%)	(%)	(%)	(%)	(%)	(%)	(%)	(%)	(%)	(%)	(%)	(%)
33								0	(%)	(%)	(%)	(%)	(%)	(%)	(%)	(%)	(%)	(%)	(%)	(%)
34								0	(%)	(%)	(%)	(%)	(%)	(%)	(%)	(%)	(%)	(%)	(%)	(%)
35								0	(%)	(%)	(%)	(%)	(%)	(%)	(%)	(%)	(%)	(%)	(%)	(%)
36								0	(%)	(%)	(%)	(%)	(%)	(%)	(%)	(%)	(%)	(%)	(%)	(%)
37								0	(%)	(%)	(%)	(%)	(%)	(%)	(%)	(%)	(%)	(%)	(%)	(%)
38								0	(%)	(%)	(%)	(%)	(%)	(%)	(%)	(%)	(%)	(%)	(%)	(%)
39								0	(%)	(%)	(%)	(%)	(%)	(%)	(%)	(%)	(%)	(%)	(%)	(%)
40								0	(%)	(%)	(%)	(%)	(%)	(%)	(%)	(%)	(%)	(%)	(%)	(%)
41																				
42	Total			16600	1950	1650														
43	============																			

Revenues or expenses that follow a seasonal pattern. *Frequently expenses or sales of a product follow a seasonal pattern such as that of the cost of heat entered on row 8 above. A seasonality supplement, linked to the general forecasting template, can help you adapt line items to their seasonal pattern. You enter expected monthly percentages of the total of the item on the supplement and formulas in the corresponding months on the template. The formulas multiply any amount entered in the total column on the template by the percentage entered on the supplement. Any changes in the total column or in the percentages on the supplement will automatically change the monthly amounts.*

Instead of developing a supplement, you could make each row seasonal by entering a formula in each monthly cell that multiplies the amount entered on the same row in the total column by the expected monthly percentage. For instance, a formula in the first column that multiplies the amount in the total column by 10 percent would result in this cell containing 10 percent of whatever amount was entered in the total column. The problem with this approach is immediately seen if changes in the seasonal pattern need to be entered. The formulas in every cell have to be revised.

ROWS 6–40 **Income or expenses that occur on a predictable seasonal basis** can be entered quickly by adding a supplement to the general forecasting template. In this step, you'll set up the supplement by entering headings and data entry spaces in which seasonal percentage figures can be entered later. You may not use all these rows for seasonal patterns, but we suggest you follow the instructions to set them up. In the next step (linking the seasonal supplement to the main template), you can select the rows you want to set up this way by entering formulas on those rows. Only the rows on the main template into which these formulas are entered will be linked to the seasonal supplement. Also, the percentages you choose will not be seen on a printout, so you might question later how your numbers were derived. Entering the percentages on a separate table not only lets you see their distribution but also makes it much easier to explore "What Ifs," since seasonal patterns can easily and quickly be changed.

To enter

a label that identifies this as the seasonal patterns supplement

column headings for the supplement that copy the months from the main template

formulas in column Q(O) that will total up all of the percentages you enter into the supplement so you can check to be sure they add up to exactly 100 percent

data entry spaces (%) in the supplement that can be used to enter the expected seasonal distribution of income or expenses

Type >Q(O)**1** and type **Seasonal** →
>R(P)**1** and type **patterns:** ⏎

>Q(O)**2** and type **/-=** ⏎

>Q(O)**3** and type **/FR Total** →
>R(P)**3** and type **+E**(C)**3** ⏎

>Q(O)**4** and type **/FR "%** →
>R(P)**4** and type **+E**(C)**4** ⏎

>Q(O)**5** and type **/--** ⏎

>Q(O)**6** and type **@SUM(R**(P)**6.AC**(AA)**6)** ⏎
>R(P)**6** and type **/FR "(%)** ⏎

To replicate

from one cell to a range

Type >Q(O)**2** and type **/R** ⏎ **R**(P)**2.AC**(AA)**2** ⏎
>R(P)**3** and type **/R** ⏎ **S**(Q)**3.AC**(AA)**3** ⏎
Prompt line will read N=No change
R=Relative
Type **R**

>R(P)**4** and type **/R** ⏎ **S**(Q)**4.AC**(AA)**4** ⏎
Prompt line will read N=No change
R=Relative
Type **R**

>Q(O)**5** and type **/R** ⏎ **R**(P)**5.AC**(AA)**5** ⏎
>Q(O)**6** and type **/R** ⏎ **Q**(O)**7.Q**(O)**40** ⏎
Prompt line will read N=No change
R=Relative
Type **RR**

>R(P)**6** and type **/R** ⏎ **R**(P)**7.R**(P)**40** ⏎

from one range to another range

Type >Q(O)**2** and type **/R.AC**(AA)**2** ⏎ **Q**(O)**43** ⏎
>Q(O)**5** and type **/R.AC**(AA)**5** ⏎ **Q**(O)**41** ⏎

from one range to a number of ranges

Type >R(P)**6** and type **/R.R**(P)**40** ⏎ **S**(Q)**6.AC**(AA)**6**
⏎

Result You have just accomplished a great deal with very little effort. Your template should have column headings on rows 3 and 4 that carry the month and year from the main template, a total percent column Q(O), and data entry spaces between columns R(P) and AC(AA) on rows 6 and 40.

Linking the seasonal supplement to the main template can be done by entering formulas on the main template that multiply the total entered in column D(B) of the main template times the percentages entered on the same rows of the supplement.

You can choose which rows on the template will be linked to the seasonal pattern supplement. You will enter formulas in the monthly columns of the main template on those rows that are to be set up this way. All typing instructions below indicate row numbers with question marks (**?**). Fill in the question marks with the rows you are using as you enter the monthly formulas.

To enter

a data entry space in column D(B) where you will enter a total for annual sales receipts or an expense *formulas* on the main template that will multiply the monthly percentages you enter on the supplement times the totals entered in column D(B) and also enter the correct percentages into each monthly column. The formulas on the main template divide the result by 100, so you can enter whole numbers on the supplement rather than decimals (i.e., 25 to indicate 25 percent).

Type >D(B)(**?**) and type **/FR "($)** →
>E(C)(**?**) and type **+D**(B)(**?**)*****R**(P)(**?**)**/100** ⏎

To replicate

from one cell to a range

Type >E(C)(**?**) and type **/R** ⏎ **F**(D)(**?**)**.P**(N)(**?**) ⏎
Prompt line will read N=No change
R=Relative
Type **NR**

from one range to a number of ranges (if you want to set up more than one row this way)

Type >D(B)(**?**) and type **/R.P**(N)(**?**) ⏎ **D**(B)(**?**)**.D**(B)(**?**)
⏎
Prompt line will read N=No change
R=Relative
Type 24 **R**s

Result A series of zeros should appear on the rows in which you entered or replicated a formula. To make the row work, you will have to enter a number in the total column, D(B), and at least one percentage on the same row of the supplement. Press the **SHIFT** and ! keys together to recalculate and watch the results. If you do this, be sure to replace the numbers you entered with blank data entry spaces before saving the template.

Forecasting sales

The sales forecast is the basis for all financial projections. It is the starting point. Since sales determine the level of operations in a firm, they determine expenses — both those that vary with sales (variable expenses), such as material purchases, and those that are fixed over a given period of time, such as salaries and depreciation.

Like any forecasting, arriving at a sales forecast is as much an art as a science. The "scientific" part of forecasting comes from the existence of hard information that is predictable, verifiable, and follows a pattern over time. For instance, a steady sales growth rate over the past five years is historical information and presents a pattern that may be useful in predicting how sales will occur in the future. But forecasting is also an art, based on personal intuition and perceptions, because the future is always uncertain. Who says that the clear trend in sales over the past five years will continue in the future? The farther into the future you are trying to forecast, the more likely it is that the actual results will differ from your forecast.

Sales forecast versus sales potential

A distinction is necessary between making a sales forecast and estimating sales potential. A sales forecast is based on past sales performance and a reckoning of known and anticipated market conditions. From these, the expected sales level is determined.

Sales potential, on the other hand, is a measure of the capacity of the business to reach a certain volume of sales. It is based on knowledge of the total market and the extent of competitive influence, and it involves the use of strategy through sales effort. Past sales performance may bear little or no resemblance to sales potential. In general, sales potential is likely to represent a higher sales level than a sales forecast.

Methods of forecasting

There are numerous techniques that can be used to forecast sales. Here are some common ones.

Project sales on the basis of key market factors. First identify factors that have affected your sales in the past and may do so in the future. These include general business and economic conditions, specific industry or trade conditions and trends, anticipated new product introductions, existing product life characteristics, effects of advertising and promotional events, and so forth. If you serve a local or regional market, the use of national economic or industry statistics and forecasts might be misleading and vice versa. Remember, numbers are not answers. They only provide information that may be useful in making a decision or forecast. (If you discuss trends with your competition, be sure you don't enter into a sit-

uation in which you could become involved in sales collusion. This is illegal.) Next, estimate the impact of these factors on sales. When there are different projections for the future, you can do one of two things. You can establish probabilities (including the relative frequencies) of each occurring. Or, you can rank each of the events in order of their likelihood of taking place. Ranking possible outcomes is the simpler approach, but generally is less accurate than establishing probabilities.

Survey buyer intentions. You can ask potential customers if they would utilize your new or expanded service, and if so, how frequently. However, keep in mind that it is best to use this information as an indication of how good the growth potential of the new venture will be, rather than forecast sales. It's not likely that you'll be able to develop the right type of survey data to obtain an accurate sales forecast unless you have considerable experience in conducting market research.

Plot past sales on a graph to obtain an indication of what future sales trends for your business will be. To use this approach effectively, you must be able to anticipate market and business changes that can be expected to occur. The advantage of the approach is that it is simple, and you can utilize information already available to you. The principal disadvantage is that your findings are tied to past performance, which may not be a good indicator of future events.

Query a cross section of company employees or sales representatives for their opinions. This approach may or may not be a good one. This method is known as the Delphi technique, and assumes that the individuals involved have the ability to judge and evaluate the factors that influence sales. Their knowledge may be limited to a particular product line or region. When salespeople and other executives are involved, forecasting often becomes a give-and-take process, with projections based on group opinion.

You, as owner or manager, may want to adjust these forecasts based on your perspective of the whole of the business. For example, one salesperson may consistently underestimate the sales he can make because he always wants to exceed his target. Over time you will recognize this characteristic and should revise this salesperson's forecast upwards.

Up to this point, we've discussed sales forecasting generally. As you've seen, sales can be estimated in a number of ways. Now we'll show you how to do some specific sales forecasting by using your computer and adapting the general forecasting templates.

Examples of forecasting: Forecasting sales by dollars (revenue)

Sales can be estimated by dollars or total revenue. These figures are often based on a review of sales history. For example, assume that sales (revenue) have been growing at a rate of 10 percent a year for the last five years. You expect that economic and industry conditions in the coming year will be much the same as in the last few years. Therefore, it would be reasonable to expect sales next year to be 10 percent greater than they were this year. That expectation, translated into dollars or revenue, gives you the total sales forecast figure.

But breaking down sales dollars by market segments or product groups is more often useful. It helps you focus attention on certain products or services, market segments, and sales regions, depending on your needs. For example, products tend to have a life cycle of their own. New products have fast growth, then over a period of years their sales flatten and decline. It is important to have products at different stages of the life cycle. If all your products are old, in the last stages of their life cycle, overall sales are likely to start falling at some point in the near future.

Another reason for these breakdowns is that they allow you to look at past activity and to make plans based on the changes you want to occur. Let's take an example. Assume that you have broken sales down into two geographic areas. Area 1 is the largest and most rapidly growing. But over the last few years sales have been higher and growing at a faster rate in Area 2. In planning for the future, you decide to make a concerted effort to generate more sales in Area 1. The actions you plan to take will be reflected in the sales forecast by geographic area.

Sales may also be forecast in terms of unit sales which will be discussed later. There are several advantages, however, to using revenue in forecasting. It is often faster and easier to forecast total dollar sales. The number you come up with is an aggregate (or summary) figure. You do not have to spend a lot of time working with detail. Additional sophistication and complexity is introduced when dollar sales are broken down into categories. The principal advantage with this approach is that your attention is focused on the parts that make up the whole. If you break down cost into the same categories as sales, you can also analyze the profitability of each breakdown such as product group or market served.

The major disadvantage to evaluating and forecasting sales revenue is that it can be misleading. Dollar sales can be rising while unit sales are declining because of price increases. Many business managers have been pleased with their firm's growth in sales revenue only to find themselves in financial difficulty because the growth was not the result of higher product or service output. As prices rise, competitive products can become more attractive and capture the market.

Forecasting sales by units

Unit sales is the other common method for sales forecasting. The number of expected units to be sold for each product is estimated. (The number of units times the net price of each unit equals the anticipated sales revenues.)

Forecasting unit sales by product or some other sales classification requires more effort and detail than simply forecasting sales revenue. But it overcomes the major weakness of the revenue method. Unit sales are the basis, directly or indirectly, for all revenue and expenses. Production, personnel, storage space, manufacturing facilities, office space, administrative requirements, financing needs, and almost any other activity a firm is involved with are all fixed to its level of operations, or unit production. For this reason unit sales are usually the starting point for financial forecasting.

By linking planning and forecasting to unit sales you will have the necessary information for estimating future profitability by comparing revenues to costs associated with either total unit sales or unit sales categories. Evaluating the forecast for product or market profitability affords you the opportunity to take the actions most likely to improve the financial performance and condition of your business in the future.

BUSINESS TIPS Market breakdowns

If you decide to use market breakdowns in your sales forecast, you might consider the following areas of distribution:

Retail
Wholesale
    Dealer
        Sales representative
Distributor
Direct response (from coupon ads)
International
Government
Domestic
Special
Catalog (from any catalogs or brochures you might mail)

	A	B(A)	C(A)	D(B)	E(C)	F(D)	G(E)	H(F)	I(G)	J(H)	K(I)	L(J)	M(K)	N(L)	O(M)	P(N)
1	Template: The general forecasting template															
3	Detail of line item:			Total	1	2	3	4	5	6	7	8	9	10	11	12
4	Sales revenue				1984	1984	1984	1984	1984	1984	1984	1984	1984	1984	1984	1984
6	Monthly service:															
8			Client # 1	1200	100	100	100	100	100	100	100	100	100	100	100	100
9			Client # 2	1200	100	100	100	100	100	100	100	100	100	100	100	100
10			Client # 3	1200	100	100	100	100	100	100	100	100	100	100	100	100
11			Client # 4	1200	100	100	100	100	100	100	100	100	100	100	100	100
12			Client # 5	1200	100	100	100	100	100	100	100	100	100	100	100	100
13			Client # 6	1200	100	100	100	100	100	100	100	100	100	100	100	100
14			Client # 7	1200	100	100	100	100	100	100	100	100	100	100	100	100
15			Client # 8	1200	100	100	100	100	100	100	100	100	100	100	100	100
16			Client # 9	1200	100	100	100	100	100	100	100	100	100	100	100	100
18	Quarterly service:															
20			Client # 11	1200	300	($)	($)	300	($)	($)	300	($)	($)	300	($)	($)
21			Client # 12	1200	300	($)	($)	300	($)	($)	300	($)	($)	300	($)	($)
22			Client # 13	1200	300	($)	($)	300	($)	($)	300	($)	($)	300	($)	($)
23			Client # 14	1200	300	($)	($)	300	($)	($)	300	($)	($)	300	($)	($)
24			Client # 15	1200	300	($)	($)	300	($)	($)	300	($)	($)	300	($)	($)
25			Client # 16	1200	300	($)	($)	300	($)	($)	300	($)	($)	300	($)	($)
26			Client # 17	1200	300	($)	($)	300	($)	($)	300	($)	($)	300	($)	($)
27			Client # 18	1200	300	($)	($)	300	($)	($)	300	($)	($)	300	($)	($)
28			Client # 19	1200	300	($)	($)	300	($)	($)	300	($)	($)	300	($)	($)
29			Client # 20	1200	300	($)	($)	300	($)	($)	300	($)	($)	300	($)	($)
31	Annual service:															
33			Client # 30	400	($)	($)	($)	($)	($)	($)	($)	($)	($)	($)	($)	400
34			Client # 31	400	($)	($)	($)	($)	($)	($)	($)	($)	($)	($)	($)	400
35			Client # 32	400	($)	($)	($)	($)	($)	($)	($)	($)	($)	($)	($)	400
36			Client # 33	400	($)	($)	($)	($)	($)	($)	($)	($)	($)	($)	($)	400
37			Client # 34	400	($)	($)	($)	($)	($)	($)	($)	($)	($)	($)	($)	400
38			Client # 35	400	($)	($)	($)	($)	($)	($)	($)	($)	($)	($)	($)	400
39			Client # 36	400	($)	($)	($)	($)	($)	($)	($)	($)	($)	($)	($)	400
40			Client # 37	400	($)	($)	($)	($)	($)	($)	($)	($)	($)	($)	($)	400
42	Total			26000	3900	900	900	3900	900	900	3900	900	900	3900	900	4100

Forecasting sales by dollars. *If you make a sales forecast in dollars, the template can be used without modification. In the example above, sales have been forecast for a service business that provides services to a number of clients. The revenues from these services are organized first by frequency of service and then by client. Rows 8 through 16 forecast sales for clients who receive regular monthly services, rows 20 through 29 for those who receive quarterly services, and rows 33 through 40 for those who receive annual services. The formulas used to enter sales patterns of these types are explained on page 102.*

VISICALC TIPS Eliminating ERROR messages on your screen display and printouts

Whenever a template is prepared that uses division formulas, the blank template will have ERROR appearing in the cells containing those formulas. The reason is that any number divided by 0 generates this message automatically. When you enter data, these messages will disappear. If you want to clean up your template so these messages don't appear when it is blank, all you have to do is to embed the formulas in @IF statements. For instance, the formula +A1/A2 will result in an error message if cell A2 has no value. By embedding the formula in an @IF statement such as @IF(A2<>0,A1/A2,0), you will see a 0 until data are entered in cell A2. The formula would read, "If A2 is less than or greater than zero, divide A1 by A2. If it isn't, show 0."

BUSINESS TIPS Selling expenses

Selling expenses generally include all expenses associated with the selling of a product. There are a variety of costs that fall into this area, from sales staff salaries and/or commissions to the cost of art used in ads. Here is a list of some items to think about:

Salespeople's salaries
Sales commissions and bonuses
Staff salaries and benefits
Telephone charges for sales calls
Cost of ads
Cost of catalogs, brochures, etc.
Premiums or other incentives
Delivery and freight
Travel
Automobiles
Depreciation

A	B(A)	C(A)	D(B)	E(C)	F(D)	G(E)	H(F)	I(G)	J(H)	K(I)	L(J)	M(K)	N(L)	O(M)	P(N)	Q(O)	R(P)	S(Q)
1 Templa:Forecasting unit sales, sales revenue, and cost of goods																		
3 Detail of line item:			Total	1	2	3	4	5	6	7	8	9	10	11	12			
4 Unit sales forecast			units	1984	1984	1984	1984	1984	1984	1984	1984	1984	1984	1984	1984			
6 Product number 1			1200	96	96	96	120	120	120	120	120	120	72	48	72			
7 Product number 2			1200	24	24	24	48	48	48	60	96	180	216	216	216			
8 Product number 3			500	(#)	(#)	250	250	(#)	(#)	(#)	(#)	(#)	(#)	(#)	(#)			
9 Product number 4			2000	(#)	(#)	(#)	(#)	(#)	(#)	(#)	(#)	(#)	(#)	(#)	2000			
10 Product number 5			4000	333	333	333	333	333	333	333	333	333	333	333	333			
11 Product number 6			100	8	8	8	8	8	8	8	8	8	8	8	8			
12 Product number 7			0	(#)	(#)	(#)	(#)	(#)	(#)	(#)	(#)	(#)	(#)	(#)	(#)			
13 Product number 8			0	(#)	(#)	(#)	(#)	(#)	(#)	(#)	(#)	(#)	(#)	(#)	(#)			
14 Product number 9			0	(#)	(#)	(#)	(#)	(#)	(#)	(#)	(#)	(#)	(#)	(#)	(#)			
15 Product number 10			0	(#)	(#)	(#)	(#)	(#)	(#)	(#)	(#)	(#)	(#)	(#)	(#)			
16 Product number 11			0	(#)	(#)	(#)	(#)	(#)	(#)	(#)	(#)	(#)	(#)	(#)	(#)			
18 Total unit sales			9000	462	462	712	760	510	510	522	558	642	630	606	2630			

A	B(A)	C(A)	D(B)	E(C)	F(D)	G(E)	H(F)	I(G)	J(H)	K(I)	L(J)	M(K)	N(L)	O(M)	P(N)	Q(O)	R(P)	S(Q)
22 Detail of line item:			Total	1	2	3	4	5	6	7	8	9	10	11	12	Net	Dis-	List
23 Sales revenue forecast			sales	1984	1984	1984	1984	1984	1984	1984	1984	1984	1984	1984	1984	price	count	price
25 Product number 1			4800	384	384	384	480	480	480	480	480	480	288	192	288	4.00	(%)	4.00
26 Product number 2			7200	144	144	144	288	288	288	360	576	1080	1296	1296	1296	6.00	(%)	6.00
27 Product number 3			1200	0	0	600	600	0	0	0	0	0	0	0	0	2.40	20	3.00
28 Product number 4			9000	0	0	0	0	0	0	0	0	0	0	0	9000	4.50	(%)	4.50
29 Product number 5			32700	2725	2725	2725	2725	2725	2725	2725	2725	2725	2725	2725	2725	8.18	50	16.35
30 Product number 6			735	61	61	61	61	61	61	61	61	61	61	61	61	7.35	(%)	7.35
31 Product number 7			0	0	0	0	0	0	0	0	0	0	0	0	0	9.25	(%)	9.25
32 Product number 8			0	0	0	0	0	0	0	0	0	0	0	0	0	0.00	(%)	($)
33 Product number 9			0	0	0	0	0	0	0	0	0	0	0	0	0	0.00	(%)	($)
34 Product number 10			0	0	0	0	0	0	0	0	0	0	0	0	0	0.00	(%)	($)
35 Product number 11			0	0	0	0	0	0	0	0	0	0	0	0	0	0.00	(%)	($)
37 Total sales revenue			55635	3314	3314	3914	4154	3554	3554	3626	3842	4346	4370	4274	13370	6.18		

Forecasting sales by units. *Most sales forecasts begin with an estimate of unit sales. These units are then multiplied times the net price to determine dollar sales revenues. There are a variety of ways to set up a worksheet to handle this approach, but most of them incorporate the linking of two or more worksheets together, one to show units and the other to show revenue.*

In the illustration above, the general forecasting template has been adapted so that it can be used to forecast unit sales. A separate worksheet to show the resulting sales revenue has then been added and linked to it. When units are forecast on the top part of the template, sales revenues are automatically calculated on the lower part. (Later, on page 115, you will see how to expand the template one additional step to calculate monthly cost of goods.) Here is how the unit and dollar template works:

1 The beginning month and year of the forecast are entered. All other monthly columns will automatically be dated.

2 Sales are broken down and listed by product or market in columns A-C (column A for Advanced Version users).

3 The expected annual units can then be entered and distributed throughout the months using one of the three techniques described starting on page 102.

4 The list price and discounts, if any, are entered for each item on the lower part of the worksheet.

5 The net price is automatically calculated by formulas that multiply the list price by 100 percent minus the discount in column Q(O).

6 Monthly sales revenue for each product or market is then calculated by formulas entered in each monthly cell of the lower template. These formulas multiply the net price times the monthly units sold in the corresponding cell of the upper portion of the worksheet. Formulas on the total row (row 37) add up total monthly sales revenue.

7 Formulas in the total column, D(B), add up the total monthly sales revenue for each product or service to give an annual total.

8 A formula on the total row (row 37) under the net price column calculates the average net price by dividing total sales revenue by total units sold. This average can be used in many cases to speed up future planning. If you find that this percentage historically follows the same pattern, it may actually be a more accurate forecasting guide than the item-by-item breakdown shown on the template.

Adapting the template to forecast unit sales

The general forecasting template can be adapted to forecast unit sales and the resulting sales revenue. The number of products that can be forecast in this way is limited only by the size of your computer's memory. Since the number of products for which businesses might want a forecast varies widely, we will not explain how to build this adapted template row by row. The step-by-step techniques given below should be sufficient to guide you in adapting the template to your use.

```
          A    B(A)   C(A)   D(B)   E(C)   F(D)   G(E)   H(F)   I(G)   J(H)   K(I)   L(J)   M(K)   N(L)   O(M)   P(N)   Q(O)   R(P)   S(Q)
 1     Templa:Forecasting unit sales, sales revenue, and cost of goods
 2     ========================================================================================================================
 3     Detail of line item:  Total (#  )    1      2      3      4      5      6      7      8      9     10     11
 4     Unit sales forecast   units (#  )    0      0      0      0      0      0      0      0      0      0      0
 5
 6     .................     0 (#  ) (#  ) (#  ) (#  ) (#  ) (#  ) (#  ) (#  ) (#  ) (#  ) (#  ) (#  )
 7     .................     0 (#  ) (#  ) (#  ) (#  ) (#  ) (#  ) (#  ) (#  ) (#  ) (#  ) (#  ) (#  )
 8     .................     0 (#  ) (#  ) (#  ) (#  ) (#  ) (#  ) (#  ) (#  ) (#  ) (#  ) (#  ) (#  )
 9     .................     0 (#  ) (#  ) (#  ) (#  ) (#  ) (#  ) (#  ) (#  ) (#  ) (#  ) (#  ) (#  )
10     .................     0 (#  ) (#  ) (#  ) (#  ) (#  ) (#  ) (#  ) (#  ) (#  ) (#  ) (#  ) (#  )
11     .................     0 (#  ) (#  ) (#  ) (#  ) (#  ) (#  ) (#  ) (#  ) (#  ) (#  ) (#  ) (#  )
12     .................     0 (#  ) (#  ) (#  ) (#  ) (#  ) (#  ) (#  ) (#  ) (#  ) (#  ) (#  ) (#  )
13     .................     0 (#  ) (#  ) (#  ) (#  ) (#  ) (#  ) (#  ) (#  ) (#  ) (#  ) (#  ) (#  )
14     .................     0 (#  ) (#  ) (#  ) (#  ) (#  ) (#  ) (#  ) (#  ) (#  ) (#  ) (#  ) (#  )
15     .................     0 (#  ) (#  ) (#  ) (#  ) (#  ) (#  ) (#  ) (#  ) (#  ) (#  ) (#  ) (#  )
16
17     _____
18     Total unit sales    4100      0      0      0      0      0      0      0      0      0      0      0
19     ========================================================================================================================
20
21     ========================================================================================================================
22     Detail of line item:  Total     0      1      2      3      4      5      6      7      8      9     10     11     Net   Dis-   List
23     Sales revenue forecast sales    0      0      0      0      0      0      0      0      0      0      0      0    price count price
24     _____
25     .................     0      0      0      0      0      0      0      0      0      0      0      0    0.00 (   %) ($   )
26     .................     0      0      0      0      0      0      0      0      0      0      0      0    0.00 (   %) ($   )
27     .................     0      0      0      0      0      0      0      0      0      0      0      0    0.00 (   %) ($   )
28     .................     0      0      0      0      0      0      0      0      0      0      0      0    0.00 (   %) ($   )
29     .................     0      0      0      0      0      0      0      0      0      0      0      0    0.00 (   %) ($   )
30     .................     0      0      0      0      0      0      0      0      0      0      0      0    0.00 (   %) ($   )
31     .................     0      0      0      0      0      0      0      0      0      0      0      0    0.00 (   %) ($   )
32     .................     0      0      0      0      0      0      0      0      0      0      0      0    0.00 (   %) ($   )
33     .................     0      0      0      0      0      0      0      0      0      0      0      0    0.00 (   %) ($   )
34     .................     0      0      0      0      0      0      0      0      0      0      0      0    0.00 (   %) ($   )
35     .................     0      0      0      0      0      0      0      0      0      0      0      0    0.00 (   %) ($   )
36     _____
37     Total sales revenue   0      0      0      0      0      0      0      0      0      0      0      0    0.00
38     ========================================================================================================================
```

Step 1. Load the general forecasting template (Template) and change the labels as shown in the illustration above. Enter the beginning month and year in column D(B). Enter labels for each of the products to be forecast in columns A-C (column A for Advanced Version users). Then enter unit sales using one of the three techniques described starting on page 102. To be sure your computer doesn't run out of memory, delete any rows on the template that aren't being used. Since this section is only a part of the completed template, you might want to check the memory indicator on the upper right-hand corner of your VisiCalc display. If after entering this section you have used more than one third of the available memory, you may not be able to complete the template to calculate both sales revenue and cost of goods (page 115). If you have used more than one third but less than one half of the available memory you should be able to complete the sales revenue forecast.

If your available memory isn't sufficient, you may have to consolidate some products. Another approach would be to build the first part of the template (the unit sales forecast) and save it. Reload and add sales revenue.

Later in the chapter you can reload the first part of the template and add the cost of goods section. The result will be one template forecasting unit sales and sales revenue and a second forecasting unit sales and cost of goods.

Step 2. Enter column headings and ruled lines for the sales revenue section of the forecast. The month and year formulas should reference the same months and year on the unit sales forecast. For example:

Type $>$**E**(C)**22** and type $+$**E**(C)**3** ⏎

Step 3. Replicate the labels of the products being forecast from columns A through C (column A for Advanced Version users) into columns A through C of this section of the template.

Step 4. Enter data entry spaces and formulas into the net price, discount, and list price columns on the sales revenue forecast. The list price and discount columns are used to enter data. You can at this point enter either your data or data entry spaces to guide you when you enter the data later on.

To enter the net price, the basic formula is:

List price × (1 − discount).

For example:

Type >**Q**(O)**25** and type **/F$ +S**(Q)**25*(1-(R**(P)**25/100))** ⏎

You should also format the list price column to display the prices out to two places. The command for this format is **/F$**.

Step 5. Enter the formulas to calculate sales revenue in the first monthly column of the forecast, column E(C). Start in the upper left-hand corner for the first product and the first month. The formula is:

Net price × units sold

For example:

Type >**E**(C)**25** and type **+Q**(O)**25*E**(C)**6** ⏎

Now replicate this formula down the column to where the last product is listed. All values are relative.

Enter a formula on the total row to add all sales calculated by the formulas for each product in the column. The formula range should be between the ruled lines so that products can be added or deleted in the future without affecting the formulas.

For example:

Type >**E**(C)**37** and type **@SUM(E**(C)**24.E**(C)**36)** ⏎

Step 6. Replicate these formulas from column E(C) to all other monthly columns. The source range would start at the first product and end at the formula used to calculate the total. The first cell reference in the formula should be **N** for No change and the second **R** for Relative. This is because the first cell reference is to the net price column, which is the same in all of the formulas. The second reference is to the monthly unit sales in the top part of the template, which are relative. When you get to the last formula that sums the column the This cell references should both be **R** for Relative.

For example:

Type >**E**(C)**25** and type **/R.E**(C)**35** ⏎ **F**(D)**25.P**(N)**25** ⏎
The prompt line would read N=No change
R=Relative
You would type **NRRR**

Step 7. Enter formulas in the total column that will calculate the total sales for the period covered for each product. For example:

Type >**D**(B)**25** and type **@SUM(E**(C)**25.P**(N)**25)** ⏎

Replicate this formula down the column with all cell references relative. You can then replicate the same formula to the cell beneath the column on the total row.

Step 8. Enter a formula on the total row below the net price column to calculate the average net price. This formula will be embedded in an IF statement so that it doesn't read ERROR on the blank template. The basic formula is:

If total units sold are greater than zero then divide total sales revenue by the total units sold.

For example:

Type >**Q**(O)**37** and type **@IF(D**(B)**18>0,D**(B)**37/D**(B) **18,0** ⏎

Now that the template has been completed, enter the same numbers shown on the example on page 111. Recalculate the worksheet a few times and see if you get the same results. If you entered your own data as you went along, check the results with a calculator to be sure the template is operating correctly. If so, save it under a new file name. *Do not save it under the file name Template* or it will erase that template from the disk as it is being stored.

VISICALC TIPS Replicating a block

When the Example is entered in Chapters 3, 4, and 5, the DIF command is used to transfer a block of data in two columns to the two adjacent columns. With the Advanced Version you can replicate the entire block in one step. To do this, type **/R** followed by the source range (the range you are replicating from), in this case the cell coordinates of the upper left-hand corner and the lower right-hand corner of the block to be replicated. The target range (the range you are replicating to) is then entered with only the upper left-hand cell coordinate specified.

Forecasting expenses

The management of costs or expenses is often the most critical area for many small businesses. As we mentioned earlier, the level of operations or unit sales directly or indirectly determines the various costs of doing business. Before you can institute measures to control expenses, you must anticipate what the expenses are likely to be. There are three general methods you can use to forecast expenses. Most businesses will use more than one of these methods, since different expenses can require different techniques.

The first method is to base expense item forecasts on unit sales. You can easily forecast some costs such as inventory expense and direct labor by examining your projected unit sales levels.

The second method is to assume expenses will be a percentage of sales revenues. You can estimate nearly every expense this way.

The third method is to forecast expenses by using a task or goal objective. Many firms need to expend funds to generate future sales. A task or objective might include research and development, product development, promotion activity, or personnel training.

	A	B(A)	C(A)	D(B)	E(C)	F(D)	G(E)	H(F)	I(G)	J(H)	K(I)	L(J)	M(K)	N(L)	O(M)	P(N)	Q(O)	R(P)	S(Q)
41	Detail of line item:			Total	1	2	3	4	5	6	7	8	9	10	11	12	Unit	C.O.G.	Gross
42	C.O.G forecast			C.O.G	1984	1984	1984	1984	1984	1984	1984	1984	1984	1984	1984	1984	cost	%	margin
44	Product number 1			2400	192	192	192	240	240	240	240	240	240	144	96	144	2.00	50	50
45	Product number 2			3240	65	65	65	130	130	130	162	259	486	583	583	583	2.70	45	55
46	Product number 3			650	0	0	325	325	0	0	0	0	0	0	0	0	1.30	54	46
47	Product number 4			4320	0	0	0	0	0	0	0	0	0	0	0	4320	2.16	48	52
48	Product number 5			30760	2563	2563	2563	2563	2563	2563	2563	2563	2563	2563	2563	2563	7.69	94	6
49	Product number 6			400	33	33	33	33	33	33	33	33	33	33	33	33	4.00	54	46
50	Product number 7			0	0	0	0	0	0	0	0	0	0	0	0	0	($)	0	0
51	Product number 8			0	0	0	0	0	0	0	0	0	0	0	0	0	($)	0	0
52	Product number 9			0	0	0	0	0	0	0	0	0	0	0	0	0	($)	0	0
53	Product number 10			0	0	0	0	0	0	0	0	0	0	0	0	0	($)	0	0
54	Product number 11			0	0	0	0	0	0	0	0	0	0	0	0	0	($)	0	0
56	Total cost of goods			41770	2853	2853	3178	3219	2966	2966	2999	3096	3323	3324	3276	7644	4.64	75	25

Forecasting cost of goods. On page 111 you saw how to expand the template so that it would automatically forecast sales revenues from a unit sales forecast. That revised template can be adapted one additional step to calculate cost of goods sold. If it is set up this way, the cost of goods monthly totals (row 56) can, in some cases, be transferred to the cost of goods line on the pro forma income statement section of the example using the DIF command.

Most firms cannot directly transfer row 56, total cost of goods, to the cash budget because of timing differences in declaring the expense (see discussion on pages 121 and 123). The two exceptions are when you use cash basis accounting and when your inventory purchases occur in the same month that the inventory is sold.

Here is how a template set up this way will work:

1 The unit cost of each product is entered in the unit cost column. These figures can be drawn from your firm's records.

2 Formulas in the monthly columns multiply the unit cost times the number of units sold that month. The units are shown on the unit sales forecast section of the template. For instance, 24 units of Product #2 were sold in January (cell E(C)7). 24 units times a unit cost of $2.70 equals $65.00. This cost is automatically calculated for Product #2 in January (cell E(C)45).

3 Total cost of goods for each product is calculated in the total column for the period covered by the forecast.

4 Cost of goods percentages and gross margins will automatically be calculated. Cost of goods percentages are derived from discounts from the list price: either those offered by your suppliers (if you are a retailer), or the percentage difference between your manufacturing costs and list price (if you are a manufacturer). Gross margin is the difference between net receipts (100 percent) and the cost of goods percentage. For instance, a product with a cost of goods percentage of 40 percent will have a gross margin of 60 percent.

5 Formulas on row 56 beneath the unit cost, discount, and gross margin columns calculate the averages of these items. These cost and gross margin percentages show how much of the price is made up of cost of goods and how much is gross profit. In the illustration above, for instance, the average cost of goods is 75 percent and the average gross margin is 25 percent (100 percent minus 75 percent). In some cases these averages can be used in subsequent forecasts to simplify planning if they are found to remain fairly constant.

Adapting the template to calculate cost of goods (Temp1A)

Here's how to adapt the general forecasting template to calculate cost of goods automatically from the unit sales forecast.

	A	B(A)	C(A)	D(B)	E(C)	F(D)	G(E)	H(F)	I(G)	J(H)	K(I)	L(J)	M(K)	N(L)	O(M)	P(N)	Q(O)	R(P)	S(Q)
40	=======																		
41	Detail of line item:			Total	(# |)	1	2	3	4	5	6	7	8	9	10	11	Unit	C.O.G.	Gross
42	C.O.G forecast			C.O.G.	(# |)	0	0	0	0	0	0	0	0	0	0	0	cost	%	margin
43	-------																		
44	....			0	0	0	0	0	0	0	0	0	0	0	0	0	($)	0	0
45	....			0	0	0	0	0	0	0	0	0	0	0	0	0	($)	0	0
46	....			0	0	0	0	0	0	0	0	0	0	0	0	0	($)	0	0
47	....			0	0	0	0	0	0	0	0	0	0	0	0	0	($)	0	0
48	....			0	0	0	0	0	0	0	0	0	0	0	0	0	($)	0	0
49	....			0	0	0	0	0	0	0	0	0	0	0	0	0	($)	0	0
50	....			0	0	0	0	0	0	0	0	0	0	0	0	0	($)	0	0
51	....			0	0	0	0	0	0	0	0	0	0	0	0	0	($)	0	0
52	....			0	0	0	0	0	0	0	0	0	0	0	0	0	($)	0	0
53	....			0	0	0	0	0	0	0	0	0	0	0	0	0	($)	0	0
54	....			0	0	0	0	0	0	0	0	0	0	0	0	0	($)	0	0
55																			
56	Total cost of goods			0	0	0	0	0	0	0	0	0	0	0	0	0	0	0	0
57	=======																		

Step 1. Load the adapted template using the file name you used to save it.

Step 2. Enter column headings and ruled lines for the cost of goods section of the forecast. Use the same formulas described for the sales revenue section of the template.

Step 3. Replicate the labels of the products being forecast into this section of the template.

Step 4. Enter unit costs in the unit cost column. You can either enter your data at this point or enter data entry spaces to guide you later. You should also format the column to display the unit costs out to two places. The command for this format is **/F$**.

Step 5. Enter the formulas to calculate cost of goods in the first monthly column (column E(C)) of the forecast. Start in the upper left-hand corner for the first product and the first month. The formula is:

Unit cost × units sold.

For example:

Type >**E**(C)**44** and type **+Q**(O)**44*E**(C)**6** ⏎

Now replicate this formula down the column to where the last product is listed. All values are relative.

Add a formula on the total row to add all cost of goods calculated by the formulas for each product in the column. The formula range should be between the ruled lines so products can be added or deleted in the future without affecting the formulas.
For example:

Type >**E**(C)**57** and type **@SUM(D**(B)**43.D**(B)**56)** ⏎

Step 6. Replicate these formulas from column E(C) to all other monthly columns. The source range would start at the first product and end at the formula used to calculate the total. The first cell reference in the formula should be **N** for No change and the second **R** for Relative. This is because the first cell reference is to the unit cost column which is the same in all of the formulas. The second reference is to the monthly unit sales in the top part of the template, which are relative. In the last formula that sums the column, both cell references are relative. In our example the replication commands would be:

Type >**E**(C)**44** and type **/R.E**(C)**55** ⏎ **F**(D)**55.P**(N)**55** ⏎

The prompt line would read N=No change R=Relative
You would type **NRRR**

Step 7. Enter formulas in the total column that will calculate the total cost of goods for each product for the period covered.
For example:

Type >**D**(B)**44** and type **@SUM(D**(B)**45.D**(B)**55)** ⏎

Replicate this formula down the column with all cell references relative. You can then replicate the same formula to the last cell in the total column, cell D(B)57.

Step 8. Enter formulas on the total row below the unit cost, cost of goods percentage, and gross margin columns to calculate the average of each column. The basic formulas are:

Average unit cost = total cost of goods divided by total units sold.
For example:

Type >**Q**(O)**57** and type **@IF(D**(B)**18>0,D**(B)**57/D**(B)**18,0** ⏎

Average cost of goods = total cost of goods divided by total sales revenue.

For example:

Type >**R**(P)**57** and type **@IF(D**(B)**37**>**0(D**(B)**57/D**(B)**37)*100,0** ⏎

Average gross margin = 100% minus average cost of goods percentage.

For example:

Type >**S**(Q)**57** and type **100-R**(P)**57** ⏎

Now that the template has been completed, enter the same numbers shown on the example on page 114. Recalculate the worksheet a few times and see if you get the same results. If you entered your own data as you went along, check the results with a calculator to be sure the template is operating correctly. If so save it under the file name you used previously. *Do not save it under the file name Template* (we use file name Temp1A) or that template will be erased from the diskette as it is being stored.

BUSINESS TIPS Cost of goods expenses

Cost of goods expenses are those directly related to the purchase or manufacture of products for sale. The items included in this category and even its name depend on the business involved. The basic terms used for this item and typical expenses included in the category are:

Retail businesses — inventory costs or cost of goods
The cost of inventory purchased less any discounts

Manufacturing businesses — cost of goods
Cost of raw materials
Direct labor costs
Supervisor's wages and other supervisory costs
Overhead
    Fuel
    Insurance
    Utilities
    Maintenance and repairs
    Property taxes
    Vehicles
    Employee benefits
    Depreciation

Service businesses — cost of services
Salaries of staff providing service
Employee benefits
Vehicle expense
Insurance

BUSINESS TIPS General and administrative expenses

General and administrative expenses (G&A) include all of the expenses connected with running an office and keeping a staff. Some companies include all salaries in this account, while others apportion part of salaries to departments and carry only management salaries in G&A. Some other items that are generally included in G&A are:

Travel and entertainment
Utilities
    Phone
    Electricity
    Water
    Gas
    Oil
Payroll taxes
    Income
    FICA
Benefits
    Medical insurance
    Life insurance
    Automobiles
    Bonuses
    Unemployment compensation
Office expenses
    Rent
    Cleaning
    Maintenance and repairs
    Stationery
    Equipment repair and maintenance
Liability and property insurance
Delivery expenses
Postage
Contributions
Dues
Subscriptions
Legal expenses
Accounting expenses
Consulting expenses
Business taxes and licences
Depreciation

Developing a budget from a forecast

Budgets are often based upon forecasts; but forecasts, particularly a detailed expense one, can also become budgets. Let's explore an example: the selling expense of advertising.

Advertising costs are a completely controllable expense. Advertising budgets are the means of determining and controlling this expense and dividing it wisely among departments, lines, or services.

If you want to build sales, it's almost certain you'll need to advertise. How much should you spend? How should you allocate your advertising dollars? How can you be sure your advertising outlays aren't out of line? The advertising budget helps you determine how much you have to spend and helps establish the guidelines for how you're going to spend it.

What you'd like to invest in advertising and what you can afford are seldom the same. Spending too much is obviously an extravagance, but spending too little can be just as bad in terms of lost sales and diminished visibility. Costs must be tied to results. You must be prepared to evaluate your goals and assess your capabilities — a budget will also help you do precisely this. Your budget will help you choose and assess the amount of advertising and its timing. It will also serve as the background for next year's financial forecast.

Like most expenses, advertising can be forecast in three ways:

- by using unit sales

- as a percentage of sales

- by objective and task

Unit sales

In the unit sales method, you set aside a fixed sum for each unit of a product to be sold, based on your experience and trade knowledge of how much advertising it takes to sell each unit. That is, if it takes two cents' worth of advertising to sell a case of canned vegetables and you want to move 100,000 cases, you'll probably plan to spend $2,000 on advertising them. Does it cost X dollars to sell a refrigerator? Then you'll probably have to budget 1,000 times X if you plan to sell a thousand refrigerators. You're simply basing your budget on unit sales rather than dollar amounts of sales.

Some people consider this method just a variation of the next method, percentage of sales. Unit sales does, however, probably let you make a closer estimate of what you should plan for maximum effect, since it's based on what experience tells you it takes to sell an actual unit, rather than an overall percentage of your gross sales estimate.

The unit sales method is particularly useful in fields where the amount of product available is limited by outside factors, such as the weather's effect on crops. If that's the situation for your business, you first estimate how many units or cases will be available to you. Then, you advertise only as much as experience tells you it takes to sell them. Thus, if you have a pretty good idea ahead of time how many units will be available, you should have minimal waste in your advertising costs.

This method is also suited for specialty goods, such as washing machines and automobiles; however, it's difficult to apply when you have many different kinds of products to advertise and must divide your advertising among these products. The unit sales method is not very useful in sporadic or irregular markets or for "style" merchandise.

Percentage of sales

The most widely used method of establishing an advertising estimate or budget is to base it on a percentage of sales. Advertising is as much a business expense as, say, the cost of labor and, thus, should be related to the quantity of goods sold.

By using the percentage of sales method, you keep your advertising in a consistent relation to your sales volume — which is what your advertising should be primarily affecting. Gross margin, especially over the long run, should also show an increase, of course, if your advertising outlays are being properly applied.

You can guide your choice of a percentage of sales figure by finding out what other businesses in your line are doing. These percentages are fairly consistent within a given category of business. It's fairly easy to find out this ratio of advertising expense to sales in your line. Check trade magazines and associations. You can also find these percentages in Census and Internal Revenue Service reports and in reports published by financial institutions such as Dun & Bradstreet, the Robert Morris Associates, and the Accounting Corporation of America.

Knowing what the ratio for your industry is will help to assure you that you will be spending proportionately as much or more than your competitors; but remember, these industry averages are not gospel. Your particular situation may dictate that you want to advertise more than or less than your competition.

Average may not be good enough for you. You may want to out-advertise your competitors and be willing to cut into short-term profits to do so. Growth takes investment.

Which sales? Your budget can be determined as a percentage of past sales, of estimated future sales, or as a combination of the two:

Developing a budget from a forecast, Continued

1 Past sales. Your base can be last year's sales or an average of a number of years in the immediate past. Consider, though, that changes in economic conditions can make your figure too high or too low.

2 Estimated future sales. You can calculate your advertising budget as a percentage of your anticipated sales for next year. The most common pitfall of this method is an optimistic assumption that your business will continue to grow. You must keep general business trends always in mind, especially if there's the chance of a slump, and hardheadedly assess the directions of your industry and your own operation.

3 Past sales and estimated future sales. The middle ground between an often conservative appraisal based on last year's sales and a usually too optimistic assessment of next year's is to combine both. It's a more realistic method during periods of changing economic conditions. It allows you to analyze trends and results thoughtfully and to predict with a little more assurance of accuracy.

Objective and task

The most difficult (and least used) method for determining an advertising budget is the objective and task approach. Yet, it's the most accurate and best accomplishes what all budgets should:

■ It relates the expense appropriation to the marketing task to be accomplished.

■ It relates the advertising expense appropriation under usual conditions and in the long run to the volume of sales, so that profits and reserves will not be drained.

To establish your budget by this method, you need a coordinated marketing program with specific objectives based on a thorough survey of your markets and their potential.

While the percentage of sales method first determines how much you'll spend without much consideration of what you want to accomplish, the task method establishes what you must do in order to meet your objectives. Only then do you calculate its cost.

You should set specific objectives: not just "Increase sales," but, for example, "Sell 25 percent more of product X or service Y by attracting the business of teenagers." Then determine what media best reach your target market and estimate how much it will cost to run the number and types of advertisements you think it'll take to get that sales increase. You repeat this process for each of your objectives. When you total these costs, you have your projected budget.

Of course, you may find that you can't afford to advertise as you'd like to. It's a good idea, therefore, to rank your objectives. As with the other methods, be prepared to change your plan to reflect reality and to fit the resources you have available.

Any combination of these methods may be employed to forecast advertising expense or your advertising budget. All of them — or simply one — may be needed to plan your advertising. However you decide to plan your budget, you must make it *flexible*, capable of being adjusted to changes in the marketplace.

The duration of your planning and budgeting period depends upon the nature of your business. If you can use short budgeting periods, you'll find that your advertising can be more flexible and that you can change tactics to meet immediate trends.

To ensure advertising flexibility, you should have a contingency fund to deal with special circumstances — such as the introduction of a new product, specials available in local media, or unexpected competitive situations.

Once you've determined your advertising budget, you can then allocate your advertising dollars. Common breakdowns for allocating are by departments, calendar periods, media, or sales areas.

Forecasting other line items

You may recall that when you entered the example, certain assumptions were made about some line items such as those dealing with tax and interest rates. To adapt the example to your own situation, you need to enter your own data, which may mean some of those assumptions should be changed. Here are some rows to examine and think about when adapting the model to your own use:

Adapting the cash budget

Row 6 — Seasonal patterns: You may want to drop this feature altogether and replace it with a detailed sales forecast using the template described earlier. If you don't need the extra detail that a product-by-product or market-by-market forecast provides, you can just enter new monthly percentage figures that reflect your own seasonal patterns.

Rows 10–13 — Receipts: You can determine your own collection pattern by keeping track of how long it takes to collect on individual sales. The easiest way to estimate your collection pattern is to track collections over several months. For example, you might have had sales of $100,000 in November. Of that, $25,000 was collected in December, $50,000 in January, and $25,000 in February. Your collection pattern was 25 percent — less than 30 days; 50 percent — 30 to 60 days; and 25 percent — 60 to 90 days.

In addition to adjusting the percentages in column D(B), you will have to revise the first month's entry on the 30 day row, the first two months' entries on the 60-day row, and the first three months' entries on the 90-day row. Your figures will come directly from your aging of accounts receivable report for the end of the last period.

Row 17 — Inventory purchases: This row assumes inventory is paid for one month before it is sold. In other words, the dollar figure shown for January inventory purchases is 60 percent of the figure entered for February sales. You may want to revise the formulas on this row to reflect the timing and cost percentage for your business. You might also want to use the general forecasting template to make a more accurate estimate of your inventory purchases. (For more explanation of this row, see TIPS, "Assumptions about inventory purchases," page 123.)

In some businesses, tracking inventory can be very complicated, requiring a great deal of detail. Most small businesses cannot afford the time and expense involved to budget and forecast hundreds of individual inventory items. The objective of planning and forecasting is to get a feel for what your future cash position (the cash budget), profitability (the income statement), and financial condition (the balance sheet) will be. It is not usually necessary to forecast in great detail. Most firms find that

their accounting records provide a reasonable point of departure for estimating inventory purchases. Inventory cost for each product can be determined from these records. Using this as a base, any anticipated increases or decreases in cost can be taken into account when planning. The expected inventory cost can then be divided by the selling price to arrive at the inventory cost percentage. When this percentage is multiplied times the selling price and unit sales, the total product inventory cost is calculated.

Manufacturers also will include direct labor costs and overhead under inventory in their cash budget. These can be estimated in the same manner as inventory purchases and the sum entered onto a new direct labor and factory overhead line.

Row 20 — Interest expense: The example calculates interest at a rate of 15 percent of loans appearing on row 29 (loans required) and row 82 (long-term debt). Many businesses, including yours, may have a variety of loans at a variety of interest rates, so you may want to change the interest percentage in cell D(B)20 to reflect your own average interest rate.

Row 22 — Taxes: These are calculated at 40 percent of net income (row 50) and paid quarterly in the example. In reality, rates vary depending on level of profitability. You might want to change the percentage on this row to incorporate a different tax rate. The tax payment entered in cell E(C)22 is a value from the period directly previous to the start of the example. You would also want to change this to reflect your own taxes due. As you become more comfortable with the VisiCalc program you can also create the appropriate tax table in a separate part of your template and use the LOOKUP function to bring the actual tax rate into the pro forma income statement.

Adapting the pro forma income statement

Row 35 — Cost of goods sold: These are calculated by multiplying the inventory percentage figure (cell D(B)17) times this month's sales (row 7).

Like inventory purchases on row 17, cost of goods sold estimates can involve a lot more detail than most small firms have time to assemble. Usually the percentage of cost of goods sold to net sales is used as an estimate.

For example:

$$\frac{\text{Cost of goods sold}}{\text{Net sales}} = \text{Percentage}$$

or

$$\frac{\$100,000}{\$200,000} = 50\%$$

	A	B(A)	C(A)	D(B)	E(C)	F(D)	G(E)	H(F)	I(G)	J(H)	K(I)	L(J)	M(K)	N(L)	O(M)	P(N)
1	Part 1: Cash budget															
2	=======															
3	Item:			What if	1	2	3	4	5	6	7	8	9	10	11	12
4				column	1984	1984	1984	1984	1984	1984	1984	1984	1984	1984	1984	1984
5																
6	Seasonal pattern*			100	8	8	8	8	8	8	8	8	8	8	8	8
7	Net sales; monthly*			450000	37500	37500	37500	37500	37500	37500	37500	37500	37500	37500	37500	37500
8																
9	Cash receipts:															
10	% collected within 30 days*			60	22500	22500	22500	22500	22500	22500	22500	22500	22500	22500	22500	22500
11	% collected within 60 days*			20	7500	7500	7500	7500	7500	7500	7500	7500	7500	7500	7500	7500
12	% collected within 90 days*			20	7500	7500	7500	7500	7500	7500	7500	7500	7500	7500	7500	7500
13	Other cash receipts*			0	($)	($)	($)	($)	($)	($)	($)	($)	($)	($)	($)	($)
14																
15	Total cash receipts				37500	37500	37500	37500	37500	37500	37500	37500	37500	37500	37500	37500
16																
17	Inventory purchases*			60	22500	22500	22500	22500	22500	22500	22500	22500	22500	22500	22500	22500
18	Gen.& admin.*			20	7500	7500	7500	7500	7500	7500	7500	7500	7500	7500	7500	7500
19	Selling expenses*			10	3750	3750	3750	3750	3750	3750	3750	3750	3750	3750	3750	3750
20	Interest expense*			15	500	500	500	500	500	500	500	500	500	500	500	500
21	Other expense*			0	($)	($)	($)	($)	($)	($)	($)	($)	($)	($)	($)	($)
22	Taxes*			40	2400			2400			2400			2400		
23																
24	Total cash disbursements				36650	34250	34250	36650	34250	34250	36650	34250	34250	36650	34250	34250
25																
26	Net cash flow				850	3250	3250	850	3250	3250	850	3250	3250	850	3250	3250
27																
28	Opening cash balance				20000	20850	24100	27350	28200	31450	34700	35550	38800	42050	42900	46150
29	Loans required			0	0	0	0	0	0	0	0	0	0	0	0	0
30	Ending cash balance*			20000	20850	24100	27350	28200	31450	34700	35550	38800	42050	42900	46150	49400
31																
32	Part 2: Pro forma income statement															
33	=======															
34	Net sales			450000	37500	37500	37500	37500	37500	37500	37500	37500	37500	37500	37500	37500
35	Cost of goods sold			270000	22500	22500	22500	22500	22500	22500	22500	22500	22500	22500	22500	22500
36																
37	Gross profit			180000	15000	15000	15000	15000	15000	15000	15000	15000	15000	15000	15000	15000
38																
39	General & administrative			90000	7500	7500	7500	7500	7500	7500	7500	7500	7500	7500	7500	7500
40	Selling expenses			45000	3750	3750	3750	3750	3750	3750	3750	3750	3750	3750	3750	3750
41	Depreciation			15000	1250	1250	1250	1250	1250	1250	1250	1250	1250	1250	1250	1250
42																
43	Operating income			30000	2500	2500	2500	2500	2500	2500	2500	2500	2500	2500	2500	2500
44	Interest expense			6000	500	500	500	500	500	500	500	500	500	500	500	500
45	Other income/expense*			0	($)	($)	($)	($)	($)	($)	($)	($)	($)	($)	($)	($)
46																
47	Income before taxes			24000	2000	2000	2000	2000	2000	2000	2000	2000	2000	2000	2000	2000
48	Taxes			9600	800	800	800	800	800	800	800	800	800	800	800	800
49																
50	Net income			14400	1200	1200	1200	1200	1200	1200	1200	1200	1200	1200	1200	1200
51																
52	Part 3: Pro forma balance sheet															
53	=======															
54	Assets:															
55																
56	<Current assets>															
57	Cash			20000	20850	24100	27350	28200	31450	34700	35550	38800	42050	42900	46150	49400
58	Accounts receivable			60000	60000	60000	60000	60000	60000	60000	60000	60000	60000	60000	60000	60000
59	Inventory			30000	30000	30000	30000	30000	30000	30000	30000	30000	30000	30000	30000	30000
60	Prepaid expenses			2000	2000	2000	2000	2000	2000	2000	2000	2000	2000	2000	2000	2000
61																
62	Total current assets			112000	112850	116100	119350	120200	123450	126700	127550	130800	134050	134900	138150	141400
63																
64	<Fixed assets>															
65	Buildings & equipment			50000	50000	50000	50000	50000	50000	50000	50000	50000	50000	50000	50000	50000
66	Less accum.depreciation			30000	31250	32500	33750	35000	36250	37500	38750	40000	41250	42500	43750	45000
67	Land			10000	10000	10000	10000	10000	10000	10000	10000	10000	10000	10000	10000	10000
68																
69	Net fixed assets			30000	28750	27500	26250	25000	23750	22500	21250	20000	18750	17500	16250	15000
70																
71	Total assets			142000	141600	143600	145600	145200	147200	149200	148800	150800	152800	152400	154400	156400
72																
73	Liabilities:															
74																
75	<Current liabilities>															
76	Accounts payable			22500	22500	22500	22500	22500	22500	22500	22500	22500	22500	22500	22500	22500
77	Accrued wages & taxes			5500	3900	4700	5500	3900	4700	5500	3900	4700	5500	3900	4700	5500
78	Other current liabilities			4000	4000	4000	4000	4000	4000	4000	4000	4000	4000	4000	4000	4000
79																
80	Total current liabilities			32000	30400	31200	32000	30400	31200	32000	30400	31200	32000	30400	31200	32000
81																
82	Long term debt			40000	40000	40000	40000	40000	40000	40000	40000	40000	40000	40000	40000	40000
83																
84	Total liabilities			72000	70400	71200	72000	70400	71200	72000	70400	71200	72000	70400	71200	72000
85																
86	<Owner equity>															
87	Common stock			50000	50000	50000	50000	50000	50000	50000	50000	50000	50000	50000	50000	50000
88	Retained earnings			20000	21200	22400	23600	24800	26000	27200	28400	29600	30800	32000	33200	34400
89																
90	Total owner equity			70000	71200	72400	73600	74800	76000	77200	78400	79600	80800	82000	83200	84400
91																
92	Total liab. & owner equity			142000	141600	143600	145600	145200	147200	149200	148800	150800	152800	152400	154400	156400
93	=======															

This is a fairly accurate estimate as long as any expected increases or decreases in cost are taken into account. For the types of items that might be included in your cost of goods estimate, see TIPS on page 116.

It is often useful to estimate cost of goods sold on the same basis as that used to forecast sales. That is, if sales are forecast by product or product group, cost of goods sold should be, too. If sales are forecast on the general forecasting template using a market breakdown, cost of goods sold should use the same breakdown. Setting up your pro forma income statement in this manner will allow you to perform gross margin analysis (gross margin equals net income minus cost of goods sold) and determine which products, product groups, or market segments are the most and least profitable.

Adapting the pro forma balance sheet

Row 57 — Cash: This line is taken directly from the ending balance (row 30) of the cash budget. You will want to change the opening cash balance figure in cell D(B)30 to reflect the correct figure.

Row 58 — Accounts receivable: This line is calculated by taking accounts receivable from the previous month, adding this month's sales (row 7), and then subtracting this month's cash receipts (row 15). Accounts receivable are always determined by the collection pattern, level of monthly sales, and the previous period's accounts receivable balance.

Row 59 — Inventory: This line is calculated by formulas which take inventory from the previous month, add inventory purchases for one month ahead (inventory arrives one month before it is paid for on row 17, two months before it is sold), and then subtract this month's cost of goods sold (row 35). The built-in assumption is that inventory purchases are made two months in advance and paid for one month in advance of their sale. You can adjust this assumption to reflect your pattern. (For more detail on this line, see TIPS on page 123.)

Row 76 — Accounts payable: Accounts payable are calculated by a formula that takes the previous month's accounts payable, adds the inventory purchases (on row 17) for the next month in the future (inventory is delivered two months before it is sold and one month before it's paid for), and then subtracts this month's inventory purchases. The built-in assumption is that inventory purchases are made two months in advance and paid for one month in advance of their sale (see Inventory, above). Inventory costs are entered in accounts payable when they are ordered and are deducted when they are paid for. (For more detail on how this row works, see TIPS on page 123.)

Accounts payable usually includes more than inventory purchases. Other items that may be included are any bills outstanding at the end of the previous month from unpaid telephone and utilities bills and so forth, or unpaid freight charges.

As on the inventory line, the formulas for the last two months of this row refer back to the first two months on the forecast, columns E(C) and F(D), instead of the coming two months since these don't appear on the forecast. As a result, the row peaks in September (column M(K)), reflecting inventory purchases in November ($54,000, in cell M(K)17) ordered for the large anticipated sales in December. Again, your pattern may be different and require additional information.

Row 77 — Accrued wages and taxes: This row is calculated by a formula that carries forward the accrued wages and taxes from the previous month, adds taxes due from the income statement (row 48) based on this month's net income, and subtracts quarterly payments shown on the cash budget (row 22). Make any necessary changes.

Row 78 — Other current liabilities: The formulas on this row carry forward the previous month's current liabilities and add to them any new loans required (from row 29 of the cash budget). Normally other current liabilities will include all liabilities that are known to be due for payment within one year. These might be notes payable (bank loans), the current portion of long-term debt, and royalties due. If any of those are significant or large, they should be listed separately.

Beyond the basics

Forecasting and planning are necessary for efficient and effective management. The level of detail you employ in developing your forecasts will depend on the size and complexity of your business. Too much planning can be counterproductive and take away from actually operating and running the business. Any forecast or plan is built on a number of assumptions about many factors, some of which you can control and some of which you can't. There are seven critical factors you should consider when you develop any of the forecasting tools discussed in this book. These variables, and your assumptions about them, will affect individual line items and the overall forecasts. The chart on the next page summarizes these factors, the line items they affect, and critical questions to ask yourself about each factor as you forecast, plan, and budget for the upcoming period.

Forecasting other line items, Continued

Factor	Line items affected	Critical questions
1. Volume The level of unit sales for a product	Sales Cost of goods sold General and administrative expense Selling expense	Do you expect volume to increase or decrease in the future? Do you expect your competition's volume to change? Why? Will it affect your volume forecast?
2. Price The charge for a product or service	Sales Selling expenses (if commissions are based on sales)	Do you anticipate price changes for any or all of your products? Are changing profit margins (i.e., changing unit costs) forcing you to consider a price change? Have your competitors changed or do you expect them to change their prices? Will changing prices reduce or increase unit sales?
3. Product mix The volume and number of different products offered by a firm	Sales Cost of goods sold Selling expense	Which products are selling well and which aren't? Do you plan to introduce new products or drop existing ones? How will a change in your product mix affect your cash flow, profits, and financial condition?
4. Wage inflation Increases in salaries and wages necessary to maintain employees' standards of living	Cost of goods sold General and administrative expense Selling expense	Do you anticipate wage and salary increases for employees? How will a change affect your profits and cash flow? How are your competitors dealing with wage inflation?
5. General inflation Rate of general cost increases	Cost of goods sold General and administrative expense Selling expense	What is the current rate of inflation, and what are future estimates about it? Have you adjusted your estimates on operating and financing costs up to account for inflation projections?
6. Cost efficiency In terms of cost or time spent	Cost of goods sold General and administrative expense Selling expense	Can you identify ways to make the firm more cost efficient? If you plan to introduce improved production measures, what do you expect their effect to be? Will increasing unit production produce economies of scale and lower average cost per unit?
7. Activity levels Number of activities not directly tied to sales in the forecast period. These are expected to increase sales or decrease costs in the long run, but their immediate effect is often higher costs resulting in lower profits and cash flow. An example is research and development for a new product.	General and administrative expense Selling expenses	Are there major new products in the development stage? Are you planning a major marketing effort to promote your company or any of its products? Are you considering the implementation of any specialized programs such as in the areas of personnel training or security?

The basic assumption in the example is that inventory is received two months prior to its being sold and is paid for one month prior to its sale. It is *added to* the inventory and accounts payable lines of the balance sheet when it is received (two months prior to its sale) and on the inventory purchases line of the cash budget when it is paid for (one month prior to its sale). It is *deducted* from the inventory line the month it is sold (the amount is taken from the cost of goods sold line on the income statement, row 35), and is deducted from the accounts payable line the month it is paid for (taken from the inventory purchases line on the cash budget, row 17).

Here is how the example works line by line:

Row 17: Inventory purchases are paid for one month before they are sold. (Since there is no "next month" for the last month on the budget, this cell refers back to the first month's sales to calculate inventory purchases. The assumption is that sales the first month of next year will be the same as those the first month of this year.)

Row 59: Inventory purchases are entered on the balance sheet when they are received, two months before they are sold and one month before they are paid for. The formulas on this row refer to one month ahead on the inventory purchases row (row 17), which is referring to one month further into the future on the net sales line (row 7); hence the two month "lead" in respect to sales.

Because there is no "one month in the future" on the inventory purchases row for the last column on the forecast, the last column on this row refers to the first month on the inventory purchases row. This means that December is referring to January on the inventory purchases row (row 17), which in turn is referring to February sales on row 7. The example assumes the first month of next year will have the same sales as the first month of the period covered by the budget.

Row 76: Accounts payable is increased by inventory purchases when they are received two months before they are sold and one month before they are paid for. The formulas on this row refer to one month ahead on the inventory purchases row (row 17), which is referring to one month further into the future; hence the two month "lead" in respect to sales.

Because there is no "one month in the future" on the inventory purchases row for the last column on the forecast, the last column on this row refers to the first month on the inventory purchases row. This means December is referring to January on the inventory purchases row (row 17) which in turn is referring to February sales on row 7. The example assumes the first month of the next year will have the same net sales as the first month of the period covered by the example.

The table below shows when inventory is added to the lines of the example:

Projected sales

	July	August	September
Add to inventory (row 59) inventory purchases equal to 60% of sales in two months	$6,000		
Add to accounts payable amount of the inventory purchases since the inventory was bought on credit	$6,000		
Subtract from cash and accounts payable the actual cash payment for the inventory purchased in the last 30 days		−$6,000	
Subtract from inventory the inventory sold during the month			−$6,000

Forecasting other line items, Continued

VISICALC TIPS Printing long templates

Many templates or worksheets are too long to print out on a standard sheet of paper, so they must be broken into pages. To do this with the VisiCalc program, you have to position the cursor in the upper left corner of the template, then specify the lower right coordinate that will identify a section of data that fits onto the sheet you are printing. When that sheet is printed, you go to cell A on the line below the last row printed to begin printing the next page.

Phantom prompts can be used to guide you. These are hidden instructions which appear when the cursor is in the correct location. When the first phantom prompt is in cell A1, specifying where to print to and where to begin the next page, the job is easier. A typical phantom prompt of this kind would read Print to K46 >A47. This identifies both the lower right-hand coordinate, K46 (so you don't have to find it with the cursor or remember it), and the cell to go to (using the Go To command >**A47**) to begin printing the next page.

The Advanced Version has a simpler technique. You can use the printer-setting option, /**PS**, followed by a pagination command to control printing automatically. The codes following the basic command give you a great deal of flexibility. For example:

L provides double spaces
B indicates a place for the printer to pause while you change paper
T prints titles for rows and columns even when other parts of the screen are scrolled under them
prints a number on each page of the printout

You can also change character width, the number of lines printed on each page, the length of lines, and margins with other, similar commands. See your VisiCalc Advanced Version user's manual for more details.

VISICALC TIPS Advanced Version layout

There are a few extras you can use to fine-tune your layouts so that printouts are clear and easy to read. Since the best layouts are determined through trial and error, the ability to refine without affecting the data and formulas on a worksheet is important. With its wide range of options, the Advanced Version gives you the ability to do this.

Do your columns print too close together? Do your reports lack that added visual refinement? If so, you can fine-tune with the Advanced Version. You can indent cell displays by any number of characters from the right or left edge of the column. /**AV**< aligns flush left, /**AV**> aligns flush right, /**AV2L** will indent two characters from the column's left edge, /**AV3L** will indent three characters, etc. /**AV2R, /AV3R** will do the same for the column's right edge. /**AVC** centers an entry in a column, useful when column headings are smaller than the column in which they are entered. Other ideas for improving layout and readability of screen displays and printouts can be found in the following TIPS boxes:

Formatting the display and printouts (page 47)
Calculating and displaying percentages (page 103)
Displaying dollar values (page 37)

Troubleshooting the Example

If you encounter any problems with your example, either when entering it or when using it to explore the "What Ifs" in Chapter 6, here are some suggestions on how to identify the problem.

If your example doesn't give results identical to those described in the book, there are several possible causes. Listed in order of their likelihood they include:

1 You didn't recalculate the worksheet enough times.

2 Values or formulas were not entered correctly when the example was entered.

3 The example was entered correctly but after changing some numbers in a "What If," you neglected to restore them before proceeding with the next step.

4 When entering changes in the example, you inadvertently typed a value into a cell containing a formula, erasing the formula in the process.

5 After making changes in a "What If," you saved the changed file on top of the original example by mistake. (You should never save a "What If" file and you should write-protect the disk containing the original example when it's finished so this can't happen. See "Write-protecting your disks" on page 49.)

Regardless of the cause of the problem, the first step is to identify it.

Step 1. Use the **SHIFT** and ! keys to recalculate the worksheet three or four times. This is a very complicated worksheet and up to four recalculations are sometimes required to carry changes throughout it.

Step 2. If the problem was first noticed when you explored "What Ifs," clear the screen and reload Example. See if the problem was cleared up. If so, it was probably caused by "3" or "4" above. If the problem still exists, however, continue.

Step 3. Check the basics. When you follow the troubleshooting steps below, first set recalculation to automatic by typing **/GRA** and always check the example from the top down. If you follow both of these suggestions any error you correct will automatically recalculate all values in the entire example. This will prevent your exploring figures that appear to be incorrect because they were caused by a previously corrected error but which haven't changed because the sheet wasn't recalculated.

Step 4. Check the example row by row against the illustration on page 85.

■ If you have to check the entire row, begin the comparison at D(B) and use the ⊝ key to scroll across the row comparing each entry with the illustration on page 85.

■ If you find a pair of figures that doesn't match, put the cursor in that space and read the entry contents line to see if the cell contains a formula or value. If it contains a formula, check it against the formulas given in the "To enter" sections for that row in Chapter 3, 4, or 5.

■ If the cell contains a value, check to see if it should. You may have inadvertently typed a value on top of the formula or erased it by using the # key to see the entire calculated value and then hitting the return key. Check the cell contents in your example against the entries you should have made listed in Chapter 3, 4, or 5.

Troubleshooting, Continued

TIPS A troubleshooting checklist

The example contains hundreds of formulas, either entered directly, or replicated from other cells on the template. When you enter a template of this complexity, it is very likely that some mistakes will be made. Identifying and correcting these mistakes is essential if you expect the template to provide you with useful information.

To be sure the example is working exactly the way you want it to, here are some things to look for:

Format errors: Do you show too many or too few digits to have ease of readability combined with the required precision? To know that your profit is 10.1001345% doesn't tell you much more than knowing your profit is 10%. In this case, formatting the display with the **/FI** command makes it easier to read and compare figures. If you use the **/FI** command, percents such as 10.4% and 10.6% will be rounded off to 10% and 11% respectively. A format of /**F$** will give you a slightly more precise answer. Using /**F$**, for instance, would display the same 10.4% and 10.6% as 10.40% and 10.60%. For maximum precision, but a difficult display to read, use /**FG**. This will display any decimals out to the maximum number of characters available in the column display. If your decimal fills the column and you want to see more, temporarily change the column width with the **/GC** command.

Formula errors: These can frequently be found only by checking the results on a completed template with the results found by calculating the same information manually. When discrepancies are found, check the cell involved and all cells to which it relates. The cell contents may, for instance, be calculated by dividing, multiplying, adding to, or subtracting from another cell's contents. You should check the other cell, because it may be the one that is wrong.

If you can't find the problem quickly, place the cursor in the cell in question and compare the cell contents, as they are displayed on the cell contents line, with the contents as described in the appropriate section of this book. Scan the step illustrations to find the section in which the row or column involved was entered. Check that section to see if the illustration and your cell contents match. If they don't, it is wise to assume some independent judgment. Although the authors have tried to be painfully accurate, mistakes do happen.

Advanced Version: When using the Advanced Version, you can display all formulas on the worksheet. This makes it easier to compare the worksheet with the formulas that should have been entered. The *attribute* command /**AE** displays formulas, rather than their calculated values. You can also make a printout of the formulas displayed in the cells in which they are entered. To display all formulas on the worksheet, type /**GAEY.** You may have to temporarily change some column widths to see complete formulas.

Replication errors: If you have a serious problem, such as an entire section that isn't functioning properly, the problem was probably caused when you replicated rows or columns. The sequence of **N**s and **R**s that you are directed to enter by the prompt line is critical. Percentages in all of the percent columns are calculated by dividing all numbers in the column to the percent column's immediate left by the same number. In the case of the income statement, the number dividing all other numbers is net sales revenue; on the balance sheet, it is total assets. Not using the **N** key to keep these divisors constant when replicating will cause wrong answers. Fortunately, errors caused in this way are frequently so bizarre that the problem is immediately obvious.

Error messages: These are usually caused by a failure to recalculate the worksheet after reloading it. If encountered when entering formulas the reason is usually failure to close brackets used in formulas, or by division of a cell by one that contains a zero value. Check any cell containing ERROR, and see if you can locate the cause. Be sure to check all cells to which the incorrect cell is related by formulas, since an error in a cell to which this cell refers will cause an ERROR to appear. Track back to the first error and correct it. This may cause other messages to disappear as well.

Printouts of "What Ifs"

WHAT IF 1

	A	B(A)	C(A)	D(B)	E(C)	F(D)	G(E)	H(F)	I(G)	J(H)	K(I)	L(J)	M(K)	N(L)	O(M)	P(N)
1	PART 1: CASH BUDGET			WHAT IF #1												
2	===
3	ITEM:			WHAT IF	1	2	3	4	5	6	7	8	9	10	11	12
4				COLUMN	1984	1984	1984	1984	1984	1984	1984	1984	1984	1984	1984	1984
5	
6	SEASONAL PATTERN*			100	5	5	5	5	5	5	10	10	10	10	10	20
7	NET SALES; MONTHLY*			450000	22500	22500	22500	22500	22500	22500	45000	45000	45000	45000	45000	90000
8	
9	CASH RECEIPTS:
10	% COLLECTED WITHIN 30 DAYS*			60	22500	13500	13500	13500	13500	13500	13500	27000	27000	27000	27000	27000
11	% COLLECTED WITHIN 60 DAYS*			20	7500	7500	4500	4500	4500	4500	4500	4500	9000	9000	9000	9000
12	% COLLECTED WITHIN 90 DAYS*			20	7500	7500	7500	4500	4500	4500	4500	4500	4500	9000	9000	9000
13	OTHER CASH RECEIPTS*			0	($)	($)	($)	($)	($)	($)	($)	($)	($)	($)	($)	($)
14	
15	TOTAL CASH RECEIPTS				37500	28500	25500	22500	22500	22500	22500	36000	40500	45000	45000	45000
16	
17	INVENTORY PURCHASES*			60	13500	13500	13500	13500	13500	27000	27000	27000	27000	27000	54000	13500
18	GEN. & ADMIN. *			20	7500	7500	7500	7500	7500	7500	7500	7500	7500	7500	7500	7500
19	SELLING EXPENSES*			10	3750	3750	3750	3750	3750	3750	3750	3750	3750	3750	3750	3750
20	INTEREST EXPENSE*			15	500	500	500	500	500	500	500	500	500	500	709	709
21	OTHER EXPENSE*			0	($)	($)	($)	($)	($)	($)	($)	($)	($)	($)	($)	($)
22	TAXES*			40	2400			-4800			-4800			6000		
23	
24	TOTAL CASH DISBURSEMENTS				27650	25250	25250	20450	25250	38750	33950	38750	38750	44750	65959	25459
25	
26	NET CASH FLOW				9850	3250	250	2050	-2750	-16250	-11450	-2750	1750	250	-20959	19541
27	
28	OPENING CASH BALANCE*				20000	29850	33100	33350	35400	32650	16400	4950	2200	3950	4200	0
29	LOANS REQUIRED			16759	0	0	0	0	0	0	0	0	0	0	16759	0
30	ENDING CASH BALANCE*			20000	29850	33100	33350	35400	32650	16400	4950	2200	3950	4200	0	19541
31	===
32	PART 2: PRO FORMA INCOME STATEMENT
33	
34	NET SALES			450000	22500	22500	22500	22500	22500	22500	45000	45000	45000	45000	45000	90000
35	COST OF GOODS SOLD			270000	13500	13500	13500	13500	13500	13500	27000	27000	27000	27000	27000	54000
36	
37	GROSS PROFIT			180000	9000	9000	9000	9000	9000	9000	18000	18000	18000	18000	18000	36000
38	
39	GENERAL & ADMINISTRATIVE			90000	7500	7500	7500	7500	7500	7500	7500	7500	7500	7500	7500	7500
40	SELLING EXPENSES			45000	3750	3750	3750	3750	3750	3750	3750	3750	3750	3750	3750	3750
41	DEPRECIATION			15000	1250	1250	1250	1250	1250	1250	1250	1250	1250	1250	1250	1250
42	
43	OPERATING INCOME			30000	-3500	-3500	-3500	-3500	-3500	-3500	5500	5500	5500	5500	5500	23500
44	INTEREST EXPENSE			6419	500	500	500	500	500	500	500	500	500	500	709	709
45	OTHER INCOME/EXPENSE*			0	($)	($)	($)	($)	($)	($)	($)	($)	($)	($)	($)	($)
46	
47	INCOME BEFORE TAXES			23581	-4000	-4000	-4000	-4000	-4000	-4000	5000	5000	5000	5000	4791	22791
48	TAXES			9432	-1600	-1600	-1600	-1600	-1600	-1600	2000	2000	2000	2000	1916	9116
49	
50	NET INCOME			14149	-2400	-2400	-2400	-2400	-2400	-2400	3000	3000	3000	3000	2874	13674
51	===
52	PART 3: PRO FORMA BALANCE SHEET
53	
54	ASSETS:
55	
56	<CURRENT ASSETS>
57	CASH			20000	29850	33100	33350	35400	32650	16400	4950	2200	3950	4200	0	19541
58	ACCOUNTS RECEIVABLE			60000	45000	39000	36000	36000	36000	36000	58500	67500	72000	72000	72000	117000
59	INVENTORY			30000	30000	30000	30000	30000	43500	57000	57000	57000	57000	84000	70500	30000
60	PREPAID EXPENSES			2000	2000	2000	2000	2000	2000	2000	2000	2000	2000	2000	2000	2000
61	
62	TOTAL CURRENT ASSETS			112000	106850	104100	101350	103400	114150	111400	122450	128700	134950	162200	144500	168541
63	
64	<FIXED ASSETS>
65	BUILDINGS & EQUIPMENT			50000	50000	50000	50000	50000	50000	50000	50000	50000	50000	50000	50000	50000
66	LESS ACCUM. DEPRECIATION			30000	31250	32500	33750	35000	36250	37500	38750	40000	41250	42500	43750	45000
67	LAND			10000	10000	10000	10000	10000	10000	10000	10000	10000	10000	10000	10000	10000
68	
69	NET FIXED ASSETS			30000	28750	27500	26250	25000	23750	22500	21250	20000	18750	17500	16250	15000
70	
71	TOTAL ASSETS			142000	135600	131600	127600	128400	137900	133900	143700	148700	153700	179700	160750	183541
72	
73	LIABILITIES:
74	
75	<CURRENT LIABILITIES>
76	ACCOUNTS PAYABLE			22500	22500	22500	22500	22500	36000	36000	36000	36000	36000	63000	22500	22500
77	ACCRUED WAGES & TAXES			5500	1500	-100	-1700	1500	-100	-1700	5100	7100	9100	5100	7016	16132
78	OTHER CURRENT LIABILITIES			4000	4000	4000	4000	4000	4000	4000	4000	4000	4000	4000	20759	20759
79	
80	TOTAL CURRENT LIABILITIES			32000	28000	26400	24800	28000	39900	38300	45100	47100	49100	72100	50276	59392
81	
82	LONG TERM DEBT			40000	40000	40000	40000	40000	40000	40000	40000	40000	40000	40000	40000	40000
83	
84	TOTAL LIABILITIES			72000	68000	66400	64800	68000	79900	78300	85100	87100	89100	112100	90276	99392
85	
86	<OWNER EQUITY>
87	COMMON STOCK			50000	50000	50000	50000	50000	50000	50000	50000	50000	50000	50000	50000	50000
88	RETAINED EARNINGS			20000	17600	15200	12800	10400	8000	5600	8600	11600	14600	17600	20474	34149
89	
90	TOTAL OWNER EQUITY			70000	67600	65200	62800	60400	58000	55600	58600	61600	64600	67600	70474	84149
91	
92	TOTAL LIAB. & OWNER EQUITY			142000	135600	131600	127600	128400	137900	133900	143700	148700	153700	179700	160750	183541
93	===

Printouts of "What Ifs," Continued

WHAT IF 2

	A B(A) C(A)	D(B)	E(C)	F(D)	G(E)	H(F)	I(G)	J(H)	K(I)	L(J)	M(K)	N(L)	O(M)	P(N)
1	PART 1: CASH BUDGET	WHAT IF #2												
3	ITEM:	WHAT IF COLUMN	1 1984	2 1984	3 1984	4 1984	5 1984	6 1984	7 1984	8 1984	9 1984	10 1984	11 1984	12 1984
6	SEASONAL PATTERN*	100	5	5	5	5	5	5	10	10	10	10	10	20
7	NET SALES; MONTHLY*	450000	22500	22500	22500	22500	22500	22500	45000	45000	45000	45000	45000	90000
9	CASH RECEIPTS:													
10	% COLLECTED WITHIN 30 DAYS*	80	22500	18000	18000	18000	18000	18000	18000	36000	36000	36000	36000	36000
11	% COLLECTED WITHIN 60 DAYS*	10	7500	7500	2250	2250	2250	2250	2250	2250	4500	4500	4500	4500
12	% COLLECTED WITHIN 90 DAYS*	10	7500	7500	7500	2250	2250	2250	2250	2250	2250	4500	4500	4500
13	OTHER CASH RECEIPTS*	0	($)	($)	($)	($)	($)	($)	($)	($)	($)	($)	($)	($)
15	TOTAL CASH RECEIPTS		37500	33000	27750	22500	22500	22500	22500	40500	42750	45000	45000	45000
17	INVENTORY PURCHASES*	60	13500	13500	13500	13500	13500	27000	27000	27000	27000	27000	54000	13500
18	GEN. & ADMIN.*	20	7500	7500	7500	7500	7500	7500	7500	7500	7500	7500	7500	7500
19	SELLING EXPENSES*	10	3750	3750	3750	3750	3750	3750	3750	3750	3750	3750	3750	3750
20	INTEREST EXPENSE*	15	500	500	500	500	500	500	500	500	500	500	539	539
21	OTHER EXPENSE*	0	($)	($)	($)	($)	($)	($)	($)	($)	($)	($)	($)	($)
22	TAXES*	40	2400			-4800			-4800			6000		
24	TOTAL CASH DISBURSEMENTS		27650	25250	25250	20450	25250	38750	33950	38750	38750	44750	65789	25289
26	NET CASH FLOW		9850	7750	2500	2050	-2750	-16250	-11450	1750	4000	250	-20789	19711
28	OPENING CASH BALANCE*		20000	29850	37600	40100	42150	39400	23150	11700	13450	17450	17700	0
29	LOANS REQUIRED	3091	0	0	0	0	0	0	0	0	0	0	3089	0
30	ENDING CASH BALANCE*	20000	29850	37600	40100	42150	39400	23150	11700	13450	17450	17700	0	19711
32	PART 2: PRO FORMA INCOME STATEMENT													
34	NET SALES	450000	22500	22500	22500	22500	22500	22500	45000	45000	45000	45000	45000	90000
35	COST OF GOODS SOLD	270000	13500	13500	13500	13500	13500	13500	27000	27000	27000	27000	27000	54000
37	GROSS PROFIT	180000	9000	9000	9000	9000	9000	9000	18000	18000	18000	18000	18000	36000
39	GENERAL & ADMINISTRATIVE	90000	7500	7500	7500	7500	7500	7500	7500	7500	7500	7500	7500	7500
40	SELLING EXPENSES	45000	3750	3750	3750	3750	3750	3750	3750	3750	3750	3750	3750	3750
41	DEPRECIATION	15000	1250	1250	1250	1250	1250	1250	1250	1250	1250	1250	1250	1250
43	OPERATING INCOME	30000	-3500	-3500	-3500	-3500	-3500	-3500	5500	5500	5500	5500	5500	23500
44	INTEREST EXPENSE	6079	500	500	500	500	500	500	500	500	500	500	539	539
45	OTHER INCOME/EXPENSE*	0	($)	($)	($)	($)	($)	($)	($)	($)	($)	($)	($)	($)
47	INCOME BEFORE TAXES	23921	-4000	-4000	-4000	-4000	-4000	-4000	5000	5000	5000	5000	4961	22961
48	TAXES	9568	-1600	-1600	-1600	-1600	-1600	-1600	2000	2000	2000	2000	1985	9185
50	NET INCOME	14352	-2400	-2400	-2400	-2400	-2400	-2400	3000	3000	3000	3000	2977	13777
52	PART 3: PRO FORMA BALANCE SHEET													
54	ASSETS:													
56	<CURRENT ASSETS>													
57	CASH	20000	29850	37600	40100	42150	39400	23150	11700	13450	17450	17700	0	19711
58	ACCOUNTS RECEIVABLE	60000	45000	34500	29250	29250	29250	29250	51750	56250	58500	58500	58500	103500
59	INVENTORY	30000	30000	30000	30000	30000	43500	57000	57000	57000	57000	84000	70500	30000
60	PREPAID EXPENSES	2000	2000	2000	2000	2000	2000	2000	2000	2000	2000	2000	2000	2000
62	TOTAL CURRENT ASSETS	112000	106850	104100	101350	103400	114150	111400	122450	128700	134950	162200	131000	155211
64	<FIXED ASSETS>													
65	BUILDINGS & EQUIPMENT	50000	50000	50000	50000	50000	50000	50000	50000	50000	50000	50000	50000	50000
66	LESS ACCUM.DEPRECIATION	30000	31250	32500	33750	35000	36250	37500	38750	40000	41250	42500	43750	45000
67	LAND	10000	10000	10000	10000	10000	10000	10000	10000	10000	10000	10000	10000	10000
69	NET FIXED ASSETS	30000	28750	27500	26250	25000	23750	22500	21250	20000	18750	17500	16250	15000
71	TOTAL ASSETS	142000	135600	131600	127600	128400	137900	133900	143700	148700	153700	179700	147250	170211
73	LIABILITIES:													
75	<CURRENT LIABILITIES>													
76	ACCOUNTS PAYABLE	22500	22500	22500	22500	22500	36000	36000	36000	36000	36000	63000	22500	22500
77	ACCRUED WAGES & TAXES	5500	1500	-100	-1700	1500	-100	-1700	5100	7100	9100	5100	7085	16269
78	OTHER CURRENT LIABILITIES	4000	4000	4000	4000	4000	4000	4000	4000	4000	4000	4000	7089	7089
80	TOTAL CURRENT LIABILITIES	32000	28000	26400	24800	28000	39900	38300	45100	47100	49100	72100	36673	45858
82	LONG TERM DEBT	40000	40000	40000	40000	40000	40000	40000	40000	40000	40000	40000	40000	40000
84	TOTAL LIABILITIES	72000	68000	66400	64800	68000	79900	78300	85100	87100	89100	112100	76673	85858
86	<OWNER EQUITY>													
87	COMMON STOCK	50000	50000	50000	50000	50000	50000	50000	50000	50000	50000	50000	50000	50000
88	RETAINED EARNINGS	20000	17600	15200	12800	10400	8000	5600	8600	11600	14600	17600	20577	34354
90	TOTAL OWNER EQUITY	70000	67600	65200	62800	60400	58000	55600	58600	61600	64600	67600	70577	84354
92	TOTAL LIAB. & OWNER EQUITY	142000	135600	131600	127600	128400	137900	133900	143700	148700	153700	179700	147250	170211

WHAT IF 3

	A	B(A)	C(A)	D(B)	E(C)	F(D)	G(E)	H(F)	I(G)	J(H)	K(I)	L(J)	M(K)	N(L)	O(M)	P(N)
1	PART 1: CASH BUDGET			WHAT IF #3												
3	ITEM:			WHAT IF	1	2	3	4	5	6	7	8	9	10	11	12
4				COLUMN	1984	1984	1984	1984	1984	1984	1984	1984	1984	1984	1984	1984
6	SEASONAL PATTERN*			100	8	8	8	8	8	8	8	8	8	8	8	8
7	NET SALES; MONTHLY*			450000	37500	37500	37500	37500	37500	37500	37500	37500	37500	37500	37500	37500
9	CASH RECEIPTS:															
10	% COLLECTED WITHIN 30 DAYS*			60	22500	22500	22500	22500	22500	22500	22500	22500	22500	22500	22500	22500
11	% COLLECTED WITHIN 60 DAYS*			20	7500	7500	7500	7500	7500	7500	7500	7500	7500	7500	7500	7500
12	% COLLECTED WITHIN 90 DAYS*			20	7500	7500	7500	7500	7500	7500	7500	7500	7500	7500	7500	7500
13	OTHER CASH RECEIPTS*			0	($)	($)	($)	($)	($)	($)	($)	($)	($)	($)	($)	($)
15	TOTAL CASH RECEIPTS				37500	37500	37500	37500	37500	37500	37500	37500	37500	37500	37500	37500
17	INVENTORY PURCHASES*			60	22500	22500	22500	22500	22500	22500	22500	22500	22500	22500	22500	22500
18	GEN. & ADMIN.*			20	7500	7500	7500	7500	7500	7500	7500	7500	7500	7500	7500	7500
19	SELLING EXPENSES*			10	3750	3750	3750	3750	3750	3750	3750	3750	3750	3750	3750	3750
20	INTEREST EXPENSE*			10	667	667	667	667	667	667	667	667	667	667	667	667
21	OTHER EXPENSE*			0	($)	($)	($)	($)	($)	($)	($)	($)	($)	($)	($)	($)
22	TAXES*			40	2400			2200			2200			2200		
24	TOTAL CASH DISBURSEMENTS				36817	34417	34417	36617	34417	34417	36617	34417	34417	36617	34417	34417
26	NET CASH FLOW				683	3083	3083	883	3083	3083	883	3083	3083	883	3083	3083
28	OPENING CASH BALANCE*				60000	60683	63767	66850	67733	70817	73900	74783	77867	80950	81833	84917
29	LOANS REQUIRED				0	0	0	0	0	0	0	0	0	0	0	0
30	ENDING CASH BALANCE*			60000	60683	63767	66850	67733	70817	73900	74783	77867	80950	81833	84917	88000
32	PART 2: PRO FORMA INCOME STATEMENT															
34	NET SALES			450000	37500	37500	37500	37500	37500	37500	37500	37500	37500	37500	37500	37500
35	COST OF GOODS SOLD			270000	22500	22500	22500	22500	22500	22500	22500	22500	22500	22500	22500	22500
37	GROSS PROFIT			180000	15000	15000	15000	15000	15000	15000	15000	15000	15000	15000	15000	15000
39	GENERAL & ADMINSTRATIVE			90000	7500	7500	7500	7500	7500	7500	7500	7500	7500	7500	7500	7500
40	SELLING EXPENSES			45000	3750	3750	3750	3750	3750	3750	3750	3750	3750	3750	3750	3750
41	DEPRECIATION			15000	1250	1250	1250	1250	1250	1250	1250	1250	1250	1250	1250	1250
43	OPERATING INCOME			30000	2500	2500	2500	2500	2500	2500	2500	2500	2500	2500	2500	2500
44	INTEREST EXPENSE			8000	667	667	667	667	667	667	667	667	667	667	667	667
45	OTHER INCOME/EXPENSE*			0	($)	($)	($)	($)	($)	($)	($)	($)	($)	($)	($)	($)
47	INCOME BEFORE TAXES			22000	1833	1833	1833	1833	1833	1833	1833	1833	1833	1833	1833	1833
48	TAXES			8800	733	733	733	733	733	733	733	733	733	733	733	733
50	NET INCOME			13200	1100	1100	1100	1100	1100	1100	1100	1100	1100	1100	1100	1100
52	PART 3: PRO FORMA BALANCE SHEET															
54	ASSETS:															
56	<CURRENT ASSETS>															
57	CASH			60000	60683	63767	66850	67733	70817	73900	74783	77867	80950	81833	84917	88000
58	ACCOUNTS RECEIVABLE			60000	60000	60000	60000	60000	60000	60000	60000	60000	60000	60000	60000	60000
59	INVENTORY			30000	30000	30000	30000	30000	30000	30000	30000	30000	30000	30000	30000	30000
60	PREPAID EXPENSES			2000	2000	2000	2000	2000	2000	2000	2000	2000	2000	2000	2000	2000
62	TOTAL CURRENT ASSETS			152000	152683	155767	158850	159733	162817	165900	166783	169867	172950	173833	176917	180000
64	<FIXED ASSETS>															
65	BUILDINGS & EQUIPMENT			50000	50000	50000	50000	50000	50000	50000	50000	50000	50000	50000	50000	50000
66	LESS ACCUM.DEPRECIATION			30000	31250	32500	33750	35000	36250	37500	38750	40000	41250	42500	43750	45000
67	LAND			10000	10000	10000	10000	10000	10000	10000	10000	10000	10000	10000	10000	10000
69	NET FIXED ASSETS			30000	28750	27500	26250	25000	23750	22500	21250	20000	18750	17500	16250	15000
71	TOTAL ASSETS			182000	181433	183267	185100	184733	186567	188400	188033	189867	191700	191333	193167	195000
73	LIABILITIES:															
75	<CURRENT LIABILITIES>															
76	ACCOUNTS PAYABLE			22500	22500	22500	22500	22500	22500	22500	22500	22500	22500	22500	22500	22500
77	ACRRUED WAGES & TAXES			5500	3833	4567	5300	3833	4567	5300	3833	4567	5300	3833	4567	5300
78	OTHER CURRENT LIABILITIES			4000	4000	4000	4000	4000	4000	4000	4000	4000	4000	4000	4000	4000
80	TOTAL CURRENT LIABILITIES			32000	30333	31067	31800	30333	31067	31800	30333	31067	31800	30333	31067	31800
82	LONG TERM DEBT			80000	80000	80000	80000	80000	80000	80000	80000	80000	80000	80000	80000	80000
84	TOTAL LIABILITIES			112000	110333	111067	111800	110333	111067	111800	110333	111067	111800	110333	111067	111800
86	<OWNER EQUITY>															
87	COMMON STOCK			50000	50000	50000	50000	50000	50000	50000	50000	50000	50000	50000	50000	50000
88	RETAINED EARNINGS			20000	21100	22200	23300	24400	25500	26600	27700	28800	29900	31000	32100	33200
90	TOTAL OWNER EQUITY			70000	71100	72200	73300	74400	75500	76600	77700	78800	79900	81000	82100	83200
92	TOTAL LIAB. & OWNER EQUITY			182000	181433	183267	185100	184733	186567	188400	188033	189867	191700	191333	193167	195000

WHAT IF 4

	A	B(A)	C(A)	D(B)	E(C)	F(D)	G(E)	H(F)	I(G)	J(H)	K(I)	L(J)	M(K)	N(L)	O(M)	P(N)
1	PART 1: CASH BUDGET			WHAT IF #4												
3	ITEM:			WHAT IF COLUMN	1 1984	2 1984	3 1984	4 1984	5 1984	6 1984	7 1984	8 1984	9 1984	10 1984	11 1984	12 1984
6	SEASONAL PATTERN*			100	8	8	8	8	8	8	8	8	8	8	8	8
7	NET SALES; MONTHLY*			450000	37500	37500	37500	37500	37500	37500	37500	37500	37500	37500	37500	37500
9	CASH RECEIPTS:															
10	% COLLECTED WITHIN 30 DAYS*			60	22500	22500	22500	22500	22500	22500	22500	22500	22500	22500	22500	22500
11	% COLLECTED WITHIN 60 DAYS*			20	7500	7500	7500	7500	7500	7500	7500	7500	7500	7500	7500	7500
12	% COLLECTED WITHIN 90 DAYS*			20	7500	7500	7500	7500	7500	7500	7500	7500	7500	7500	7500	7500
13	OTHER CASH RECEIPTS*			0	($)	($)	($)	($)	($)	($)	($)	($)	($)	($)	($)	($)
15	TOTAL CASH RECEIPTS				37500	37500	37500	37500	37500	37500	37500	37500	37500	37500	37500	37500
17	INVENTORY PURCHASES*			60	22500	22500	22500	22500	22500	22500	22500	22500	22500	22500	22500	22500
18	GEN.& ADMIN.*			20	7500	7500	7500	7500	7500	7500	7500	7500	7500	7500	7500	7500
19	SELLING EXPENSES*			10	3750	3750	3750	3750	3750	3750	3750	3750	3750	3750	3750	3750
20	INTEREST EXPENSE*			18	1200	1200	1200	1200	1200	1200	1200	1200	1200	1200	1200	1200
21	OTHER EXPENSE*			0	($)	($)	($)	($)	($)	($)	($)	($)	($)	($)	($)	($)
22	TAXES*			40	2400			1560			1560			1560		
24	TOTAL CASH DISBURSEMENTS				37350	34950	34950	36510	34950	34950	36510	34950	34950	36510	34950	34950
26	NET CASH FLOW				150	2550	2550	990	2550	2550	990	2550	2550	990	2550	2550
28	OPENING CASH BALANCE*				60000	60150	62700	65250	66240	68790	71340	72330	74880	77430	78420	80970
29	LOANS REQUIRED			0	0	0	0	0	0	0	0	0	0	0	0	0
30	ENDING CASH BALANCE*			60000	60150	62700	65250	66240	68790	71340	72330	74880	77430	78420	80970	83520
32	PART 2: PRO FORMA INCOME STATEMENT															
34	NET SALES			450000	37500	37500	37500	37500	37500	37500	37500	37500	37500	37500	37500	37500
35	COST OF GOODS SOLD			270000	22500	22500	22500	22500	22500	22500	22500	22500	22500	22500	22500	22500
37	GROSS PROFIT			180000	15000	15000	15000	15000	15000	15000	15000	15000	15000	15000	15000	15000
39	GENERAL & ADMINSTRATIVE			90000	7500	7500	7500	7500	7500	7500	7500	7500	7500	7500	7500	7500
40	SELLING EXPENSES			45000	3750	3750	3750	3750	3750	3750	3750	3750	3750	3750	3750	3750
41	DEPRECIATION			15000	1250	1250	1250	1250	1250	1250	1250	1250	1250	1250	1250	1250
43	OPERATING INCOME			30000	2500	2500	2500	2500	2500	2500	2500	2500	2500	2500	2500	2500
44	INTEREST EXPENSE			14400	1200	1200	1200	1200	1200	1200	1200	1200	1200	1200	1200	1200
45	OTHER INCOME/EXPENSE*			0	($)	($)	($)	($)	($)	($)	($)	($)	($)	($)	($)	($)
47	INCOME BEFORE TAXES			15600	1300	1300	1300	1300	1300	1300	1300	1300	1300	1300	1300	1300
48	TAXES			6240	520	520	520	520	520	520	520	520	520	520	520	520
50	NET INCOME			9360	780	780	780	780	780	780	780	780	780	780	780	780
52	PART 3: PRO FORMA BALANCE SHEET															
54	ASSETS:															
56	<CURRENT ASSETS>															
57	CASH			60000	60150	62700	65250	66240	68790	71340	72330	74880	77430	78420	80970	83520
58	ACCOUNTS RECEIVABLE			60000	60000	60000	60000	60000	60000	60000	60000	60000	60000	60000	60000	60000
59	INVENTORY			30000	30000	30000	30000	30000	30000	30000	30000	30000	30000	30000	30000	30000
60	PREPAID EXPENSES			2000	2000	2000	2000	2000	2000	2000	2000	2000	2000	2000	2000	2000
62	TOTAL CURRENT ASSETS			152000	152150	154700	157250	158240	160790	163340	164330	166880	169430	170420	172970	175520
64	<FIXED ASSETS>															
65	BUILDINGS & EQUIPMENT			50000	50000	50000	50000	50000	50000	50000	50000	50000	50000	50000	50000	50000
66	LESS ACCUM.DEPRECIATION			30000	31250	32500	33750	35000	36250	37500	38750	40000	41250	42500	43750	45000
67	LAND			10000	10000	10000	10000	10000	10000	10000	10000	10000	10000	10000	10000	10000
69	NET FIXED ASSETS			30000	28750	27500	26250	25000	23750	22500	21250	20000	18750	17500	16250	15000
71	TOTAL ASSETS			182000	180900	182200	183500	183240	184540	185840	185580	186880	188180	187920	189220	190520
73	LIABILITIES:															
75	<CURRENT LIABILITIES>															
76	ACCOUNTS PAYABLE			22500	22500	22500	22500	22500	22500	22500	22500	22500	22500	22500	22500	22500
77	ACCRUED WAGES & TAXES			5500	3620	4140	4660	3620	4140	4660	3620	4140	4660	3620	4140	4660
78	OTHER CURRENT LIABILITIES			4000	4000	4000	4000	4000	4000	4000	4000	4000	4000	4000	4000	4000
80	TOTAL CURRENT LIABILITIES			32000	30120	30640	31160	30120	30640	31160	30120	30640	31160	30120	30640	31160
82	LONG TERM DEBT			80000	80000	80000	80000	80000	80000	80000	80000	80000	80000	80000	80000	80000
84	TOTAL LIABILITIES			112000	110120	110640	111160	110120	110640	111160	110120	110640	111160	110120	110640	111160
86	<OWNER EQUITY>															
87	COMMON STOCK			50000	50000	50000	50000	50000	50000	50000	50000	50000	50000	50000	50000	50000
88	RETAINED EARNINGS			20000	20780	21560	22340	23120	23900	24680	25460	26240	27020	27800	28580	29360
90	TOTAL OWNER EQUITY			70000	70780	71560	72340	73120	73900	74680	75460	76240	77020	77800	78580	79360
92	TOTAL LIAB. & OWNER EQUITY			182000	180900	182200	183500	183240	184540	185840	185580	186880	188180	187920}	189220	190520

WHAT IF 5

	A	B(A)	C(A)	D(B)	E(C)	F(D)	G(E)	H(F)	I(G)	J(H)	K(I)	L(J)	M(K)	N(L)	O(M)	P(N)
1	PART 1: CASH BUDGET			WHAT IF #5												
2																
3	ITEM:			WHAT IF	1	2	3	4	5	6	7	8	9	10	11	12
4				COLUMN	1984	1984	1984	1984	1984	1984	1984	1984	1984	1984	1984	1984
5																
6	SEASONAL PATTERN*			100	8	8	8	8	8	8	8	8	8	8	8	8
7	NET SALES; MONTHLY*			450000	37500	37500	37500	37500	37500	37500	37500	37500	37500	37500	37500	37500
8																
9	CASH RECEIPTS:															
10	% COLLECTED WITHIN 30 DAYS*			60	22500	22500	22500	22500	22500	22500	22500	22500	22500	22500	22500	22500
11	% COLLECTED WITHIN 60 DAYS*			20	7500	7500	7500	7500	7500	7500	7500	7500	7500	7500	7500	7500
12	% COLLECTED WITHIN 90 DAYS*			20	7500	7500	7500	7500	7500	7500	7500	7500	7500	7500	7500	7500
13	OTHER CASH RECEIPTS*			0	($)	($)	($)	($)	($)	($)	($)	($)	($)	($)	($)	($)
14																
15	TOTAL CASH RECEIPTS				37500	37500	37500	37500	37500	37500	37500	37500	37500	37500	37500	37500
16																
17	INVENTORY PURCHASES*			65	24375	24375	24375	24375	24375	24375	24375	24375	24375	24375	24375	24375
18	GEN. & ADMIN. *			20	7500	7500	7500	7500	7500	7500	7500	7500	7500	7500	7500	7500
19	SELLING EXPENSES*			10	3750	3750	3750	3750	3750	3750	3750	3750	3750	3750	3750	3750
20	INTEREST EXPENSE*			15	500	500	500	500	500	500	500	500	500	500	500	500
21	OTHER EXPENSE*			0	($)	($)	($)	($)	($)	($)	($)	($)	($)	($)	($)	($)
22	TAXES*			40	2400		150			150				150		
23																
24	TOTAL CASH DISBURSEMENTS				38525	36125	36125	36275	36125	36125	36275	36125	36125	36275	36125	36125
25																
26	NET CASH FLOW				−1025	1375	1375	1225	1375	1375	1225	1375	1375	1225	1375	1375
27																
28	OPENING CASH BALANCE*				20000	18975	20350	21725	22950	24325	25700	26925	28300	29675	30900	32275
29	LOANS REQUIRED			0	0	0	0	0	0	0	0	0	0	0	0	0
30	ENDING CASH BALANCE*			20000	18975	20350	21725	22950	24325	25700	26925	28300	29675	30900	32275	33650
31																
32	PART 2: PRO FORMA INCOME STATEMENT															
33																
34	NET SALES			450000	37500	37500	37500	37500	37500	37500	37500	37500	37500	37500	37500	37500
35	COST OF GOODS SOLD			292500	24375	24375	24375	24375	24375	24375	24375	24375	24375	24375	24375	24375
36																
37	GROSS PROFIT			157500	13125	13125	13125	13125	13125	13125	13125	13125	13125	13125	13125	13125
38																
39	GENERAL & ADMINSTRATIVE			90000	7500	7500	7500	7500	7500	7500	7500	7500	7500	7500	7500	7500
40	SELLING EXPENSES			45000	3750	3750	3750	3750	3750	3750	3750	3750	3750	3750	3750	3750
41	DEPRECIATION			15000	1250	1250	1250	1250	1250	1250	1250	1250	1250	1250	1250	1250
42																
43	OPERATING INCOME			7500	625	625	625	625	625	625	625	625	625	625	625	625
44	INTEREST EXPENSE			6000	500	500	500	500	500	500	500	500	500	500	500	500
45	OTHER INCOME/EXPENSE*			0	($)	($)	($)	($)	($)	($)	($)	($)	($)	($)	($)	($)
46																
47	INCOME BEFORE TAXES			1500	125	125	125	125	125	125	125	125	125	125	125	125
48	TAXES			600	50	50	50	50	50	50	50	50	50	50	50	50
49																
50	NET INCOME			900	75	75	75	75	75	75	75	75	75	75	75	75
51																
52	PART 3: PRO FORMA BALANCE SHEET															
53																
54	ASSETS:															
55																
56	<CURRENT ASSETS>															
57	CASH			20000	18975	20350	21725	22950	24325	25700	26925	28300	29675	30900	32275	33650
58	ACCOUNTS RECEIVABLE			60000	60000	60000	60000	60000	60000	60000	60000	60000	60000	60000	60000	60000
59	INVENTORY			30000	30000	30000	30000	30000	30000	30000	30000	30000	30000	30000	30000	30000
60	PREPAID EXPENSES			2000	2000	2000	2000	2000	2000	2000	2000	2000	2000	2000	2000	2000
61																
62	TOTAL CURRENT ASSETS			112000	110975	112350	113725	114950	116325	117700	118925	120300	121675	122900	124275	125650
63																
64	<FIXED ASSETS>															
65	BUILDINGS & EQUIPMENT			50000	50000	50000	50000	50000	50000	50000	50000	50000	50000	50000	50000	50000
66	LESS ACCUM.DEPRECIATION			30000	31250	32500	33750	35000	36250	37500	38750	40000	41250	42500	43750	45000
67	LAND			10000	10000	10000	10000	10000	10000	10000	10000	10000	10000	10000	10000	10000
68																
69	NET FIXED ASSETS			30000	28750	27500	26250	25000	23750	22500	21250	20000	18750	17500	16250	15000
70																
71	TOTAL ASSETS			142000	139725	139850	139975	139950	140075	140200	140175	140300	140425	140400	140525	140650
72																
73	LIABILITIES:															
74																
75	<CURRENT LIABILITIES>															
76	ACCOUNTS PAYABLE			22500	22500	22500	22500	22500	22500	22500	22500	22500	22500	22500	22500	22500
77	ACRRUED WAGES & TAXES			5500	3150	3200	3250	3150	3200	3250	3150	3200	3250	3150	3200	3250
78	OTHER CURRENT LIABILITIES			4000	4000	4000	4000	4000	4000	4000	4000	4000	4000	4000	4000	4000
79																
80	TOTAL CURRENT LIABILITIES			32000	29650	29700	29750	29650	29700	29750	29650	29700	29750	29650	29700	29750
81																
82	LONG TERM DEBT			40000	40000	40000	40000	40000	40000	40000	40000	40000	40000	40000	40000	40000
83																
84	TOTAL LIABILITIES			72000	69650	69700	69750	69650	69700	69750	69650	69700	69750	69650	69700	69750
85																
86	<OWNER EQUITY>															
87	COMMON STOCK			50000	50000	50000	50000	50000	50000	50000	50000	50000	50000	50000	50000	50000
88	RETAINED EARNINGS			20000	20075	20150	20225	20300	20375	20450	20525	20600	20675	20750	20825	20900
89																
90	TOTAL OWNER EQUITY			70000	70075	70150	70225	70300	70375	70450	70525	70600	70675	70750	70825	70900
91																
92	TOTAL LIAB. & OWNER EQUITY			142000	139725	139850	139975	139950	140075	140200	140175	140300	140425	140400	140525	140650
93																

WHAT IF 6

	A	B(A)	C(A)	D(B)	E(C)	F(D)	G(E)	H(F)	I(G)	J(H)	K(I)	L(J)	M(K)	N(L)	O(M)	P(N)
1	PART 1: CASH BUDGET			WHAT IF #6												
2																
3	ITEM:			WHAT IF	1	2	3	4	5	6	7	8	9	10	11	12
4				COLUMN	1984	1984	1984	1984	1984	1984	1984	1984	1984	1984	1984	1984
5																
6	SEASONAL PATTERN*			100	8	8	8	8	8	8	8	8	8	8	8	8
7	NET SALES; MONTHLY*			450000	37500	37500	37500	37500	37500	37500	37500	37500	37500	37500	37500	37500
8																
9	CASH RECEIPTS:															
10	% COLLECTED WITHIN 30 DAYS*			60	22500	22500	22500	22500	22500	22500	22500	22500	22500	22500	22500	22500
11	% COLLECTED WITHIN 60 DAYS*			20	7500	7500	7500	7500	7500	7500	7500	7500	7500	7500	7500	7500
12	% COLLECTED WITHIN 90 DAYS*			20	7500	7500	7500	7500	7500	7500	7500	7500	7500	7500	7500	7500
13	OTHER CASH RECEIPTS*			0	($)	($)	($)	($)	($)	($)	($)	($)	($)	($)	($)	($)
14																
15	TOTAL CASH RECEIPTS				37500	37500	37500	37500	37500	37500	37500	37500	37500	37500	37500	37500
16																
17	INVENTORY PURCHASES*			65	24375	24375	24375	24375	24375	24375	24375	24375	24375	24375	24375	24375
18	GEN.& ADMIN.*			15	5625	5625	5625	5625	5625	5625	5625	5625	5625	5625	5625	5625
19	SELLING EXPENSES*			10	3750	3750	3750	3750	3750	3750	3750	3750	3750	3750	3750	3750
20	INTEREST EXPENSE*			15	500	500	500	500	500	500	500	500	500	500	500	500
21	OTHER EXPENSE*			0	($)	($)	($)	($)	($)	($)	($)	($)	($)	($)	($)	($)
22	TAXES*			40	2400			2400			2400			2400		
23																
24	TOTAL CASH DISBURSEMENTS				36650	34250	34250	36650	34250	34250	36650	34250	34250	36650	34250	34250
25																
26	NET CASH FLOW				850	3250	3250	850	3250	3250	850	3250	3250	850	3250	3250
27																
28	OPENING CASH BALANCE*				20000	20850	24100	27350	28200	31450	34700	35550	38800	42050	42900	46150
29	LOANS REQUIRED			0	0	0	0	0	0	0	0	0	0	0	0	0
30	ENDING CASH BALANCE*			20000	20850	24100	27350	28200	31450	34700	35550	38800	42050	42900	46150	49400
31																
32	PART 2: PRO FORMA INCOME STATEMENT															
33																
34	NET SALES			450000	37500	37500	37500	37500	37500	37500	37500	37500	37500	37500	37500	37500
35	COST OF GOODS SOLD			292500	24375	24375	24375	24375	24375	24375	24375	24375	24375	24375	24375	24375
36																
37	GROSS PROFIT			157500	13125	13125	13125	13125	13125	13125	13125	13125	13125	13125	13125	13125
38																
39	GENERAL & ADMINSTRATIVE			67500	5625	5625	5625	5625	5625	5625	5625	5625	5625	5625	5625	5625
40	SELLING EXPENSES			45000	3750	3750	3750	3750	3750	3750	3750	3750	3750	3750	3750	3750
41	DEPRECIATION			15000	1250	1250	1250	1250	1250	1250	1250	1250	1250	1250	1250	1250
42																
43	OPERATING INCOME			30000	2500	2500	2500	2500	2500	2500	2500	2500	2500	2500	2500	2500
44	INTEREST EXPENSE			6000	500	500	500	500	500	500	500	500	500	500	500	500
45	OTHER INCOME/EXPENSE*			0	($)	($)	($)	($)	($)	($)	($)	($)	($)	($)	($)	($)
46																
47	INCOME BEFORE TAXES			24000	2000	2000	2000	2000	2000	2000	2000	2000	2000	2000	2000	2000
48	TAXES			9600	800	800	800	800	800	800	800	800	800	800	800	800
49																
50	NET INCOME			14400	1200	1200	1200	1200	1200	1200	1200	1200	1200	1200	1200	1200
51																
52	PART 3: PRO FORMA BALANCE SHEET															
53																
54	ASSETS:															
55																
56	<CURRENT ASSETS>															
57	CASH			20000	20850	24100	27350	28200	31450	34700	35550	38800	42050	42900	46150	49400
58	ACCOUNTS RECEIVABLE			60000	60000	60000	60000	60000	60000	60000	60000	60000	60000	60000	60000	60000
59	INVENTORY			30000	30000	30000	30000	30000	30000	30000	30000	30000	30000	30000	30000	30000
60	PREPAID EXPENSES			2000	2000	2000	2000	2000	2000	2000	2000	2000	2000	2000	2000	2000
61																
62	TOTAL CURRENT ASSETS			112000	112850	116100	119350	120200	123450	126700	127550	130800	134050	134900	138150	141400
63																
64	<FIXED ASSETS>															
65	BUILDINGS & EQUIPMENT			50000	50000	50000	50000	50000	50000	50000	50000	50000	50000	50000	50000	50000
66	LESS ACCUM.DEPRECIATION			30000	31250	32500	33750	35000	36250	37500	38750	40000	41250	42500	43750	45000
67	LAND			10000	10000	10000	10000	10000	10000	10000	10000	10000	10000	10000	10000	10000
68																
69	NET FIXED ASSETS			30000	28750	27500	26250	25000	23750	22500	21250	20000	18750	17500	16250	15000
70																
71	TOTAL ASSETS			142000	141600	143600	145600	145200	147200	149200	148800	150800	152800	152400	154400	156400
72																
73	LIABILITIES:															
74																
75	<CURRENT LIABILITIES>															
76	ACCOUNTS PAYABLE			22500	22500	22500	22500	22500	22500	22500	22500	22500	22500	22500	22500	22500
77	ACRRUED WAGES & TAXES			5500	3900	4700	5500	3900	4700	5500	3900	4700	5500	3900	4700	5500
78	OTHER CURRENT LIABILITIES			4000	4000	4000	4000	4000	4000	4000	4000	4000	4000	4000	4000	4000
79																
80	TOTAL CURRENT LIABILITIES			32000	30400	31200	32000	30400	31200	32000	30400	31200	32000	30400	31200	32000
81																
82	LONG TERM DEBT			40000	40000	40000	40000	40000	40000	40000	40000	40000	40000	40000	40000	40000
83																
84	TOTAL LIABILITIES			72000	70400	71200	72000	70400	71200	72000	70400	71200	72000	70400	71200	72000
85																
86	<OWNER EQUITY>															
87	COMMON STOCK			50000	50000	50000	50000	50000	50000	50000	50000	50000	50000	50000	50000	50000
88	RETAINED EARNINGS			20000	21200	22400	23600	24800	26000	27200	28400	29600	30800	32000	33200	34400
89																
90	TOTAL OWNER EQUITY			70000	71200	72400	73600	74800	76000	77200	78400	79600	80800	82000	83200	84400
91																
92	TOTAL LIAB. & OWNER EQUITY			142000	141600	143600	145600	145200	147200	149200	148800	150800	152800	152400	154400	156400
93																

WHAT IF 7

	A	B(A)	C(A)	D(B)	E(C)	F(D)	G(E)	H(F)	I(G)	J(H)	K(I)	L(J)	M(K)	N(L)	O(M)	P(N)
1	PART 1: CASH BUDGET			WHAT IF #7												
3	ITEM:			WHAT IF	1	2	3	4	5	6	7	8	9	10	11	12
4				COLUMN	1984	1984	1984	1984	1984	1984	1984	1984	1984	1984	1984	1984
6	SEASONAL PATTERN*			100	8	8	8	8	8	8	8	8	8	8	8	8
7	NET SALES; MONTHLY*			600000	50000	50000	50000	50000	50000	50000	50000	50000	50000	50000	50000	50000
9	CASH RECEIPTS:															
10	% COLLECTED WITHIN 30 DAYS*			60	22500	30000	30000	30000	30000	30000	30000	30000	30000	30000	30000	30000
11	% COLLECTED WITHIN 60 DAYS*			20	7500	7500	10000	10000	10000	10000	10000	10000	10000	10000	10000	10000
12	% COLLECTED WITHIN 90 DAYS*			20	7500	7500	7500	10000	10000	10000	10000	10000	10000	10000	10000	10000
13	OTHER CASH RECEIPTS*			0	($)	($)	($)	($)	($)	($)	($)	($)	($)	($)	($)	($)
15	TOTAL CASH RECEIPTS				37500	45000	47500	50000	50000	50000	50000	50000	50000	50000	50000	50000
17	INVENTORY PURCHASES*			60	30000	30000	30000	30000	30000	30000	30000	30000	30000	30000	30000	30000
18	GEN.& ADMIN.*			20	10000	10000	10000	10000	10000	10000	10000	10000	10000	10000	10000	10000
19	SELLING EXPENSES*			10	5000	5000	5000	5000	5000	5000	5000	5000	5000	5000	5000	5000
20	INTEREST EXPENSE*			15	500	500	500	500	500	500	500	500	500	500	500	500
21	OTHER EXPENSE*			0	($)	($)	($)	($)	($)	($)	($)	($)	($)	($)	($)	($)
22	TAXES*			40	2400			3900			3900			3900		
24	TOTAL CASH DISBURSEMENTS				47900	45500	45500	49400	45500	45500	49400	45500	45500	49400	45500	45500
26	NET CASH FLOW				−10400	−500	2000	600	4500	4500	600	4500	4500	600	4500	4500
28	OPENING CASH BALANCE*				20000	9600	9100	11100	11700	16200	20700	21300	25800	30300	30900	35400
29	LOANS REQUIRED			0	0	0	0	0	0	0	0	0	0	0	0	0
30	ENDING CASH BALANCE*			20000	9600	9100	11100	11700	16200	20700	21300	25800	30300	30900	35400	39900
32	PART 2: PRO FORMA INCOME STATEMENT															
34	NET SALES			600000	50000	50000	50000	50000	50000	50000	50000	50000	50000	50000	50000	50000
35	COST OF GOODS SOLD			360000	30000	30000	30000	30000	30000	30000	30000	30000	30000	30000	30000	30000
37	GROSS PROFIT			240000	20000	20000	20000	20000	20000	20000	20000	20000	20000	20000	20000	20000
39	GENERAL & ADMINSTRATIVE			120000	10000	10000	10000	10000	10000	10000	10000	10000	10000	10000	10000	10000
40	SELLING EXPENSES			60000	5000	5000	5000	5000	5000	5000	5000	5000	5000	5000	5000	5000
41	DEPRECIATION			15000	1250	1250	1250	1250	1250	1250	1250	1250	1250	1250	1250	1250
43	OPERATING INCOME			45000	3750	3750	3750	3750	3750	3750	3750	3750	3750	3750	3750	3750
44	INTEREST EXPENSE			6000	500	500	500	500	500	500	500	500	500	500	500	500
45	OTHER INCOME/EXPENSE*			0	($)	($)	($)	($)	($)	($)	($)	($)	($)	($)	($)	($)
47	INCOME BEFORE TAXES			39000	3250	3250	3250	3250	3250	3250	3250	3250	3250	3250	3250	3250
48	TAXES			15600	1300	1300	1300	1300	1300	1300	1300	1300	1300	1300	1300	1300
50	NET INCOME			23400	1950	1950	1950	1950	1950	1950	1950	1950	1950	1950	1950	1950
52	PART 3: PRO FORMA BALANCE SHEET															
54	ASSETS:															
56	<CURRENT ASSETS>															
57	CASH			20000	9600	9100	11100	11700	16200	20700	21300	25800	30300	30900	35400	39900
58	ACCOUNTS RECEIVABLE			60000	72500	77500	80000	80000	80000	80000	80000	80000	80000	80000	80000	80000
59	INVENTORY			30000	30000	30000	30000	30000	30000	30000	30000	30000	30000	30000	30000	30000
60	PREPAID EXPENSES			2000	2000	2000	2000	2000	2000	2000	2000	2000	2000	2000	2000	2000
62	TOTAL CURRENT ASSETS			112000	114100	118600	123100	123700	128200	132700	133300	137800	142300	142900	147400	151900
64	<FIXED ASSETS>															
65	BUILDINGS & EQUIPMENT			50000	50000	50000	50000	50000	50000	50000	50000	50000	50000	50000	50000	50000
66	LESS ACCUM.DEPRECIATION			30000	31250	32500	33750	35000	36250	37500	38750	40000	41250	42500	43750	45000
67	LAND			10000	10000	10000	10000	10000	10000	10000	10000	10000	10000	10000	10000	10000
69	NET FIXED ASSETS			30000	28750	27500	26250	25000	23750	22500	21250	20000	18750	17500	16250	15000
71	TOTAL ASSETS			142000	142850	146100	149350	148700	151950	155200	154550	157800	161050	160400	163650	166900
73	LIABILITIES:															
75	<CURRENT LIABILITIES>															
76	ACCOUNTS PAYABLE			22500	22500	22500	22500	22500	22500	22500	22500	22500	22500	22500	22500	22500
77	ACRRUED WAGES & TAXES			5500	4400	5700	7000	4400	5700	7000	4400	5700	7000	4400	5700	7000
78	OTHER CURRENT LIABILITIES			4000	4000	4000	4000	4000	4000	4000	4000	4000	4000	4000	4000	4000
80	TOTAL CURRENT LIABILITIES			32000	30900	32200	33500	30900	32200	33500	30900	32200	33500	30900	32200	33500
82	LONG TERM DEBT			40000	40000	40000	40000	40000	40000	40000	40000	40000	40000	40000	40000	40000
84	TOTAL LIABILITIES			72000	70900	72200	73500	70900	72200	73500	70900	72200	73500	70900	72200	73500
86	<OWNER EQUITY>															
87	COMMON STOCK			50000	50000	50000	50000	50000	50000	50000	50000	50000	50000	50000	50000	50000
88	RETAINED EARNINGS			20000	21950	23900	25850	27800	29750	31700	33650	35600	37550	39500	41450	43400
90	TOTAL OWNER EQUITY			70000	71950	73900	75850	77800	79750	81700	83650	85600	87550	89500	91450	93400
92	TOTAL LIAB. & OWNER EQUITY			142000	142850	146100	149350	148700	151950	155200	154550	157800	161050	160400	163650	166900

Save time and energy

✄

Disk order form

To:
Curtin & London, Inc.
6 Vernon Street
Somerville, MA 02145

☐ Yes . . . I want to save time. Rush me the disk to accompany **Planning and Budgeting.**

My computer is an:

☐ IBM Personal Computer
☐ IBM Personal Computer XT

My VisiCalc version is:

☐ VisiCalc
☐ VisiCalc Advanced Version

Send to: (Please print)

Name _____

Street _____

City _____ State_____ Zip Code _____

The method of payment of **$29.95**
(Mass. residents add 5%—**$31.45**) is checked below:

☐ My check to **Curtin & London, Inc.** is enclosed

☐ Bill to my Master Card # _____

☐ Bill to my Visa Card # _____

The expiration date for my card is _____

Signature: _____

☐ Please add me to your mailing list for announcements of other new books and disks in the **Business User's Guide** series

Return policy:
No returns accepted unless disk is defective. If defective, return disk within 10 days of receipt and we will mail you a replacement disk immediately. Sorry, no refunds.

✄

A special disk containing the completed example and templates used throughout this book is available. Although this disk isn't mandatory, it will save you time and energy because you don't have to enter the example and templates yourself and it eliminates the possibility of introducing errors. You can begin immediately to explore the principles and problems of business. Since Curtin & London disks are not write-protected, you can adapt or customize the templates and make copies for use on more than one computer.

If you did not purchase the Disk Edition of this book, write directly to the publisher at the address on the order form. It will be shipped by first class mail the day your order and payment are received. To assure delivery of the correct disk, be sure to check the appropriate boxes and mail your order form with payment to Curtin & London, Inc.

Curtin & London, Inc.
6 Vernon Street
Somerville, MA 02145